"I found this to be a great read; no, a MUST read for all beginning investors. Simple, yet thorough, I was informed, educated, and motivated to continue investing in real estate. If you thumb through the pages, you WILL need to buy the book to get the entire message!"

> RK KLIEBENSTEIN
> Author, *How To Invest In Self-Storage*

"This Real Estate Investor's Handbook *provides a roadmap for both the new and experienced Real Estate investor. The subtleties of real estate investing are explained in an easy to understand format, allowing the reader to assimilate years of experience for the cost of a good 'read'."*

> JIM BABINSKI
> Managing Realtor
> Best Western Real Estate Services
> 15437 Anacapa Rd., Suite 3
> Victorville, CA 92392
> (760) 953-7814
> jimbabinski@verizon.net
> www.BestWesternRealEstate.com

THE
REAL ESTATE
INVESTOR'S
HANDBOOK:

The Complete Guide for the Individual Investor

By Steven D. Fisher

The Real Estate Investor's Handbook:
The Complete Guide for the Individual Investor

Copyright © 2006 by Atlantic Publishing Group, Inc.
1210 SW 23rd Place • Ocala, Florida 34474 • 800-814-1132 • 352-622-5836–Fax
Web site: www.atlantic-pub.com • E-mail sales@atlantic-pub.com
SAN Number: 268-1250

ISBN-13: 978-0-910627-69-6   ISBN-10: 0-910627-69-X

Library of Congress Cataloging-in-Publication Data
Fisher, Steven D., 1944-
  The real estate investor's handbook : the complete guide for the individual investor / Steven D. Fisher.
      p. cm.
  Includes bibliographical references and index.
  ISBN 0-910627-69-X (978-0-910627-69-6 : alk. paper)
  1. Real estate investment. I. Title.

  HD1382.5.F57 2006
  332.63'24--dc22
                              2006012577
Printed in the United States

ART DIRECTION, FRONT COVER & INTERIOR DESIGN: Meg Buchner • megadesn@mchsi.com
BOOK PRODUCTION DESIGN: Just Your Type Desktop Publishing • JustYourType.biz

TABLE of CONTENTS

CHAPTER 1:
INVESTING WITH LITTLE MONEY   27

CHAPTER 2: TYPES OF MORTGAGES   39

CHAPTER 3: INVESTING IN RESIDENTIAL
AND COMMERCIAL PROPERTIES   57

CHAPTER 4: FLIPPING   69

CHAPTER 5: FORECLOSURES AND REOS   79

CHAPTER 6: THE TEAM APPROACH 95

CHAPTER 7: FINDING AND EVALUATING PROPERTIES 115

CHAPTER 8: UNDERSTANDING LEASES AND VALUE — 137

CHAPTER 9: ENSURING A RETURN ON YOUR INVESTMENT — 151

CHAPTER 10: NEGOTIATIONS   173

CHAPTER 11: ESCROW, DUE DILIGENCE, AND OTHER VITAL MATTERS   193

THE LANDLORD PATH   233

CHAPTER 12: CHOOSING THE RIGHT LANDLORD PATH   235

CHAPTER 13: KEEPING RECORDS   287

CHAPTER 14: TAX ADVANTAGES AND EXIT STRATEGIES 297

CONCLUSION: THE SECRET TO BUILDING REAL ESTATE WEALTH 327

GLOSSARY 341

RECOMMENDED READING 381

INDEX 383

FIABCI-USA MEMBERSHIP 390

For more than 20 years as a licensed real estate broker, I have enjoyed a wonderful, exciting career, and I have always been amazed that more people don't take advantage of all this business has to offer. Real estate can be the ticket to financial independence, which is especially important in these times of downsizing, pension cutoffs, outsourcing of jobs, and other economic uncertainties.

A career in real estate offers so many benefits you simply can't find in other occupations. Embarking on a real estate career is easy. You don't need years of study or a university degree, and you don't even have to be a broker to be a successful investor. All you really need is a willingness to take action and work hard.

It's also a great way to meet people from all walks of life while earning a good income. Plus, as a real estate investor, you can get great, predictable returns over time without the volatility of the stock market.

And don't forget the tax benefits! The government encourages real estate investment and allows you to reduce your taxes through acquisition of assets. It doesn't get much better than that. But, wait a minute! Yes, it does! Because through careful investment in real estate, you can build both income and wealth. There aren't many other careers on the planet that offer you those kinds of advantages!

So with all these benefits, why don't more people invest in real estate? In my opinion, it's due to fear. And that fear comes from lack of knowledge. At first glance, the subject seems so

complicated because of the intimidating language used —
leverage, capital gains, Tax Deferred 1031 exchanges, escrow,
due diligence. We tell ourselves, "How can I learn this subject
when nobody seems to speak English!"

Well, *The Real Estate Investor's Handbook* takes care of that problem
for you. It explains every aspect of real estate investment in
the clearest possible terms and takes the mystery out of the
subject. It outlines the best possible course to take in each area of
investment. At the same time, the book doesn't offer a simplistic
"feel good" approach to a real estate career. It also identifies
pitfalls to avoid so you can always keep yourself on a profitable
path. In this book, you'll learn not only about the "nuts and
bolts" of investment (mortgages, leases, negotiating, landlording)
but also how to achieve the most important objective of all,
particularly in times of uncertainty — financial security.

The Real Estate Investor's Handbook lays a solid foundation for
your success in property investment. All you need to do is learn
and apply the knowledge in this book to build a house upon
a steady foundation. And that house will have a wonderful
address on it: A Secure Future.

I wish you much happiness as you embark on this exciting and
profitable voyage!

> John D. Pinson
> Chairman, John D. Pinson, Inc.
> CIPS, CRS, GRI, cert FIABCI
> (International Real Estate Federation)

*John is an experienced licensed real estate broker who offers the
best in real estate not only in Florida and New York but also
internationally. Visit his Web site at: **www.johnpinson.com**, and
he can be contacted at John@Pinson.com.*

ADVANTAGES & DISADVANTAGES OF REAL ESTATE

Investing in real estate is a time-tested strategy for building wealth. Like any investment, it should be approached with the most valuable weapon in your arsenal—knowledge. The purpose of this book is to provide that knowledge through proven guidelines and principles of wise investment. In addition, this book will help you decide if real estate investment is the right strategy for your personality and your goals. Real estate is often touted as the path to great wealth and security, and the first step is to take an objective look at real estate as an investment, considering its advantages and disadvantages.

ADVANTAGES OF REAL ESTATE INVESTMENT

It Offers Good Returns

Historically, real estate has given investors an average annual return of 8 to 10 percent. This rate is comparable to historic returns in the stock market without the accompanying volatility. As a general rule, real estate investments outpace inflation and create real wealth for investors.

It's Relatively Easy to Begin

Anyone can get into real estate. Even if you have only modest means, there is a property that will fit your needs and allow you to get started.

It Provides the Ability to Use Leverage

Leverage is the ability to use credit to finance a portion of the costs of purchasing or developing a real estate investment. Simply put, this means borrowing money to buy a property while investing only a small portion of the purchase price. In other words, you can buy a property for dimes on the dollar. This, in turn, allows you to convert equity gains into cash—without selling the asset. By exercising self-discipline to build savings, you can acquire a minimum of capital, allowing you to enter the real estate market.

It Provides Long-Term Appreciation

A great advantage of real estate investments is that the properties themselves increase in value over time. This happens for two reasons. First, inflation tends to drive up the replacement cost of housing. Second, as the population increases, so does the demand for ownership. Appreciation puts dollars in your pocket.

It's Stable

Compared to other investments, such as the stock market, real estate is stable. It tends to be both slow to rise and slow to fall, which means it's more predictable in terms of the investments you make. Over the past 30 years, real estate values have gone up or down by only 4 percent or so. During that same period of time, the stock market bounced up and down by nearly 17 percent in terms of daily risk. Clearly, real estate can be a solid part of any investment portfolio.

It Provides Tax Benefits

The government provides the real estate investor with three tax advantages: deductibility, depreciation, and deferability.

- As an investor, you can deduct for such routine expenses as maintenance, improvement, property upkeep, and even mortgage interest. These deductions offset your investment income and, in some cases, your personal income, reducing overall taxes in both instances.

- Tax laws also require you to depreciate your investments; that is, account for the "wear and tear" of a property by claiming an annual decline in the value of a building. This allows you to reduce taxable income through depreciation at the same time the property is most likely appreciating in value.

- The final tax advantage is deferability. By using IRAs and 1031 Exchanges to buy and sell investment real estate, taxes are deferred to a time when they will take a smaller bite out of your income. A good example is the use of your Individual Retirement Arrangement (IRA). You can invest your IRA money in real estate, and as long as the profits remain in your account, they're tax-deferred. You can also take advantage of the Tax-Deferred 1031 Exchange law. This tax law allows you to sell one property and buy another without incurring capital gains taxes. You simply have to reinvest all your profits into the next property (or properties) within a specific timeline.

All successful real estate investors use these tax benefits to build wealth.

It Allows You to Build Income and Wealth

Real estate makes use of the principle of synergy. In other words, the investments work together to create a whole greater than the sum of their parts. For example, if you have a rental property, this gives you monthly income. At the same time, that property is likely appreciating in value while you're paying down the mortgage. Over time (say, a 30-year mortgage), your mortgage payment stays the same, but the compounding of rental interest results in a greater and greater cash flow for you. Factor in depreciation, and your cash flow and return get even better. By the thirtieth year, the mortgage is paid off, your monthly expenses drop, and your cash flow really takes off. And that's just with one property! Imagine the further synergy you get when you invest in multiple properties (single-family homes, apartment buildings, etc.).

It Rewards Sweat Equity

Real estate is a physical asset made of wood, bricks, stucco, glass, and so on. Add some do-it-yourself improvements, or sweat equity, and increase a property's value. All you need is a little home-improvement knowledge, a few tools, and a lot of elbow grease. Sweat equity costs nothing but time.

You Can Live in Real Estate

You can buy a home, fix it up, live in it, and then rent it out when you move to a second home. That first home gives you a foundation for building wealth in the real estate market. Many real estate investors have begun their careers this way.

DISADVANTAGES OF REAL ESTATE INVESTMENT

It Requires Capital

No matter what self-styled gurus say in books and infomercials, no one gets into the real estate market without money. Investment can occur through the use of savings, Real Estate Investment Trusts (REITs), IRAs, and so on, but capital is required to start the process. In their early years, many successful real estate investors practiced that old-fashioned virtue: fiscal discipline. In other words, they scrimped and saved and poured every penny into their investments in order to reap the rewards later. They also learned everything they could about real estate and tax laws so they could maximize income and growth while minimizing costs.

Transaction Costs Can Reduce Your Returns

If you are not knowledgeable about real estate, profits can be greatly diminished by such costs as commissions, points, title insurance, closing costs, and other fees. Typically, the costs run around 15 percent of the transaction whether buying or selling. Analyze purchases or sales carefully to realize a good return on investment. Study the market and get practical experience in the buying and selling of properties.

It Ties Up Capital

For the most part, real estate investment is not a "quick in, quick out" kind of investment. Capital is tied up for a considerable amount of time. If you are impatient or need money quickly, real estate investment is not for you.

Returns May Vary

As stated earlier, real estate is a stable investment compared to the more volatile stock market. That, however, does not mean real estate prices remain the same. If you invest in poor areas of the market, you may find declining values rather than appreciating ones. You can avoid or minimize these fluctuations in two ways. First, analyze markets to choose desirable properties. Second, investing for the long haul will smooth out the bumps in the profit road, while you reap the reward of long-term appreciation.

Taxes Can Slash Profits (If You Are Unprepared)

Tax laws are favorable to real estate investment, but you must know how to apply them legally. Ignorance is expensive. Study the laws with care, and the state and federal government tax bites will be much smaller.

THE IMPORTANT QUESTION: IS REAL ESTATE INVESTING YOUR GAME?

Weighing the advantages and disadvantages of real estate investment can help you decide if it is the right market for you. Only you can decide that, of course, but here are some questions to consider:

Does the Prospect of Investing in Real Estate Truly Excite You?

Everybody wants great wealth, but few people are truly passionate about achieving it. The passionate ones are those who succeed. Initially excited at the prospect of learning everything they can about real estate, they continue learning because they know that great knowledge will reap great rewards. They are also committed, willing to overcome any obstacle using legal and moral means.

Are You Prepared to Sacrifice?

If you are new to real estate and have little money to invest, are you prepared to scrimp and save, forgoing niceties in order to put money into investments? In other words, are you prepared to sacrifice part of the present to achieve future success? If so, real estate is for you because you can take the necessary long view.

Do You Have the Personality and Time to Deal with People and Problems?

Real estate investment requires dealing successfully with people. It demands the ability to negotiate fairly and expertly with lenders, real estate agents, mortgage brokers, and so on. Professional investors often enjoy this process, seeing it as a wonderful game to play. If, however, you are averse to the time-consuming task of negotiating, it will cause you nothing but stress. If you own rental properties, there is the job of dealing with tenants. Are you prepared to handle leaky faucets, tenant complaints, vacancies, and many of the other problems associated with rentals? It calls for a combination of tact and toughness. Do you already have those qualities or are you prepared to develop them?

Consider the answers to these questions carefully. If you answer yes to all of these questions, then it's time to take the next step: getting financially healthy.

GET AND STAY FINANCIALLY HEALTHY!

Before you make any kind of investment, you need to check your financial pulse to make sure you are healthy and disciplined enough to tread the real estate path.

Check Your Credit Rating

One of the first things lenders will check is your credit rating. If it is good to excellent, chances of borrowing money are good. To find out your credit score, check with one of the three major credit reporting agencies. These companies act as a clearinghouse for lenders. They collect financial information and sell it to banks, credit card companies, mortgage companies, and other lending agencies. Lenders use that information to decide if an applicant is a good risk. The "big three" credit reporting agencies in the United States are the following:

Equifax Information Services LLC

P.O. Box 740256
Atlanta, GA 30374
800-685-1111
www.equifax.com

Experian

National Consumers Assistance Center
P.O. Box 2002
Allen, TX 75013
888-397-3742
www.experian.com

TransUnion Consumer Solutions
P.O. Box 2000
Chester, PA 19022-2000
800-916-8800
www.transunion.com

Eliminate Debt

The best way to raise your credit rating is to pay off credit cards and any other debt. So if you have considerable debt, pay it off before even considering any kind of real estate investment. If you have a not-so-great credit score and you would like to improve it, there are three steps to take. The first is to pay your bills on time—all the time. The second step is don't open unneeded credit card accounts to increase available credit. The third, and most important step, is to figure out where you stand financially by budgeting. In other words, reduce unnecessary expenditures so you can apply that saved money to your debt, improving your credit score. To do this, you must analyze your current financial situation. The first question to ask yourself is, How much debt is too much?

The easy way to answer that question is called the debt- to-income ratio, a simple method of measuring your net monthly income against your debt. For example, assume the following: Your net monthly income is $2,000. Your monthly debt payments are $500. Divide $500 by $2,000, and the result is your debt-to-income ratio:

$$500 \div 2000 = .25 \ (25\%)$$

Financial gurus generally agree that debt expenses should be 25 percent or less of your income. A ratio of 10 percent or less is even better. Anything above 25 percent is a red flag, signaling that you definitely need to reduce or eliminate debt.

So what is your debt-to-income ratio? Answer that question by doing the following:

- Look at last month's bills. Add all the fixed expense items (rent, mortgage, car payments, child support, loan payments, and so on).

- Check credit card bills, adding up the minimum payments owed on each card.

- Figure out your monthly take-home pay (net salary).

- Now divide monthly fixed expenses by monthly income.

What percentage did you get? If it is 25 percent or greater, it's time to take action to reduce your debt. You need to budget carefully so you can save money for your real estate investment. If it seems difficult, use a strategy often used by athletes and successful people in all walks of life called visualizing. Visualize your ultimate objective—a house needing renovation, a series of income-producing properties that will give you the freedom to travel or to be your own boss. Now visualize that goal every day. On a mirror, refrigerator, or other highly visible place, tape notes that read, "My budgeting will lead to a life of financial freedom" or "Short-term budgeting pain creates great financial gain," and so on. Repeating these positive assertions creates a change in thinking—one of optimism and a willingness to see big rewards.

Get Complete Insurance Coverage

The fastest way to derail your real estate investment career is to incur unexpected expenses—hospital bills, house fires, auto accidents, and so on. Insurance coverage is required in the following areas:

- **Auto.** Most states require insurance. Even if your state does not, make sure you have it. Liability coverage will prevent major financial loss if you are in an accident.

- **Disability.** For most, future earning power is the biggest asset we have. Protect that asset with disability insurance. It will protect a portion of employment earnings should you be incapacitated for a long time due to illness or injury.

- **Health.** Skyrocketing medical expenses can ruin your financial life if you or a member of your family should suffer a major illness or accident. Pay the money for major medical coverage; it is well worth the expense.

- **Homeowners.** This provides liability protection as well as protection against home-damaging events (fire, flood, hail, and so forth).

- **Life.** If you have a family or other loved ones who are dependent on you, buy term life insurance that provides a lump-sum death benefit. That benefit will replace your employment earnings in the event of your death.

- **Umbrella (excess liability).** This is a type of insurance that protects you against claims above and beyond the amount covered by your primary policies or for claims not currently covered.

Keep Your Current Job

At this point, you may be wondering whether you should plunge full time into real estate or take the more cautious approach and make it a part-time occupation while retaining your present job. Take the second approach. Think of the income from your current job as a form of leverage. That is, the more you save from your salary to invest in real estate, the sooner you will build wealth. As you accumulate properties, growth and income accelerate and, eventually, you will have the financial muscle to quit your current job and become a full-time real estate investor. If this option seems as if it will take too long, remember that you are teaching yourself discipline by cutting expenses and saving money to achieve your financial goals. This acquired discipline will serve you well in your real estate investment career. Research has shown that one of the universal characteristics of entrepreneurs is that they set a specific goal and then discipline themselves to achieve it. In other words, they sacrifice, save, and invest, always keeping their eyes on their ultimate objective. There are no shortcuts to wealth, only hard work, dedication, and a love of what they do. If that is the kind of attitude you have, keep reading. Apply your grit and determination to the study and understanding of the techniques covered in this book. Once you put these techniques into action, you will find the path to success easier, more rewarding, and less stressful.

1

INVESTING
WITH LITTLE MONEY

Have you seen the infomercials and books that proclaim you do not need any money to buy real estate? It is simply not true. As stated in the Introduction, it is possible to buy property for "dimes on the dollar," but some capital is required. Lenders must have reasonable assurance that they will get their money back as well as some interest. For that reason, lenders examine your credit rating and your ability to provide the necessary down payment.

YOUR CREDIT RATING

Two terms often heard are "credit rating" (or "credit score") and "FICO" score. A credit rating, or score, is the result of a complicated formula for rating credit worthiness. In 1955, two men named Fair and Isaac founded a company called the Fair Isaac Corporation, shortened to "FICO" over the years. The FICO formula is an objective way to predict how likely an applicant is to repay a new loan. The formula is based on experience with millions of consumers. A good credit score depends on the credit-scoring model and the lender. FICO models look at past delinquencies, derogatory payment behavior, current debt level, length of credit history, types of credit, and number of inquiries. The formula is based on:

- 35 percent on a borrower's payment history

- 30 percent on debt

- 15 percent on how long the applicant has had credit

- 10 percent on credit type

- 10 percent on the pattern of credit use

The higher the FICO score, the better the credit rating. A high credit score provides the best loan opportunities at the lowest rates. Here is an example of how lenders categorize a borrower in terms of risk:

- A borrower with a score of 680 and above will probably be qualified for an "A+" loan, meaning a lower rate of interest and the convenience of closing the loan within a few days.

- If the score is below 680 but above 620, lenders will probably take a closer look at the file in determining potential risks. In this range, a borrower may get "A" pricing, but the loan closing may take several days or weeks.

- If the score is below 620, the lender may still offer a loan but with a higher interest rate.

There are several different models for determining credit score. Depending on the credit-scoring model used, a score may range from 300 to 900.

As part of the rating process, lenders look carefully at an applicant's history of timely payments and other financial information. A solid record of on-time payments tells them the borrower can be counted on to repay the loan and interest. Red flags are missed payments, late payments, or unpaid debts. It is well worth your time to obtain your credit report and review it for errors. Omissions and errors do occur, adversely affecting your credit rating. Review the report carefully, particularly if you have a common name. Here are guidelines for reviewing the report:

- Search for anything that's out of date. This may include items like paid tax liens older than seven years, bankruptcies older than ten years, settled lawsuits, and so on.

- Identify misleading or incorrect information such as the following:

  — Incorrect name, address, or Social Security number

  — Incorrect account histories

  — Duplicate accounts

  — Taxes or liens listed as unpaid

An important point to remember is that you have the right to have mistakes corrected at no charge. If you do find mistakes and want them corrected, here are the options to use when correcting credit agency errors:

- Option 1: If the credit report has online instructions on how to correct errors, follow those instructions.

- Option 2: Call the credit-reporting agency and alert the company to the errors. If additional information is needed to correct the error, the credit-reporting agency will ask you to send proof (cancelled checks, etc.).

- Option 3: Explain the problem in a brief letter. By law in most states, the credit agency must respond within 30 days. If the credit bureau does not get back to you within 30 days, then the information must be removed.

If the credit-reporting agency does not find an error but you still believe the report is inaccurate, you will need to contact the creditor directly to resolve the dispute. You also have the right to explain your side of the story on the credit report (a brief 100-word summary). The shorter the statement, the more likely the credit bureau will include it in unedited form. Here are the guidelines to follow when contacting creditors:

- First, ask the creditor to remove the incorrect information and to contact the credit bureaus to delete the incorrect items. Write to the customer-service department, president, CEO, or someone at the company with the authority to take action on your complaint.

- If the information was reported by a collection agency, send the agency a copy of your letter as well.

- If a creditor is local, visit him or her personally. Be calm and firm while you explain the situation. Ask to see a manager, supervisor, CEO, or president. Do not leave until someone agrees to meet with you. You have a right to a meeting because this creditor has verified incorrect information, and it needs to be removed from your credit report. Prepare yourself for the meeting by knowing the general rules of the Fair Credit Reporting Act (FCRA). This act specifies rules for how and when creditors report information to credit bureaus. Creditors must:

  — Not report information they know is false.

  — Not ignore information they know contradicts what they have on file.

  — Refrain from reporting incorrect information when they learn that this information is, indeed, incorrect.

They also must:

  — Supply credit bureaus with the correct information when they learn that the information they have been supplying is incorrect.

  — Notify credit bureaus when information is disputed.

  — Record when accounts are "closed by the consumer."

  — Supply credit bureaus with the month and year of the delinquency of all accounts marked for collection, charged off, and so on.

  — Complete their investigation of the dispute within the 30- to 45-day period.

If you are concerned about mistakes slipping into your credit reports, visit the myFICO service on the Web at **www.myfico. com/tv/sweztv1.aspx**. For a monthly or yearly fee, myFICO monitors changes on your reports and alerts you to those changes.

OPTIONS FOR OBTAINING DOWN PAYMENT MONEY

So what if you have a great credit rating and little or no debt but still do not have sufficient money for a typical 20 percent down payment? There are several options to pursue.

Option 1: Save the Money

In these days of easy credit, it may seem a little old-fashioned to save the money necessary for a down payment on a property, but it is still the most satisfying method. Not only do you have the satisfaction of doing it on your own, but it also teaches the fiscal discipline necessary to be successful in the real estate market. In addition, it is low risk because you are not incurring debt in the process. You can increase your savings even more by cutting spending. Use budgeting to identify areas of discretionary spending that can be reduced or eliminated. Adopt an entrepreneurial mindset: *If it is not moving me toward my goal, I do not need it because I am willing to suffer short-term pain for long-term gain.*

Option 2: Increase Your Income

Education is the key to this option. Gain the knowledge needed to increase income through training that will advance your present career. At the same time, educate yourself in real estate. Earn a real estate license, home inspector license, or any other license that will deepen your understanding of the market.

Option 3: Tap Into Your Home Equity

Using home equity as a means of obtaining money for a down payment has one distinct advantage: You will most likely get a lower interest rate because lenders consider this a small risk. No one wants to lose the roof over their heads, so they will move heaven and earth to retain it, and lenders know this. If you choose this option, refinance the first loan (unless it is locked in at a lower rate than currently available). This releases the equity money and will usually be less expensive than a home equity loan or a line of credit. Some investors also use a strategy of renting out their first home. It works this way: After you have built substantial equity in your first home, buy another home. Refinance the first home and convert it into a rental. The tax-free proceeds from the refinance can be used as a down payment on the new home. This method provides income and increases equity at the same time. More than a few investors have started this way, continuing to buy homes until they have established enough "financial muscle" to move into such multiple-unit investment properties as apartments or such commercial properties as strip malls, grocery stores, and so on. As with any option (other than building savings), there are potential downsides. Be sure not to borrow more than the value of the home.

- Do not believe the hype about borrowing 120 to 125 percent of the home's value. It is easy to get in over your head with this kind of debt. Foreclosure is a real possibility if you cannot make your mortgage payments.

The more you borrow, the greater this possibility.

- Make sure the borrowing you do is tax deductible. Under current tax laws, the interest you pay on home mortgages (first and second homes) is tax deductible up to $1 million. You also can deduct home equity loan interest up to $100,000. However, if you refinance and borrow more than the outstanding amount on the previous loan, the deductibility of the interest on the excess amount borrowed is limited if it isn't used to buy, build, or improve your primary or secondary residence. To be more specific, you cannot deduct the interest on the extra amount borrowed that exceeds the $100,000 home equity limit.

Option 4: Individual Retirement Arrangement (IRA)

If you are a first-time home buyer, you can make penalty-free withdrawals of as much as $10,000 from IRA accounts — subject to eligibility requirements. Those requirements are set by your employer and have the condition that you repay the loan within a specified number of years. You still have to pay regular income tax rates on the withdrawn amount. Keep in mind that an IRA is a savings program for the future, and you are reducing those savings by withdrawing money.

Option 5: Scale Down

If you lack the capital for the property you want, try looking at lower-priced properties or properties that need work. With a little "sweat equity," you can buy a low-priced property and improve its value while having the satisfaction of working with your hands to make the home shine. If you are not handy or do not have the time to work on a house, consider a duplex. Live in one unit while you rent the other.

Option 6: Find a Partner

If you prefer to invest in higher-priced properties rather than lower-priced ones, consider finding a partner. This helps reduce risk and gives you greater borrowing power for down payments and capital improvements. The key is to find a partner who works well with you, so choose carefully. If personalities are not compatible, things can get quite stressful. On the other hand, when personalities do mesh, partnerships can form an exceptionally smooth business machine. Partnerships often work best when each partner specializes in areas that complement each other well.

Option 7: Use a Bank or Credit Union

More than likely, you already have a relationship with a local bank or credit union. These are good places to get mortgages because having a local relationship helps you build a solid financial reputation in the community. Nevertheless, shop around for the best rates and the best loan officers. Ask for referrals from lawyers, real estate agents, tax planners, and local businesspeople. Get as many different referrals as possible to get a 360-degree view of the lenders in your area. Be straightforward and ask two questions: "What do you like about this lender?" and "What don't you like?" That way, you have an idea of the positives and negatives of each lender before committing your real estate future to any one of them.

Option 8: Mortgage Brokers

Mortgage brokers are loan officers for wholesale lenders. Lenders offer a lower rate to the broker, and the broker then adds on his or her compensation before offering a loan to you.

The interest rate is usually comparable to what is charged by a mortgage banker.

Using brokers has three advantages:

1. Brokers know lenders well and can package deals with them to suit particular needs.

2. Brokers can repackage a loan if it is rejected and submit it to another lender.

3. Mortgage brokers attract a high number of the most qualified loan officers. However, this is not always true.

This leads to the disadvantages of using mortgage brokers:

1. Sometimes, loan officers are new and inexperienced and may not anticipate problems that an experienced officer would spot.

2. Mortgage brokers are weakly regulated or not regulated at all. Virtually anyone can become a broker. If you are not careful, you can end up with an incompetent person or, worse, a predatory one.

If you decide to use mortgage brokers, check them out carefully. Go to your state regulatory office to see if they have been blacklisted, fined, or otherwise censured for bad business practices. Also, follow the established rule: If a mortgage plan seems too good to be true, it most likely is.

K Kemper
K Kemper Realty
Phoenix, Arizona

It was a real estate course in college that gave me my start in real estate. When I first started investing, my biggest mistake was I did not walk through a four-plex. Instead, the agent performed dual agency and was to manage the property. I also learned that ROI is misunderstood. Hard money is a critically important commodity. Ninety-five percent of real estate agents have no clue how to guide investors.

If you're considering investing in real estate, you want to read everything you can about investing; find fixer-upper properties and foreclosures. You have to want to do hard-money lending.

I find my investment properties with the help of a seller's agent, and I prefer long-term investment properties. I also use a tax professional to handle the paying of taxes on rental properties.

One of the drawbacks of investing is everything takes three times longer than necessary. It also takes so many people to make the investment actually happen. However, there are also advantages, such as you have leverage and holding guarantees equity gain.

CHAPTER

TYPES OF MORTGAGES

Hundreds of types of mortgages are available today, but there are still only two major categories — fixed-rate loans and adjustable-rate loans.

FIXED-RATE MORTGAGES

A fixed-rate, fully amortizing loan usually has two distinct features. First, the interest rate remains fixed for the life of the loan. Second, the payments remain level for the life of the loan and so are structured to repay the loan at the end of the loan term. The most common fixed-rate loans are 15-year and 30-year mortgages. You may have noticed the term "amortization" used in conjunction with a fixed-rate loan. This simply means that the mortgage is gradually eliminated in regular payments over a specified period of time. During the early amortization period, a large percentage of the monthly payment is used for paying the interest. As the loan is paid down, more of the monthly payment is applied to the principal. Typically, a 30-year fixed-rate mortgage takes 22.5 years of level payments to pay half of the original loan amount. One advantage of a fixed-rate mortgage is just as the name suggests — the rate does not change, providing the security of knowing it will not increase and cost more. A second advantage is that it allows you to plan your finances carefully. Fixed-rate mortgages also have several disadvantages:

- **Refinancing costs.** If interest rates fall, you must refinance to take advantage of them. Refinancing may cost as much as a few thousand dollars in closing costs as well as another trip to the title company's office.

- **Too expensive.** In high-interest-rate environments, a fixed-rate mortgage can cost too much because there is no early-on payment and rate break. Also, if you plan to sell a property within five to ten years, you could be losing money by taking a locked-in interest rate.

- **Lack of flexibility.** Fixed-rate mortgages are virtually the same from lender to lender, limiting creative financing options. Adjustable-rate mortgages, on the other hand, can be customized to meet individual needs.

- **Acceleration clauses (also in ARM mortgages).** If you miss a monthly payment, this clause allows the lender to speed up the rate at which your loan comes due or even to demand immediate payment of the entire outstanding loan balance.

Be sure to compare rates among lenders. This is important, not only for the fixed rate, but also because lenders charge "points," which can vary. Points are an upfront fee that covers various expenses for a lender—salaries, building lease, employee benefits, unexpected expenses, and so on. They are most often a percentage of the amount you borrow. For example, if you borrow $300,000 and the points are 1.5, this equals 1.5 percent of the total. This means a $4,500 upfront interest payment. Points can add quite a bit to the cost of borrowing money. This is especially true if you do not plan to keep the loan for a long period of time. In general, the more points paid on a loan, the lower the interest rate the lender charges on the loan. How you deal with points depends upon your financial situation and your ultimate investment goals. The first option is to keep points to a minimum. Choose this option if you lack sufficient cash to close on a mortgage or if you don't plan to hold the property or the loan for long. The second option is to "buy down the loan rate," which means paying more points. Use this option if you want to keep your ongoing costs low, plan to hold the property for a long time, or if you are not cash-strapped to close on the loan right away. This option lowers the overall costs of borrowing while increasing the property's cash flow and equity buildup.

To make fair and accurate comparisons, ask lenders for interest rate quotes at the same point level.

ADJUSTABLE-RATE MORTGAGES (ARMS)

The interest rate on this type of mortgage varies over time although with a cap. A "cap" simply means that the interest rate can fluctuate only so far either up or down. For example, an ARM that starts out at, say, 4.75 percent can decrease by a percent or two or it can increase to as high as 11.75 percent, depending on market conditions. Never buy an ARM without a cap. Otherwise, a predatory lender can charge you any amount of interest. ARMs have several advantages:

- Early in the loan term, they have lower rates and payments, allowing you to make a lower down payment and to buy a larger property than with a fixed-rate mortgage.

- You can take advantage of falling interest rates without refinancing. Instead of having to pay a whole new set of closing costs and fees, you can sit back and watch your rates fall, which, of course, saves money.

- You can save and invest more money. For example, if you have a payment that is $100 less with an ARM than with a fixed-rate mortgage, you can invest that money in a higher-yielding instrument.

- If you do not plan to keep or live in your property for a long time, ARMs are a less expensive way to buy that property.

This type of mortgage also has disadvantages:

- They can cost you significantly more than fixed-rate mortgages because rates and payments can rise dramatically over the life of the loan. If rates rise, a 5 percent ARM can end up at 10 percent in just three years.

- ARMs have initial fixed rates that are set artificially low ("teaser rates"). The initial low rate will adjust to a level higher than the going fixed-rate level in almost every case.

- The first rate adjustment can be an unpleasant surprise because some annual caps don't apply to the initial change. For example, if you had an annual cap of 2 percent and a lifetime cap of 6 percent, theoretically you could see the rate shoot from 6 percent to 12 percent twelve months after closing.

- ARMs are more difficult to understand than fixed-rate mortgages. Lenders can be much more flexible when determining margins, caps, adjustment indexes, and other factors.

- Certain ARMs called are "negative amortization" loans, in which you can end up owing more money at the end of the term than you did at closing. How can this happen? The payments on these loans are set so low (to make the loans more affordable) that they only cover part of the interest due. The interest expense not covered by the mortgage payment is added your loan balance. **Avoid this type of loan.**

Before deciding on a mortgage, consider these questions:

- **How long do you plan to keep or stay in the property?** If you plan to keep or live in the property for only a few years, it makes sense to take the lower-rate ARM, especially if current rates are reasonable. Your payment and rate will be low, allowing you to build more savings for a larger property in the future. In addition, you will never be exposed to huge rate adjustments because you will be out before the adjustable rate period begins.

- **How often does the ARM adjust, and when is the adjustment made?** After the initial fixed period, most

ARMs adjust every year on the anniversary of the mortgage. The new rate is actually set about 45 days before the anniversary, based on the specified index. Some, however, adjust as frequently as every month. If that is too volatile for you, then you should go with a fixed-rate mortgage.

- **What is the current interest rate environment?** If rates are relatively high, ARMs make sense because their lower initial rates allow you to get the benefits of property ownership. Also, chances are good that rates will fall, meaning that you will have a chance of lower payments even if you do not refinance. When rates are relatively low, however, a fixed-rate mortgage makes more sense. For example, if the current rate is 6 or 7 percent, those are great rates at which to borrow money for 30 years!

- **Could you still afford your monthly payment if interest rates rise significantly?** Assume you qualify for a $150,000, one-year adjustable-rate mortgage at 5.75 percent with 2/6 caps. It is possible that your 5.75 percent ARM could end up at 11.75 percent. You would have to provide the cash to cover the increase.

Remember the definition of an adjustable-rate mortgage: it is a mortgage with an interest rate linked to an economic index. The interest rate — and your payment — is periodically adjusted up or down as the index fluctuates. When you talk to a lender, he or she will use the following terms:

- **Index** — An index is what the lender uses to measure interest-rate changes. Common indexes used by lenders

include one-, three-, and five-year Treasury securities
(Treasury bills, Treasury notes, and so on), but there
are many others (Certificates of Deposit or CDs, 11th
District Costs of Funds or COFI, among others). Every
ARM is linked to a specific index. Some indexes
respond quickly to market changes (those tied to CDs)
while others are slow moving. An index tied to CDs
has higher risk because rates can increase rapidly in
a short term, but lenders may offer a break by setting
lower caps. The COFI index is an example of an index
that lags behind general market interest-rate changes.
In other words, it continues rising after interest rates
reach their peak and falls more slowly after rates drop.
Thus, a COFI-type index provides greater security, but
you pay for that security with a higher start rate, caps,
margin, or points.

- **Margin** — The margin is the lender's markup. It is an
  interest rate that represents the lender's cost of doing
  business plus the profit they will make on the loan. The
  margin is added to the index rate to determine the total
  interest rate, which usually stays the same for the life of
  the loan.

- **Adjustment period** — The adjustment period is the
  period between rate adjustments.

In simplest terms, the formula works this way: For the first year
only, the lender uses a teaser rate to get you in the door. In the
second year, he starts tying the rate to a publicly known index
such as Treasury bills or the 11th District Cost of Funds Index.
To that, he adds his margin, perhaps 2.75 percent, to arrive
at your ARM rate for the new adjustment period. That rate,

however, is capped at the 2 percent maximum per year. Overall caps have been required by law since 1987.

An interest-rate cap places a limit on the amount the interest rate can increase, but interest caps come in two versions:

1. **Periodic caps,** which limit the interest-rate increase from one adjustment period to the next, and

2. **Overall caps,** which limit the interest-rate increase over the life of the loan.

Nearly all ARMs are required by law to have an overall cap. Avoid any lender offering ARMs without a cap. Many lenders also have a periodic cap. To follow is an example of how a period cap works: Assume you have an ARM with a periodic interest-rate cap of 2 percent. At the first adjustment, the index rate goes up 3 percent. The example shows what happens. The first year the interest rate is 10 percent, and the monthly payment is $570.42. The second year the interest rate is 13 percent without a cap, and the monthly payment is $717.12. But if there is a cap in the second year, then the interest rate is 12 percent and the monthly payment is $667.30. With a periodic cap, you have a savings of $49.82 per month.

PERIOD CAP EXAMPLE

Monthly Payment 1st year@ 10% =	$570.42
2nd year @ 13% (*without* cap) =	$717.12
2nd year @ 12% (*with* cap) =	$667.30
Difference =	$49.82 per month

LENGTH OF MORTGAGE

Generally speaking, mortgages are considered short-term (15 years) or long-term (30 years). Twenty- and forty-year options are sometimes offered. So which should you choose, short-term or long-term? Thirty-year mortgages are easier on the wallet because the monthly payments are lower than with 15-year options. Although you can pay the 15-year mortgage off more quickly, the higher payments can be a burden if your financial situation worsens or if your property declines in value. Also, the money saved by not taking on a 15-year mortgage can be invested in instruments with higher rates of return like stocks or bonds. One great advantage of a 30-year mortgage is that you can pay it off faster by making larger payments as you have the money to do so. In effect, you turn a long-term mortgage into a short-term one without all the negatives. Avoid mortgages with prepayment penalties (a penalty for paying off the loan ahead of time). Usually, these penalties do not apply if you sell the property, but when you refinance a loan with prepayment penalties, you do have to pay the penalty. Ask the lender if there is a prepayment penalty and, if so, how long it lasts (usually one to five years).

OTHER FEES

There are certain common fees associated with the mortgage process. It pays to know what these fees are before entering into any agreement because they can add up quickly. Make sure the lender discloses exactly what fees will be charged. Below is a description of common fees:

- **Discount points** are different from loan origination points. Discount points represent additional money paid to the lender at closing. The more points paid, the lower the interest rate. Usually, for each point paid for a 30-year loan, the interest rate is reduced by about one-eighth (or .125) of a percentage point. Discount points are a good idea if you plan to keep or live in a property for more than five years.

- **The application fee** covers the lender's cost to process the information on your loan. Usually, it is in the $200 to $300 range. You pay this charge when you file the application. Some lenders may apply the cost of the application fee to certain closing costs. Generally, there is no refund from lenders if you are not approved for the loan or if you decide not to take it.

- **The appraisal fee** pays for an independent appraisal of the home you want to buy. Fees vary depending on the price of the home. Typically, they can range from $150 to $1,000 or more for larger investment properties. The lender requires this estimate because they need to know the market value of the house for purposes of determining the size of the loan. Factors to be considered in determining market value include present cash value, use, location, replacement value of improvements, condition, income from property, net proceeds if the property is sold, and so on. After the appraisal is completed, the borrower is entitled to a copy of the appraisal from the lender.

- **The environmental assessment** applies to residential properties with five or more units and to commercial properties. It determines "recognized environmental conditions." In plain English, this means an engineering company looks for hazardous substances or pollutants (petroleum products, for instance) that may pose a threat to the environment. The company visually inspects the site, does a comprehensive photographic log, interviews owners or managers of adjacent properties, and reviews all property records. It then provides its findings in a comprehensive written report. The cost of this report is related to the location, type, size, and previous use of the property and can range from $300 to many thousands of dollars.

- **Credit report fee.** Three major national credit bureaus (Equifax, TransUnion, and Experian) supply lenders with the information on your credit behavior. Lenders may charge around $50 for this service. As stated earlier, you should have a copy of the report and have reviewed it so you are aware of what is included. Currently, you can get a joint report from all three agencies for around $35.

- **The title search** is a detailed examination of the historical records concerning a property. Such records include deeds, court records, property and name indexes, and many other documents. The purpose of the search is to make sure the buyer is purchasing a house from the legal owner and there are no liens, overdue special assessments, or other claims or outstanding restrictive covenants filed in the record, which would adversely affect the marketability or value of the title. A title search can show a number of title defects. Among these are unpaid taxes, unsatisfied mortgages, and judgments against the seller.

- **A certificate of title** is issued by the title company that did the title search.

- **Title insurance** protects against any tax liens, unpaid mortgages, or judgments missed in the research of the history of the title on the property. If a claim is made against your property, title insurance will, in accordance with the terms of your policy, assure you of a legal defense and pay all court costs and related fees. Also, if the claim proves valid, you will be reimbursed for your actual loss up to the face amount of the policy. There are two different types of policies: a lender's policy and an owner's policy. The lender's policy protects the lender's interest in the property as security for the outstanding balance under your mortgage. The owner's policy safeguards your investment or equity in the property up to the face amount of the policy. The cost of the policy is usually based on the loan amount. Although, only a lender's title insurance policy is required, but you should make sure you get the protection of title insurance by purchasing a buyer's title policy. The cost is a one-time premium, and the least expensive rate is offered by the company doing the title search.

- **Survey fee.** The title insurance company or lender may require a survey of the property. This is to verify official boundaries of the property and to ensure that your lot has not been encroached upon by any structures. Cost depends on the size of the property and the state in which you live.

- **Escrow account.** Most lenders require you to pay for some items that are due after closing. These prepaid items usually include insurance premiums for homeowners' insurance, private mortgage insurance, and real estate taxes.

- **Flood certification.** Depending on the state and location, some homes require flood certification fees. The certification verifies that the property is not in a flood zone. If the property is located within a defined flood zone, then the lender will require a flood insurance policy.

- **Recording and transfer charges.** A small fee (from $50 to $150) is charged to cover the cost of the paperwork required to record the property purchase.

- **Documentary stamp tax** on the mortgage varies from state to state and usually amounts to about 35 cents per $100 borrowed.

- **Interim interest** is the interest accrued from the closing date until the end of the month.

- **Lender's and buyer's attorney fee.** This fee (from $500 to $1,500) is used to pay for preparing and reviewing all of the documents needed to close your loan.

Usually the application fee, credit report fee, and appraisal fee will have to be paid when you submit the mortgage application.

MORTGAGES TO AVOID

Two mortgages to avoid are balloon mortgages and interest-only mortgages. Each has benefits, but each also has potentially dangerous disadvantages.

Balloon Loans

A balloon loan offers a lower fixed-interest rate for a set number of years (usually in the three- to ten-year range), followed by a longer-term mortgage. For example, you have level payments on a long-term schedule for 15 or 30 years, but within that initial three- to ten-year period, the remaining balance comes due, requiring you to refinance. Serious danger can occur at this point. If your income drops because of illness or loss of a job, you could end up losing your home. Another possibility is that your property value drops, and the appraisal shows you do not qualify for the new loan. A third possibility is that interest rates will rise and you cannot qualify for those higher rates. A balloon loan is acceptable in the following circumstances:

- You have a windfall coming and that money will cover the mortgage.

- You are absolutely certain you can refinance when that balloon payment comes due.

- You plan to move within the three- to ten-year period.

If you absolutely have to get a balloon mortgage, obtain one for as long a period as possible (seven to ten years) to give yourself time to save the money necessary to cover the balance.

Interest-Only Mortgages

The concept of interest-only mortgages is simple: The first mortgage payments are used to pay only the interest that is owed, which keeps your payments lower because no money is repaying the principal. Unfortunately, this also means that you are not paying down the loan balance. In addition, after a set period of time (seven to ten years), that mortgage payment leaps upward. To use a simple example, it may jump from $600 (interest-only) to $773 (fully amortized), a 29 percent increase. Avoid this kind of mortgage even if it means you have to stay out of real estate for a while. If you have heard that real estate investors take risks, you are only half right. They take risks, but they take intelligent ones. Interest-only mortgages are not a smart risk, especially if you are just getting started in the market.

Linda Rike
Linda Rike Real Estate
1410 Arendell Street
Morehead City, NC 28557
Phone: 800-240-6922
Local: 247-6922
www.lindarike.com

In 1985, after having sold a couple of personal residences and having received less-than-satisfactory service, I decided to get into the real estate business. I knew I could do a better job than those real estate agents had done for me.

The biggest mistake I made when I was just starting out was not buying more rental properties sooner. However, I also learned the importance of following up; of having systems in place; and of getting advanced designations, such as ABR, CRS, GRI, etc. It's also just as important to continue getting advanced designations.

I always look for good buys in neighborhoods that are increasing in value. One measure I use is if the same amount of money was deposited in the bank, would the return be greater from the rent? I prefer long-term investments, and I currently have several properties. One is right across the street from my office; it was in terrible shape when I bought it, so I completely renovated it. The second property is a furnished, older home, close to my own home, and the price was right. The third property is a two-bedroom townhouse in excellent condition near the sports center.

There are several ways you, as an investor, can tell if you've made a good investment:

1. You can sleep at night.

2. You can ride by and look at the property once in a while.

3. You get use and enjoyment from the property.

4. You don't have to feed it too much. For example, there's not too much negative cash flow.

While there aren't many drawbacks to real estate investing, you must keep in mind that when a rental property is empty, you must be prepared to cover the payment out of pocket. You'll also be responsible for any needed repairs.

Among the many advantages of real estate investing are constant appreciation; and investors enjoy tax advantages including 1031 Exchanges when selling. On properties with mortgages, the renters make the payments for you, and repairs are tax deductible. You can refinance properties, and you can take out equity for various needs, such as college tuition, medical emergencies, travel, and renovations.

INVESTING IN RESIDENTIAL
AND COMMERCIAL
PROPERTIES

R eal estate investments are either residential or commercial/industrial. Many investors start with residential properties because it is a market that is easier to understand and to enter. It also provides appreciation, stability, and the opportunity to build net worth. This, in turn, can give investors the financial muscle to move into multi-family properties like apartments. Apartment properties generate multiple streams of income and build cash flow. Keep in mind that the single-family and multi-family markets tend to operate in opposite directions. That is, when housing is affordable, rents tend to fall and vacancies increase. When housing is expensive, however, then people choose apartments and rents rise.

SINGLE-FAMILY RESIDENTIAL INVESTMENTS

Generally speaking, there are four types of single-family investments available: the traditional single-family home, condominiums, town homes, and cooperatives. Not all of these may be available in your area, but you should be aware of the advantages and disadvantages of each as part of your overall market knowledge.

Single-Family Homes

Many investors start by buying single-family homes for good reason. The purchase process is not as complicated as buying such commercial properties as retail or office space or industrial properties. Prices tend to rise over time, increasing the property's appreciation. In terms of demand, this market is reliable.

Condominiums

Usually, condominiums are apartment-style units. In fact, many times, they are actually converted apartments. When you buy a condo, you buy not only a specific unit but also a share of such common areas as the pool, laundry room, recreation facilities, and so on.

Town Homes

Town homes can be considered attached or row houses. Often, the owners have to meet requirements regarding exterior paint colors, parking, pets, and gardens.

Cooperatives

Cooperatives are similar to both apartments and condominiums.

The difference is that when you buy a share in a cooperative, you own a share of the entire building. Generally speaking, you must obtain approval from the cooperative association if you want to remodel or rent your unit. Also, in some co-ops, you must get approval from the association to sell your unit to a buyer. It is generally more difficult to get a loan for a co-op unit than for other single-family housing.

Town homes, condos, and co-ops are called "shared housing," and they offer the following advantages:

- Because an owner is not buying land, shared housing offers the most living space for the dollar.

- Individual owners are not responsible for general maintenance. The building's association is responsible for maintenance and repairs.

- Owners may feel more secure, knowing that neighbors are only a wall's width away.

- Owners have access to recreational facilities like swimming pools, exercise rooms, and tennis courts.

- In terms of investments, condos have the lowest maintenance costs because the condominium association arranges and negotiates fees for such matters as roofing and landscaping. Often, an association is able to get lower prices because of its ability to make quantity purchases.

Of course, shared housing has its disadvantages as well:

- Shared housing seldom appreciates as well as single-family homes.

- There is a smaller pool of potential buyers because most prefer a stand-alone home.

- A greater supply of this type of housing exists, meaning that prices tend to stay depressed.

- Some shared housing associations have tough restrictions, and many forbid rentals. Carefully review the governing documents before you buy the property.

MULTI-FAMILY RESIDENTIAL INVESTMENTS

If you have sufficient money saved or available, apartment buildings are a good investment because they generate cash flow even in the early years (even though that early flow is small). As time goes on, that cash flow gets better because the mortgage expense stays fixed while your rents increase faster than your expenses. A multi-family dwelling also has a great advantage over owning, say, five different single-family homes. It's much simpler to manage and maintain one building than several separate ones. A multi-family property also tends to have greater dollar amounts of appreciation simply because they cost more in the first place. A single-family home worth $200,000 appreciating at 10 percent generates $20,000 worth of appreciation. A multi-family dwelling worth $750,000 will generate $75,000 worth of appreciation. That's $55,000 more in your pocket. With apartment buildings, you can also generate extra cash through such amenities and services as coin-operated laundries, pet fees, storage, parking, and lawn care. It is highly recommended to have the tenants take care of their own utilities. The downside of owning an apartment building is management and upkeep of the property. If you plan to manage it yourself, be prepared to deal with tenant concerns, to handle the bookkeeping and paperwork, to take care of maintenance and repairs, and, in general, handle the many details that come with a larger property. Most investors hire a property manager as soon as possible. Also, if you are a serious investor, concentrate on the investment side, not the daily management and maintenance, which does not make you money.

RECOMMENDATIONS ON RESIDENTIAL PROPERTIES

Choose detached single-family homes or an apartment building or a mix of both, if you can afford it. Shared housing tends to be overbuilt in areas where there is undeveloped land, depressing prices. If you do buy shared housing, make sure it is in fully developed urban environments.

If you choose single-family homes, how can you make the most of your investment? First, look for soundly built homes that require inexpensive cosmetic changes, such as the following:

- Fresh paint

- Upgraded landscaping

- Replacement of garage doors

- Upgraded kitchens

These kinds of changes cost relatively little money while increasing the curb appeal and overall value of the home, allowing you to raise the rent.

If you are considering an apartment building and are just beginning in the market, try for smaller buildings with four or fewer units. These are considered residential properties and will qualify for more favorable mortgage terms. A rental property with five or more units is considered a commercial property and will require a more expensive commercial mortgage.

COMMERCIAL PROPERTIES

Commercial real estate includes office, retail, and industrial properties. This market includes malls, grocery stores, office buildings, self-storage, retail space, and so on. If its purpose is for business, it's a commercial property. Investing in these properties is complicated and requires a great deal of knowledge of markets, tax laws, and the like and, thus, is a much greater risk than buying a residential property. Knowledge is definitely power in the commercial market.

- Know the area in which you want to invest. Check out supply and demand. Know how much total space is available for rent. Determine the price per square foot. Find out vacancy rates and the rate of change in those rates over time.

- Understand the concept of **absorption**. You want positive absorption; that is, a situation in which the demand for space is greater than the supply. Avoid negative absorption, the situation in which the supply of space is too great, which leads to vacancies, falling rent rates, and disappointing investment returns.

The more you know, the better position you will be in to make good commercial real estate investments. If you feel you are ready to tackle this market, the key is location. Look for a prime location surrounded by successful businesses. Typically, these locations have good foot traffic and are next to banks and supermarkets and the like. It also helps if they are located near affluent suburbs. Retail shops, shopping centers, and the like are often good choices.

UNDEVELOPED LAND

Why buy undeveloped land? Well, it has several advantages. You do not have to deal with tenants or handle property maintenance. You can also make a good return on your investment if you buy in the path of progress. In other words, identify an area into which a community will expand. If you buy wisely, the price of the land you bought will increase or even soar if a major company decides to build on your property. The downside of buying undeveloped land is if you are wrong, you have property earning nothing for a long time. Meanwhile, you still have to pay property taxes and liability insurance as well as keep the land looking neat and attractive. Taxes and insurance create a cash drain of money that could be invested elsewhere. Another disadvantage is that lenders see buying undeveloped land as a speculative investment, so they require higher down payments (generally in the 30 to 40 percent range) and charge higher fees and interest rates.

A final disadvantage is that raw land has no tax depreciation write-offs. If you are an experienced investor, follow the same rules as with other real estate investments: First, know your market. Do extensive research. Take your time and find areas that are attracting solid companies and have a shortage of housing as well as land for development. Second, total your expenses, called **annual carrying costs** (property taxes, etc.), before you buy. You definitely want to know how much cash will be flowing out of your pocket on a yearly basis to make sure you can afford the purchase. Third, if you plan to develop the land, figure out what improvements the land may need. Typically, these include building roads, running utility, sewer and water lines, and landscaping. Never underestimate these costs. Fourth, make sure you have ingress and egress to the land by checking with the appropriate local authority. Ingress/egress simply means that you have the easements that allow access to your property. If you have do not have these rights, your investment is wasted. Fifth, be sure to understand the environmental and zoning laws regarding the property.

To use a simple example, if you buy land for purposes attracting a commercial or industrial business and then find out it is zoned only for residential use, you could lose significant value. To avoid this kind of surprise, research the local planning departments and take the pulse of the community in which you are planning to buy land. Is it anti-development or pro-development? Are there environmental issues roiling the development waters? If so, proceed carefully to avoid being tangled up in endless litigation over use of the land.

REAL ESTATE INVESTMENT TRUSTS

If you want to avoid the headaches of owning rental property, then consider a Real Estate Investment Trust, or REIT. REITs are for-profit companies established by Congress in 1960 to give small investors the opportunity to invest in large, income-producing properties. The stocks of most public REITs are available on major stock exchanges. REITs present investors with an efficient method of investing in real estate; each shareholder earns a pro-rata percent of the REIT profits. REITs own and operate such income-producing real estate property as shopping centers, apartments, offices, warehouses, hotels, and other rental buildings. The companies that hold such properties are known as equity REITs. The companies that concentrate on the financing end of the business are known as mortgage REITs. They lend to real estate property owners and operators, or they provide indirect credit through buying loans (mortgage-backed securities such as Government National Mortgage Association instruments, or Ginnie Maes). In addition to other criteria, to qualify as a public REIT, the company must:

- Pay at least 90 percent of its taxable income to its shareholders every year.

- Have at least 100 shareholders.

- Invest at least 75 percent of its total assets in real estate.

- Derive at least 75 percent of its income from rent or mortgage interest from properties in its portfolio.

There are also private REITs that do not have to meet the strict Securities and Exchange Commission's criteria listed above. Research these carefully. Because these companies do not have the same disclosure rules as the public REITs, the company can make changes that adversely affect your returns while rewarding its sponsors or affiliates.

So what kind of returns have REITs provided their shareholders? According to the National Association of Real Estate Trusts (NAREIT) all REITs had provided an average

10.68 percent return over the past 20 years as of 2005 (**www.nareit.com/nareitindexes/web3.htm**). This is comparable to the stock market in general without the volatility. REITs diversify so their values do not always move up and down with other investments. Another benefit to such trusts is that they generally pay good dividends. Note, however, that these dividends are fully taxable, so avoid holding REITs outside your retirement account if you are still in your working years. An additional benefit is that you can sell your REIT investment as easily as other securities, furnishing considerably more liquidity than actual land or property ownership.

To buy REITs, you can purchase shares in individual companies or you can invest in a mutual fund that invests in a diversified mixture of these trusts. This latter strategy reduces risk and provides easy investment through your retirement account (IRA, Keogh, etc.). You can also use borrowed money (in non-retirement accounts) to buy REITs on margin (paying 50 percent down). Professionally managed mutual funds also provide consolidated financial reports so you can keep tabs on fund performances.

If you are set on becoming a professional investor and want to select your own stocks, use such publications as *Morning Star* (**www.morningstar.com**), *Value Line* (**www.valueline.com**), or financial magazines like *Forbes* (**www.forbes.com**).

Mary Martinson
439 Congaree Road
Greenville, SC 29607
864-380-6488
www.marymartinson.com

Real estate investing has always been an interest of mine. It's important for those interested in investing that they just start; don't delay. When I first began investing, I learned quickly that buying in the wrong location can be costly. However, I also realized that it was best to start by buying small houses worth $50,000 or less, and to do good research of comps. I prefer long-term investment properties.

Real estate investors all have their own investment strategies that work best for them. Those that I've found that work best for me include:

1. Always be realistic about the profit you are going to make. Some people wait to find a house that will make them $30,000 but pass up the chance on a house that could have made them $10,000.

2. If you see a bargain, jump on it, or someone else will.

3. Don't put too much money in the house and price yourself out of that area's market.

4. Buy in areas where they are having road expansions, which indicates growth is coming.

Because I'm a Realtor, I find investment properties on my own. If you're not a Realtor, find one with whom you work well. Sign

a client agreement with a Realtor, and the realtor will be fully dedicated to you. Realtors have access to all the homes that other Realtors have access to, and they have connections with other investors.

You'll also have to pay taxes on rental properties; I use a tax professional.

Keep in mind that sometimes it takes time to find the right house. However, if you do it right, you cannot lose. It's not risky like investing in stocks and bonds.

CHAPTER

4

FLIPPING

"Flipping" is the strategy of buying property, fixing it up, waiting for a few months, and then selling it for a quick profit. Essentially, it is a speculative strategy in which you bet that the market value will rise to the point where you can make a fast profit before you close on the deal. Flipping works best in areas where the demand for housing is great, resulting in a limited supply and rapidly rising prices. As with any investment strategy, there are advantages and disadvantages. The main advantage of flipping is investing little money for great gains. For instance, assume you put down 5 percent ($12,500) on a $250,000 home. You then spend $5,000 and two months fixing up the house, and another $3,500 in payments. Your cash investment totals $21,000. If you sell the home for an $80,000 profit, then the return on your investment of $21,000 for two months exceeds most other types of investments. You've made $59,000 within sixty days!

You can also use flipping to supplement your income or, if you find that you enjoy the strategy, make it a full-time job. Be aware of the disadvantages of flipping. If too many speculators get into the market, prices can drop quickly, leaving you with the property, which you may have to rent until the market rebounds. Another possible disadvantage is that interest rates rise, dampening the demand for housing. A third disadvantage is hidden property problems. If you do not inspect a property carefully, faulty plumbing, roofing problems, or other structural damage can reduce or eliminate expected profits. To follow are some guidelines to help you navigate successfully the waters of this speculative adventure.

COMMON-SENSE FLIPPING GUIDELINES

The following guidelines work well not only for flipping but also for any area of the real estate market.

Guideline #1: Know the Markets

Knowing the markets means physically studying the neighborhoods. Drive them yourself or with a Realtor. Find out what kinds of homes are selling well. Learn the comparable worth of homes. Know the property taxes, the crime rates, the quality of school systems, and so on.

Guideline #2: Prepare and Plan

Think ahead before you enter the market. Establish goals for turn-around time and profit. Evaluate how much work a property needs to make it a great market value.

Guideline #3: Form a Team

Few people have expertise in every aspect of the real estate market. That is why they need support teams to help them evaluate properties, handle taxes, and the like. Members of your team may include a Realtor, a property inspector, contractors, a tax accountant, an attorney, and others. Be sure to evaluate their expertise and reputation before including them in your team. You want the best and most reliable advice possible.

Guideline #4: Expect Problems

Problems will occur with properties, so be prepared. A foundation can crumble or interest rates can shoot up unexpectedly. The house may not sell or may go into foreclosure. You need a financial cushion to deal with these potential problems. A good rule of thumb: If you cannot handle the financial risks, do not flip.

Guideline #5: Think Long-Term

Over the long-term, real estate performs well. If you find you cannot sell a property, live in it or rent it out. These options may not be profitable in the short-term, but they may be a good investment over time.

TYPES OF FLIPPERS

If you want to be a "flipper," be aware that there are several different types, and each type has different goals in mind.

Scouts

Scouts gather information. Their goal is to find potential deals and then sell information to other investors. Fees vary, depending upon the property price and its profit potential. A scout may make from $250 to $1,000 on each lead that results in a purchase by another investor. Why become a scout? It's a great way to get started in this market because it does not require any cash or any previous knowledge to look at properties. It is also the fastest way to earn cash. The disadvantage of being a scout is that the money you earn per transaction is the least in the market. The main requirements for becoming a scout are time and motivation. Here are some search techniques:

- Post flyers at grocery stores, laundromats, or other locations with lots of foot traffic and high visibility.

- Check the newspaper for such ads as "Handyman Special," "Fixer Upper," and so on.

- Advertise in the local newspapers and online. Run an ad in the "Real Estate Wanted" section of the newspaper.

- Drive around and note houses in disrepair.

- Get a job as a property inspector. An inspector evaluates homes that are going into foreclosure. Inspectors are paid by the bank and possibly again by the investor. This is a good way to get to know the market and the properties that are available.

- Know your investor's goals and do your best to meet them. His or her goals will determine your strategy in locating deals.

Dealers

Like scouts, dealers also find properties for other investors, but they go beyond just providing information. When a dealer locates a bargain property, he or she signs a purchase contract with the owner. The dealer then has two options: Close on the property and sell it outright or simply sell the contract to another investor. Dealers are essentially controlling the property with a binding purchase contract. On a full-time basis, a dealer may make more than $15,000 a month—all without ever improving the property or dealing with tenants. Even on part-time basis, dealers can make $2,000 to $3,000 a month by flipping one or two properties. Working as a dealer has several advantages: You have greater profit potential because you can flip as many deals as you can find. You also have negotiation power and better potential margins. In addition, of course, it is an entrepreneurial lifestyle. If you enjoy the freedom of working for yourself, then being a dealer can be a good life.

Retailers

The goal of retailers is to fix up properties so they can sell them for full retail price to an owner or occupant. Retailers buy properties with the aid of scouts, dealers, or real estate agents. Retailers tend to make the largest profits, but they also put up the most money and take greater risks. It may also take months to realize profits.

THE FLIPPING PROCESS

The process of finding properties to flip may vary from region to region, but in general you will need to accomplish the following objectives:

- Have a clear goal. Determine the market in which you want to concentrate. Decide what kind of "flipper" you would like to be—a scout, a dealer, or a retailer.

- Put your real estate investment team together.

  - Investors or buyers

  - Title company to close contract

  - A lawyer

  - Contractors

- Identify investors and then seek the properties they want to buy. Do your research:

  - Read newspaper ads.

  - Attend REI (Real Estate Investment) club meetings.

  - Attend foreclosure auctions, tax sales, trustee sales.

  - Tour neighborhoods.

  - Look within a 10- to 20-mile radius of your home.

  - Seek out vacant houses, houses in need of repair, and houses with at least 50 percent equity.

  - Learn the details of houses (square footage and so on).

  - Contact owners, talk with neighbors.

  - Check sources (county court house, tax office, and other municipal offices) for code violations, divorce, probate, evictions, bankruptcy, criminal act, out-of-state owner, and liens or judgments for possible leads.

- Keep track of all opportunities through telephone logs, tracking software, and so on.

- Network—ask other investors.

- Understand the appropriate agreements and contracts.

- A contract provides written instructions for the title company. Here are some basic rules to follow:

    — All real estate contracts must be in writing and be done in consultation with a lawyer.

    — Make sure every contract or agreement has a clause that protects your interests. For example, "This contract is subject to inspection and approval of the property by the buyer's partner."

    — Everything you and the seller agree upon must be written in the contract or agreement.

Make sure the contract does not have any clauses that would prevent you from assigning the contract. Add a phrase such as, "Buyer may assign contract."

Michael Gallagher, R.A.
Prudential Locations L.L.C.
116 B Hekili St.
Kailua, HI 96734
808-262-2727 office
808-384-9015 mobile
808-254-2826 fax
Mike.Gallagher@pruhawaii.com
Top 7% Nation Wide
Prudential Agents Award

I got started in real estate in 2002 after 23 years in retail sales and retail sales management. I was tired of that career and wanted to do something different, something that would allow me to make as much money as I wanted and to set my own hours.

When I first started out, I didn't invest in a higher appreciating market, which was a mistake. However, I learned quickly that you must have the determination and the drive to succeed as an investor. It's also essential to find a mentor. You must purchase a good cell phone, a quality computer, and a printer for your home office. Canon offers excellent home office equipment, such as printers.

In addition to having that determination to succeed, you want to find successful investment strategies, such as:

1. Invest in a tight market where the density is great; you want properties where there is little or no land left to expand.

2. Invest in a highly desirable market that is appreciating above the norm.

3. Buy in the best neighborhood at the lowest price.

4. If you follow the above advice, it will be about the land value, not the structure.

I find properties to purchase in numerous ways. I conduct Internet searches; do Multiple Listings searches for property; and I speak to those agents in the area with the most transactions. When I invest, I believe long-term is always the best strategy. Preservation of cash is equally important.

Investing in properties also means paying taxes, and unless you're a tax professional, you want to hire one.

To succeed in business, you must understand that timing is everything. You want to buy and sell at the right time. I do not invest in ways other than 401's, etc. Long-term holding in a tight, popular market is the best plan as the results will give you more cash gains than any other form of investment.

CHAPTER

5

FORECLOSURES AND REOS

I f you are willing to accept a bit more risk for a better return than with a conventional real estate purchase, then consider foreclosures and REOs (Real Estate Owned). Foreclosures are properties on which the loans are in default. Several common reasons for this include the following:

- The owners fail to meet their loan payments or other obligations. This happens with homeowners who did not make a down payment on the property and assumed 100 percent financing.

- The owners borrowed too much in the refinancing process. Seeking to take advantage of low interest rates, some owners fall for the 110-plus percent loans offered by lenders. In essence, this loan pulls all the equity out of the home. Then a personal disaster—divorce,

unemployment, serious illness — leads to missed
mortgage payments and, ultimately, to foreclosure.

- Other loan requirements are not met. If an owner fails
  to maintain adequate insurance coverage or is unable
  to keep the property in good physical condition, then a
  foreclosure can occur.

- Absentee owners neglect the property.

- Serious problems cause "walk-aways." This occurs in
  cases in which the property is in such bad shape that the
  owner chooses to walk away from the problems rather
  than deal with them. Problems can include cracked
  foundations, structural damage, and environmental
  problems, among others.

Foreclosures can occur in all property types — residential,
commercial, or industrial. In these cases, the lender is forced
to "take title"; that is, to take over legal ownership and control
of the property. After the foreclosure process is completed, the
lender owns the property and has to maintain and manage it.
This often means that the property is turned over to the lender's
REO department. This department has asset managers whose
job it is to inspect the property, make the necessary repairs, and
operate it until it is sold.

As you might expect, you can get good deals at foreclosure sales
because, in essence, you are buying the property at a wholesale
price rather than a retail price. Good deals aside, be sure to
perform "due diligence" before buying any property:

- **Physically inspect the property.** Determine the

problems, if any, and how much it will cost for repairs. Be particularly alert for any environmental problems.

- **Review the title report.** Do not buy any property with tax liens or other encumbrances.

- **Do an objective appraisal of the property.** Then set a price and stick to it.

Be familiar with the foreclosure processes used in your state, and follow procedures correctly.

TYPES OF STATE FORECLOSURES

The first type of foreclosure is the **deed of trust** state. These states require that the property title be held in the name of a third party. The trustee is empowered to foreclose or take back the property in the case of default or late payments. Because no judicial action is required, it's called **non-judicial** foreclosure, and foreclosures can occur in a range of approximately 60 to 120 days. The second type of foreclosure occurs in **mortgage** states. When mortgage goes in default in these states, the mortgage holder has to go to court to seek legal redress. This is called a **judicial** foreclosure and can take much longer than with a deed of trust foreclosure.

Foreclosures are a matter of public record in any state, so it is not difficult to find opportunities in a Notice of Default or a judicial foreclosure lawsuit. They are filed with the county recorder or equivalent of that position. They also must be published in a local newspaper. However, it can be difficult to track many different opportunities, so look for local services that can provide this information to you, preferably on a daily or weekly basis.

THE FOUR STEPS TO FORECLOSURE

To be a player in the foreclosure market, you need to know the four steps to be able to motivate the owner or lender to sell at wholesale, or even below-market, prices.

The Pre-foreclosure

This is the period of time between when an owner misses a payment or is notified in writing by the lender that he or she is not meeting the terms. It is the period of time before the formal Notice of Default is filed and offers good opportunities for you as a buyer. You can often "rescue" grateful owners from a bad situation. Most are eager not only to preserve their credit status but also to reduce their debt. This is the time to offer fair compensation, creating a win-win situation for both of you.

Notice of Default (NOD)

This is the first step in the formal legal process, and it is one in which the owner may not be aware of legal and late fees and penalties. This is also your opportunity to help stressed owners within 60 to 90 days following NOD.

Your benefit is that you can buy the property quickly at a discount. The benefits to the homeowner are many. Your action can prevent default or pay off the mortgage. In turn, this prevents a report of foreclosure or bankruptcy to the credit-reporting agencies. Instead, the homeowner will likely have only a "slow payment" report. In this situation, be sure that the owner has equity. Determine the loan balance and the property value. Obviously, the more equity you build, the better it is for both of you. It gives you more profit potential, and the owner receives fast cash so he or she can find and move to a new place.

Another option is to offer the owner a small amount of cash and then take over the payments. This is called "subject to" the current loans. To prevent the lender from not allowing you to assume the payments and then declaring the loan in default, have your attorney look for an **assumption** clause to make sure you can legally assume the loan. Also, watch out for a **Due on Sale** clause. This clause makes the full loan balance due immediately upon transfer of the loan.

The Foreclosure Sale

As stated earlier, loans are secured with a mortgage that requires a judicial foreclosure (a mortgage state) or a non-judicial foreclosure (a deed of trust state). As an investor, you need to be aware of the procedures involved in each so you can determine when the best opportunities occur for buying properties.

- **Judicial foreclosure**

  In this case, the lender has to file a lawsuit against the borrower to get the property. It begins with the serving of a summons and complaint against the borrower and any other parties who have junior liens or encumbrances against the property. The court holds a hearing (if the borrower responds) and makes a ruling. The judge may rule that the borrower has a legitimate issue and will arrange alternative payment terms, or the judge may order foreclosure. Often, the borrower does not respond. This means that the lender receives a default judgment. A referee is appointed by the court, and the lender then advertises the property for approximately four to six weeks. Then, if full payment is not forthcoming, the public sale is held, often on the courthouse steps. The

entire process can take from 3 to 12 months, depending
on the state and the circumstances.

- **Non-judicial foreclosure**

    In this case, lenders do not need a lawsuit to foreclose.
    They simply use the power of sale provisions in the
    deed of trust, which has three parties — the borrower
    (grantor), the lender (beneficiary), and the trustee — who
    hold the title during the pendency of the loan. If the
    borrower defaults on the loan, the trustee files a Notice
    of Default and a Notice of Sale in a legal newspaper.
    If the loan is not fully reinstated before the date and
    time of the trustee's sale, then a public auction occurs
    on the courthouse steps or other public location. Such
    auctions can be a fun and exciting experience, especially
    when you get the property you want. Be sure to do your
    research ahead of time and do not let emotion stampede
    you into buying a lemon. Be sure to get a clear title and
    an owner's title insurance policy.

Redemption Period

Some states allow a redemption period. This is a period of
time in which the owner can redeem his or her property. In
order to get the title back, he or she has to pay the full amount
owed — loan balance, late charges, legal fees, costs of the sale,
and so on. The period of time for redemption varies from state
to state. This period is also an opportunity for the investor, who
can buy the deed from the owner. In essence, this gives you the
redemption rights of the borrower, and thus the right to redeem
the property. Keep in mind that even if you buy the property
at the foreclosure sale, you still have to give the borrower the

opportunity to redeem the property as per the state-required period of redemption. That means you should not make any significant improvements because the borrower can redeem the property and your improvements right along with it.

REO OPPORTUNITIES

An REO is a property that goes back to the lender after unsuccessful forclosure auction. The REO departments of lenders specialize in handling foreclosed properties. The advantage of dealing with these departments is the lender can restructure the loan for you with favorable terms, provide lower interest rates, and offer long payment schedules. You can also negotiate for lower down payments and for a waiver of points and fees. The lender may even offer a discounted purchase price. Another distinct advantage is that you do not have to handle emotional owners. A disadvantage is that you are dealing with professionals who probably already have many arrangements with real estate brokers. That can make it difficult to gain a toehold in the market. Another disadvantage is that sales are "as is." Also, there may be exemptions from the usual disclosure rules, so *caveat emptor* — buyer beware. In general, it pays to learn the details of each lender's policies and procedures regarding disposal of REOs. Keep in mind that good properties may become available at lower prices when lenders have a large number of REOs on their hands. At that time, lenders may be more flexible. But the number of offerings may be limited by the Office of Thrift Supervision (OTS). It is the primary regulator of all federally chartered and many state-chartered thrift institutions, which include savings banks and savings and loan associations. A bureau of the U.S. Department of the Treasury, OTS is funded by assessments and fees levied on the institutions it regulates. One of its functions is to routinely audit lender portfolios and their REOs.

THE LEASE-OPTION STRATEGY

A lease option is a combination real estate rental, sales, and finance technique that creates a property lease for a fixed time period (usually 12 or 24 months) with an option for the tenant to buy the property at an agreed option price during the lease term. In essence, a lease option obligates the owner to sell the property, but it does not require the tenant to buy. It is a unilateral contract. Lease options have considerable advantages for each party to the lease:

Seller Advantages

- **As a seller, you have strong buyer demand.**

  There is usually a strong demand from lease-option buyers no matter how slow the market. Many potential home buyers can afford the monthly payments but often lack money for a down payment. The lease option solves this problem. It gives the tenant-buyer a rent credit toward the down payment. In effect, it is a forced savings account. Also, the tenant-buyer normally pays up-front, nonrefundable consideration for the option, usually several thousand dollars.

- **You get a top-dollar option price.**

  Because of strong buyer demand, a person can get top dollar for his or her property. Usually, the option price is set at the market value when signing the lease option. If the home's market value increases during the lease-option term, then the buyer benefits. Should the property drop in value, then the tenant usually does not complete the purchase.

- **You can get above-market rent.**

  Another seller advantage is earning above-market rent. If you're a landlord, you can charge tenants 10 to 20 percent above market rent.

- **You retain the tax deductions.**

  During the lease-option period, if you are the seller, you retain all the property income tax deductions.

Advantages for Buyers

Lease-option benefits are not one-sided. Advantages for buyers include the following:

- **You only need a small amount of cash up front.** Often, as a buyer, you may need only a few thousand dollars for the first month's rent plus a nonrefundable option consideration in order to acquire a home or other property. This option money is in lieu of a security deposit.

- **Your monthly rent credit builds a down payment.** One of the unique characteristics of a lease option is that the rent builds credit toward the buyer's down payment. That rent credit may be from 10 to 100 percent of the monthly rent, depending on the strength of the seller's motivation. The higher the rent credit percentage, the greater the chance the tenant will buy.

- **You can test the property before buying it.**
  Another special lease-option benefit for the tenant is the
  ability to "try out" the property before buying. If it is not
  the right choice, the tenant has not lost a large amount of
  cash in a home that might be difficult to resell.

- **You can control property through leverage.**
  As stated previously, leverage is the ability to control a
  property and profit from its market value appreciation
  with little cash. This is an important advantage for lease-
  option buyers.

- **Greater profitability results from longer terms.**
  Most residence lease options are for short terms, perhaps
  only a year or two. Savvy investors seek lease options
  with the longest possible term for the simple reason that
  the property is likely to appreciate in market value over
  the longer period.

Perhaps the one disadvantage of lease options for investors is
that they are seldom advertised and, thus, have to be actively
pursued.

The option, or purchase, price is the important feature of a lease
option. It can be either a fixed price based on current market
value or a projected value based on expected appreciation with
time restrictions for exercising the option. Here is an example:
Assume a home is valued at $300,000 in the current market. It
can be offered as a lease option with an option price of $315,000
that can be exercised any time in the next 12 months, during
which the seller expects appreciation of 5 percent per year. If the
option price exceeds the market value of the property, then a
smart buyer does not exercise the option.

REAL ESTATE AUCTION AND PROBATE SALE OPPORTUNITIES

Although somewhat uncommon, these real estate investments do offer opportunities.

Real Estate Auctions

Real estate auctions are public affairs in which real estate as well as antiques, collectibles, and other valuables may be sold. This method of selling is used by the government, private individuals, companies, or anyone who has real estate to sell. There are many different reasons for sellers to have an auction:

- Immediate cash needed

- Financial problems

- Retirement

- Divorce

- Out-of-state move

- Estate liquidation

- High property carrying costs

There are two types of auctions. An **absolute** auction is one in which the property is sold to the highest bidder regardless of price. From the auctioneer's point of view, the advantage of this auction is that bidders know the property is going to sell, which usually generates more interest among potential buyers. A **reserve** auction is one in which a minimum, or reserve price, is put on the property. From the seller's point of view, the advantage is that the property is not sold if it does not bring the minimum price. Of course, this is a disadvantage for a buyer. If the reserve price is set so near to the actual market value of the property, then it is no bargain at all. A second disadvantage of auctions is that there is a lot of competition for good properties, which can drive prices up. If you plan to attend auctions, be sure to do your research so you can identify profitable real estate. Then, when you attend an auction, keep in mind that the purpose of an auction (from the seller's point of view) is to generate lots of excitement to drive up prices. Stay objective during the process, and do not let the thrill of competition override your judgment. Real estate auctions are easy to find. Look in the newspaper or the Yellow Pages, listen to the radio, or watch TV. Remember to thoroughly research the property ahead of time.

Probate Sales

Legally speaking, probate is a court process that includes:

- Proving the authenticity of the deceased person's will.

- Appointing someone to handle the deceased person's affairs.

- Identifying and inventorying the deceased person's property.

- Paying debts and taxes.

- Identifying any heirs.

- Distributing the deceased person's property according to the will or, if there is no will, according to state law.

As with real estate auctions, probate sales can occur for many reasons:

- Need to satisfy creditors

- Need for cash

- Negative emotional ties to a property

Because probate laws vary from state to state, know the rules and regulations regarding sales in your area. If you buy at a sale, a waiting period and court confirmation may be required before your purchase is finalized, meaning you can do nothing with the property until these actions occur. Also be aware of the possibility of an overbid. This occurs when a buyer appeals directly to the court to buy the property for more than the offer you made. Generally speaking, an overbid must exceed your offer by at least 5 percent. If this situation occurs, you have to decide whether or not you want to raise your bid. Avoid getting caught up in a bidding war by setting a maximum limit for bidding and sticking to it.

Richard Belliveau
Richard@thenotedetective.com
www.thenotedetective.com

My emergence into real estate began with studying courses and then getting into the note business. Once I learned the concepts of cash flow, I bought my first properties. I then fixed them and prepared them for resale.

Although I've just started with my first few properties, I learned quickly that location is extremely important. I bought properties in undesirable areas. To compensate for my mistake, I'm fixing up and selling the properties at a discount. I bought really low to offset the location problem. Fortunately, I've already found several qualified buyers who have been approved for mortgages for my properties.

I also learned some invaluable investment strategies, including:

1. Buy low. You make your money going in.

2. Understand exit strategies.

3. You must understand financing, hard money, points, interest rates, total holding costs, etc.

Finding investment properties is essential, and I have "bird dogs," or wholesalers, bring them to me. I also spread the word via the Internet and at professional meetings. I let people know what type of property I want. My goal right now is to make a quick profit; perhaps later on, things will be different.

For those considering real estate investment, they should understand that there are some disadvantages. For example, holding costs on the selling end can get a little hairy. Furthermore, it's always good to know the demographics of the market you are targeting.

One of the biggest advantages to real estate investment is you can get instant equity if you purchase right. You can also develop a niche in the market and capitalize on it. The bottom line is you make your money when you buy.

CHAPTER

THE TEAM APPROACH

R eal estate investment is definitely not an individual endeavor. It requires a team, and you are the person who needs to carefully assemble that team. A team approach is important for three reasons:

1. Real estate is a complex field in terms of the knowledge required about mortgages, markets, taxes, and so on. As an investor, you do not have the time to master every aspect of real estate, nor should you try. It is your job to invest and to use the expertise of others to achieve that objective.

2. By building a team, you build a network, and that network generates leads, which, in turn, produce more opportunities for you. In effect, a team is a money-making machine for everyone involved.

3. A team allows you to seize opportunities. By putting together a great team, you stay ahead of your competition.

Who should be members of your team? They should include most or all of the following individuals:

- Lender or mortgage broker

- Tax advisor

- Financial consultant

- Real estate broker or agent

- Property appraiser

- Lawyer

- Contractors, repairpeople, and so on

Each of these individuals has a specific role to play. The lender advises you on mortgages. The tax advisor advises you on legal issues regarding federal, state, and local tax laws. The appraiser evaluates properties for you and lets you know if they are worth investing in or not. Each of these team members supplies you with valuable information based on their expertise, preventing you from wasting time on properties that do not meet your investment goals. Also, keep in mind that each team member should receive benefits from working with you. In return for their expertise, they expect you to refer business and clients to them.

Building a team takes time. It is well worth your time and effort to assemble the best people you can find. Select them for both expertise and reputation. Ideally, you want people with high standing in the community because, as an investor, your reputation is everything. People want to deal with honest, trustworthy, and reliable individuals. If you are associated with someone who lacks those qualities and has a questionable reputation, your investment opportunities will be limited.

First, you must build your reputation as a professional. People have to see you in action in order to form an opinion of your abilities and your character. Once you have made deals and worked with people you would like to become members of your team, start communicating with them on a regular basis. Send them useful articles that may help their business. Meet with them for coffee or at local functions. If you sincerely admire their expertise, ask them for advice. Refer business to them. Above all, keep your word and do what you say you will do from the simplest act like keeping an appointment to the most complex, meeting the obligations of a contract.

Now, let's look at the team members you need and their roles.

THE TAX ADVISOR

One of the great benefits of real estate investment is the tax benefit it offers. However, you have to be aware of those benefits before you can take advantage of them. Tax laws can be complex and, sometimes, downright unfathomable to a layperson, which is why a tax advisor is needed. It is his or her job to know IRS rules and regulations and to make sure you are in compliance with them. Equally important, a tax advisor can help you refine your investment goals and form an overall strategy.

The advisor you choose should specialize in real estate investing or have considerable experience in the field. Check references and reputations of local tax advisors and interview them to get a sense of their expertise. They should demonstrate an understanding of your goals and provide specific ideas on how to achieve those goals. For example, if you're an investor looking for quick cash from your properties, the tax advisor should provide you with specific knowledge on how to minimize your tax liabilities and maximize your investment. On the other hand, if you are an investor looking to build your wealth over time, that same advisor should be able to offer long-term strategies that will help you achieve growth and income for a secure future.

A tax advisor should also be able to steer you toward specific types of properties that will help you achieve your goals. In addition, he or she should recommend specific types of ownership (direct or indirect).

THE LENDER OR MORTGAGE BROKER

As an investor, you will need to borrow money, which means you need to know the loans available. Both the lender and mortgage broker are in the business of making money by making loans. In effect, they give you cash and charge rent for it. However, each operates in different ways:

Lenders

A lender is any public or private firm that directly lends you the money you need to buy your property. Often called direct lenders, the list includes banks, credit unions, and private lenders. Some lenders may offer loans in a variety of areas (automobile, personal, and so on) or they may specialize in a specific type of loan (mortgages only).

Mortgage Brokers

Mortgage brokers are considered indirect lenders. Their role is to present your loan request to a number of different lenders in order to find the best financing for you.

Keep in mind that neither lenders nor mortgage brokers are objective. They want to find the maximum amount of money you can borrow, not necessarily the amount you can afford. So work with them in an equally objective manner. Also, remember that loans can sometimes be difficult to get because lenders calculate risk before loaning money. They want reasonable assurance that they will get their money back as well as interest. They are in it for the profit, and that means they look at your credit rating before making a loan. Banks and credit unions are using depositors' money, so they must be careful about the loans they make. That's where **collateral** comes in. Collateral is real or personal property that you pledge to secure the loan or mortgage. If you fail to pay the debt, then the lender has the right to take the collateral and sell it to recover the outstanding principal and interest on the loan. Usually, the purchased property is the pledged collateral for real estate loans or mortgages.

From this information, you can see that it is important to build solid relationships with lenders or mortgage brokers. To begin the process, seek out lenders who specialize in the type of properties you would like to target. Then, meet with them and give them your latest personal financial statement. This should include your income and expenses as well as assets, liabilities, and net worth. Be honest about your financial position. First of all, it is the right thing to do. Second, exaggerating the truth about your financial situation is the quickest way to break trust—the one asset you need to establish from the beginning. Third, the lender will require supporting documents about your income and assets and will do a credit check to verify your status. These tight controls are a result of the early 1990s savings-and-loan scandals and are designed to prevent abuse of the system. So before you meet with a lender, be prepared to provide the necessary verification.

It is a good idea to seek out experienced lenders who truly understand the real estate market and its ups and downs. They maintain an objective eye and, particularly if you are inexperienced, they can prevent you from making serious mistakes. There are times when the market heats up, creating absurd prices that have no economic support. A good lender will cast a wary eye on this market and be more conservative in his or her approach, saving you both money and heartache.

THE REAL ESTATE BROKER AND AGENT

Because you will be investing in real estate, you want the best and most experienced broker or agent available. A real estate broker is the highest level of state-licensed professional. The broker supervises licensed real estate agents who are qualified to handle real estate listings and transactions.

Most of the time, you will deal with real estate agents unless you are involved in large and complicated transactions. Whether you deal with a broker or an agent, be sure the person has a solid track record with investment property transactions in the area you have targeted. When working with a real estate agent, know what kind of agency he or she represents. It can make a difference in your profits. The two types of agencies are:

- **The single agency.** In this type of agency, the agent represents only the buyer or the seller, not both. For example, the buyer's agent only has a fiduciary responsibility to the buyer. He has the responsibility of promoting the buyer's interests and keeping all information confidential unless he is legally required to disclose it. When you work with a single agency agent, he should not be passing any information to the seller without your knowledge or permission.

- **The dual agency.** With this type of agency, the same agent represents both buyer and seller or two different agents from the same agency represent the buyer and seller, creating a potential conflict of interest. The agent owes fiduciary loyalty to each client, which is difficult, if not impossible, to achieve. Avoid this situation, and choose an agent from a single agency. Of course, keep in mind that brokers and agents like the dual-agency arrangement because it generates more commissions. Most states, but not all, do not allow dual agency. If you are in a state that does permit it, the state will most likely require agents to disclose the dual relationship before taking on a client.

Compensating the Broker or Agent

Real estate agents or brokers are only compensated when a sale is made, which motivates them to see a transaction completed. Typically, their compensation is calculated as a percentage of the sales price of a property. These commissions vary according to the property and the amount of the transaction:

- 5 to 6 percent for individual residential properties (single-family homes, condos, and co-ops)

- 3 to 5 percent for small multi-family and commercial properties

- 1 to 3 percent for larger investment properties

- 10 percent or more for undeveloped land

Generally speaking, the commissions are split between the seller (the firm listing the property for sale) and the agent representing the buyer. In actual practice, the commission is paid to the broker who then pays a share to the agent based on employment or commission agreement.

Because commissions can be costly for an investor, keep in mind that they are always negotiable. At the same time, remember that a good agent will introduce you to many potentially profitable investments, which may well be worth the commission. If you still object to paying commissions, one option is to get a real estate license yourself. That way you can eliminate at least half of the expense of commissions. You can also represent yourself, reducing transaction expenses.

Finding a Great Broker or Agent

The real estate broker or agent you choose should personify professionalism. You want experienced professionals who are passionate about their careers and dedicated to them. In other words, you are looking for agents or brokers who have demonstrated excellence over time. You will also want to choose a professional who is an expert in the market in which you have chosen to invest. If you have decided to concentrate on single-family residential homes, find agents or brokers who have demonstrated knowledge of such real estate properties. By the same token, if you have decided to concentrate on commercial properties, choose an expert in that field. Ask for evidence in terms of sales and verify the following important items:

- **Licensure.** Make sure the agent is fully licensed by checking with online state databases. This simple step will establish that no citations or disciplinary actions appear on the agent's record. Also, make sure the agent's broker is in full compliance with state regulations.

- **References.** Ask for several references from the agent or broker. These references should be in your geographical area. Call each of these individuals to get a more complete picture of the agent.

- **Reputation.** A broker or agent's reputation reflects on you. An agent with a great reputation can enhance your success, especially in complicated or adversarial negotiations. Particularly, look for an agent with a reputation for honesty, the bedrock of all virtues. Honesty is not only the right thing to do, it is also good business sense. When an agent or broker is straightforward, buyers and sellers appreciate it and let others know, resulting in more prospects and more business. Also, look for fairness, integrity, and patience—particularly in commercial agents who deal in complicated negotiations.

- **Good communication skills.** Any agent or broker you choose should be a good listener and should keep you informed about transactions on a regular basis. In other words, they should have time for you. They should listen carefully to what you have to say and be able to understand what your needs are.

- **Strong interpersonal and negotiating skills.** Real estate deals are essentially about bringing people together and, hopefully, making everyone happy. Seek out agents or brokers who have the wit, charm, and patience to handle participants and move them toward the objective of the deal. Check out an agent's negotiating skills by asking former clients how well he or she handled bargaining sessions.

Once you find a great agent or broker, work with him or her only in your targeted geographic area. These individuals are a key element in your investment strategy, so maximize their expertise and contacts. Treat them fairly so your name will be the first one to come to mind when good properties come on the market. Be a serious buyer, remembering that agents only get paid for closed deals. No one wants to waste time and lose money on "ghost" buyers. Also remember that the best properties do not always make it into the Multiple Listing Service (MLS) directories or into the newspaper. Information often comes from insiders, and the only way to be on the inside is by developing close relationships with agents or brokers.

THE APPRAISER

The job of real estate appraisers is to evaluate a property and tell you its condition. They are licensed by the state and are often independent contractors associated with appraisal firms headed by a Certified Appraiser or equivalent. They negotiate compensation with their firm. It is usually a percentage of the fee that the appraisal company charges its clients. The appraiser's value lies in two areas: First, an appraiser can uncover hidden problems that could cost money. Second, they can uncover hidden opportunities that can increase your return on investment. An example would be a fixer-upper that is structurally sound. Appraisers can alert you to the fact that a minimum investment on your part could lead to a significant increase in value. Appraisers also can provide the history of a particular geographic area and let you know if it is in the path of progress.

Most appraisers will give a written report that consists of the following:

- A description of the property and its location based on a visit to the property by the appraiser. He or she evaluates the condition; overall livability based on design, layout, and appeal to the market; and other external factors.

- An evaluation of the "highest and best use" of the land.

- An evaluation of sales of comparable properties as similar to the appraised property as possible.

- Information regarding current real estate activity and market area trends.

- New construction cost and analysis of income potential may be included in the report.

If you are working with a bank, it may give you a list of approved appraisers to use. If not, you can use any appraiser you choose, after making sure the appraiser has not been blacklisted by the bank for inflating appraisal amounts.

THE REAL ESTATE ATTORNEY

If you are just starting out in real estate investment, you may not need an attorney, but as you grow, you will definitely need the services of an experienced real estate lawyer. Investment transactions can be complex, and a good attorney can save you money and hassle by reviewing all documents before a deal is finalized. It is money well-spent. As with other members of your team, check references. Look for attorneys who have the knack of explaining legal terminology in laymen's terms. Also, seek out attorneys who have expert knowledge in tenant-landlord laws, leases, and so on.

CONTRACTORS OR REPAIRPEOPLE

As with other members of your team, you want the highest quality contractors or repairpeople. When upgrading properties, you may need contractors in one or more of the following areas: heating and air-conditioning, plumbing, electricity, roofing, flooring, painting, and general repair. Keep in mind that there are licensed and unlicensed contractors. Be sure to use licensed contractors for the specialized areas (heating/air-conditioning, plumbing, electrical work, roofing, and flooring). These areas require extensive knowledge and experience. Unlicensed workers are often used for painting, installing light fixtures, and other relatively low-skill jobs simply because it costs less to use them. However, most insurance policies do not cover injuries to unlicensed workers, meaning that you could be liable for damages. To find the best contractors and repairpeople, ask around in the business community, check the "Services Available" section in the newspaper, and simply watch for repair trucks on the street. Check contractors' references and licensing. Talk to customers who have used their services to find out if they have done a quality job on time and within budget. Also, check with the Better Business Bureau to see if any complaints have been filed against them.

RK Kliebenstein
RK@ASKRK.com

My journey in real estate began over 30 years ago. As a young man making $500-$1,500 loans, the company I was working for (a division of Citibank), opened a second mortgage division where I became a manager. I specialized in loans to self-employed individuals, many of whom owned income-producing property, and I began to see the benefits of real estate ownership. I knew from that time forward that my career would always involve real estate in some way.

Undoubtedly, the biggest mistake I made when I was starting out was not investing in real estate earlier in my income potential. I did not exercise sufficient self-discipline. I didn't deny myself pleasures when I was young, so I could most afford the highest risk. I now regret spending money on "toys," and not using capital resources to invest in real estate. Now, at a point in life where I am willing to make sacrifices, I am not willing to take the risks associated with the highest rewards in real estate ownership.

When I first started in real estate investing, I learned some very valuable lessons that new real estate investors should keep in mind:

1. Every transaction must create the "win-win" solution for parties on both side of the table. Greed and selfishness are the easiest ways to derail a transaction. I consistently try to understand the issues of the other party. I try to analyze the deal points from their perspective, so I can negotiate a transaction that has the highest probability of closing.

2. Proper capitalization and the ability to close quickly are key strategies for driving the best price and negotiating the best

deal. The most difficult transactions to put together are those where the money to close the deal is not in the bank, and the funding for both the equity and the debt has not been pre-arranged.

3. Rarely is real estate a passive investment. Commencing with the prospecting of properties, moving through the due diligence, completing the close, and taking possession of a property is only the beginning of a lot of hard work. Application of personal skills, tireless hours dedicated to managing property, understanding the marketplace, and properly positioning the asset are hardly passive interests.

Every investor has his own successful investment strategies; when you find strategies that work for you, stick with them:

Be consistent yet flexible. Underwriting a transaction is simplified, and a standardized approach to analysis and deal structure is applied. That does not mean that the criteria may not change depending on market conditions, sellers, and buyers. You must be willing to adjust methodology annually to keep strategy static.

Learn that due diligence is your greatest friend. Not taking the time to do your homework can cause credibility problems with your investors, buyers or sellers and third parties to your transaction. Taking the time to investigate, verify, and confirm is as important of an investment in the transaction as is the capital.

Understand what the other party has at risk and has to gain from closing the transaction. If you understand what the motivations are on the other side of the table, you can always

negotiate from a position of strength. When one party in the transaction is imbalanced in terms of benefit, the transaction is least likely to close. Minimizing the risks of my opponent and maximizing their profits allow me to structure transactions that are easier to sell and easier to close.

Relationships close deals. Creating the "win-win" situation in a transaction can not only result in repeat transactions but can also transcend much bigger issues and provide political capital when needed. I have found that treating my opponent with dignity and respect, even in transactions that were not going to close, has been a huge benefit in closing transactions that happened several years later. The creating of good relationships not only can be a credibility builder, but you may be surprised, particularly if you stay within a niche industry, when you meet the same buyer or seller again.

I am an extensive user of the Internet in identifying markets and properties. Finding my properties is not done at the expense of brokers or agents in the transaction. While I would always prefer a principal-to-principal transaction, it is often easy to underestimate the value of a broker.

The most valuable broker in a transaction will have a relationship with a buyer or a seller. Those agents and brokers who are "name passers" or who do not work very hard understand the listing, the product, motivations of buyer and seller, the market, or the transaction will lend little value to the deal. The broker who has known the buyer or seller for a long time can add tremendous value to the deal. The less familiar the broker is with the parties he represents, the more they intend to be an impediment to getting the deal to closing.

I often joke that every real estate transaction I'm involved in I am doing for my wife's next husband. She is younger than I, in better shape, and takes better care of herself. She has the actuarial tables on her side. All kidding aside, looking at deals on a long-term basis should never be done at the sacrifice of all short-term goals. Life has too many unexpected turns, hills, and valleys that can make a short-term, weak deal a disaster. While some transactions may not be as sweet in the short run, it is not a good strategy unless you have very deep pockets to buy deals only with benefits far in the future. This is particularly true when you have investors or no heirs to your estate. By the way, I only ask of my wife to wait until I am gone, buried in the ground, and body cold, as I do not want to see her next husband's Mercedes in the driveway!

Of course, there are some disadvantages to real estate investing, such as:

- Real estate has a tendency to be a better long-term investment than a short-term investment. Because typically large costs of a transaction will be front-loaded, and unless you are buying below market to create equity of closing, you may need some seasoning in the investment to recoup closing costs.

- Most investors are surprised at the actual return on investment. Fortunately, many of them do not accurately account for the time and money truly invested in any given project.

- Liquidity takes on a different meaning. As in the first drawback, few people realize how much time investing in real estate requires, not only on the acquisition but also on the disposition

side. Naturally, the larger the transaction and the more complex it is, the longer the marketing and closing takes.

- Not all buyers and sellers are entirely honest. This creates the need for accurate and exhaustive due diligence, for which the criteria and the process should be established well ahead of the transaction.

- Sometimes, it takes a village… Investing in real estate may require the assembly of a professional team. The team would include:

  — Lawyers

  — Bankers

  — Accountants

  — Environmental Engineers

  — Structural Engineers

  — Civil Engineers

  — Insurance Brokers

  — Real Estate Brokers

  — Accountants

  — Books and Records Inspectors

  — Market Analysts

— Title Companies

— Surveyors

— Management Companies

— And a host of others, most of whom
  do not work on a contingency basis, have to be paid up
  front, and have difficult time schedules

On the other hand, there are a plethora of advantages to real
estate investing:

- Why bricks and mortars are the real deal. Typically, I can see,
  touch, smell, hear, and even feel the investment. A piece of paper
  is a poor substitution for the former.

- I can personally have an effect on the transaction. When I buy
  stock in a company, the company does not typically allow me to
  set the course of destiny for that entity. I am at the mercy of the
  board of directors, a chairman, and a management team that
  I may have had little or no input deciding who they are, what
  they stand for, and how they run a company. Oftentimes, in the
  ownership of real estate, even if I have a management company,
  I likely have the right and the opportunity to get intimately
  involved in the day-to-day operation of the property. If I lose my
  primary tenant, very little gets in the way of my ability to find a
  tenant and get the job done myself.

FINDING AND EVALUATING PROPERTIES

The key to finding properties and evaluating them is homework. That's right, homework. To be successful in real estate investment, you must gain experience that will enable you to find the best properties at the best value in the best locations.

Most likely, you have heard the three most important rules of real estate: location, location, location. Although this phrase is overdone, it contains a great deal of truth. Location is vitally important, both in terms of the regional big-picture economics as well as in the local economy.

THE REGION

The first question you must ask concerning the region is this: Is it economically healthy? To answer that question, look at economic indicators. It is relatively easy to "Google" this information on the Internet. It also can be obtained from government agencies, academic sites, and private firms. If you do not have access to the Internet, then check with the local chamber of commerce, economic development agencies, and the public library. Your broker and lender also should have access to this information. Another resource is your appraiser, who needs to know economic information to make accurate judgments on the value of the properties he or she inspects.

The U.S. government divides the country into geographic areas for the purpose of data collection and analysis. This is handled by the Office of Management and Budget (OMB) which "defines metropolitan and micropolitan statistical areas according to published standards that are applied to Census Bureau data. The general concept of a metropolitan or micropolitan statistical area is that of a core area containing a substantial population nucleus, together with adjacent communities having a high degree of economic and social integration with that core." These areas are usually referred to as Standard Metropolitan Statistical Areas, or SMSAs.

When you look at one of the SMSAs, check the numbers, but look beyond them to gauge the spirit and attitude of a community. Ask yourself such questions as: Is it committed to job creation and development? Are community leaders providing focused leadership in all areas of development? Does it have a diverse economic base, or is it centered on just a few industries?

Population Growth

This is a crucial factor in determining your real estate investment future. As the population grows, the need for residential and commercial properties grows, and so do opportunities. There is a greater demand for housing, retail shopping, office space, and service providers.

Deciding what, where, and when to buy real estate should be driven by your investment objectives and by the standards you set for the properties you want to purchase:

- Single-family residential

- Multi-family

- Commercial

- Industrial

Standards are important because they help you to buy the best properties at the lowest risk. They also assist you in determining the geographic area in which you want to invest. In addition, standards help you sift through leads quickly, enabling you to eliminate the unqualified ones and concentrate on the money-making properties. Five major categories must be analyzed in order to make the best investment choices.

THE FIVE CATEGORIES

Category 1: Location

This is the first category, of course, because it is one of the most important. The location where you buy does matter, so study geographic areas carefully before investing in any property. It is usually best to choose a local area for the following reasons:

- It is easier to gain knowledge about it and increase expertise rapidly.

- It is easy to visit and search for properties.

- It keeps costs down. This is the first area in which to narrow your search. It keeps the process manageable and affordable, and it allows you to become an expert quickly.

Think of yourself as specialized within one area of the real estate investment. Learn everything you can about the location to be become that specialist — property values, rental, rates, school systems, and so on. The more knowledge you gain, the better you'll be at evaluating properties and making good decisions.

Finding good locations is a process of elimination. Look for growing cities with strong economic engines. Check out neighborhoods that are in the path of progress or are otherwise desirable, with high-quality retail shops, recreational centers, and excellent schools, and be easily accessible to work. Look for neighborhoods in transition from run-down status to gentrification status. Many people love to move into these areas, driving up both residential and business property prices. If you decide to specialize in residential housing, then look for features that attract buyers.

Category 2: Type

Property type is the second essential category. You need to know what you are looking for — single-family homes or multi-family homes, urban or suburban, resort or ranch, and so on. Both single-family and multi-family properties have their advantages:

- **Single-family** — As discussed earlier, these properties appreciate well over time, and there is always a demand for them.

- **Multi-family** — These investments generate the benefit of cash flow, plus rents tend to rise over time.

- **Commercial/Industrial** — These properties offer greater potential growth and appreciation, but also much greater risk. Unemployment, slow economic conditions, and overbuilding can affect your returns on this type of investment.

Category 3: Property Worth

You absolutely must know what properties are worth within your chosen geographic area, so study property values closely. It will save you money — and help you make it — in the long run. First, decide your price range and then figure out the discount you will require in order to purchase the property. Next, estimate the cash flow you expect from the investment as well as the appreciation.

Once you have those figures firmly in mind, learn property values and rents by doing the following leg work:

- Talk to your broker or agent.

- Browse newspaper and Internet listings.

- Visit your targeted area. Check out open houses and look at rental properties.

- Look for "FOR RENT" signs and call to ask for details.

The more you research the properties in your target area, the better your understanding of property value will be and the easier it will be formulate your economic criteria.

- Are there favorable rental laws?

- Is the neighborhood attractive to families with school-age children?

- What is the crime rate?

- Do nearby work, retail, and recreational centers make the property more marketable?

Category 4: Population

If an area has steady population growth, then the need for residential and commercial retail properties will grow as will the opportunities for you as an investor. Look closely at local communities and neighborhoods to see the direction the demographics appear to be moving. In fact, it is wise to do as all successful real estate developers and lenders do. Examine net population growth in submarkets to see where there are positive trends for investment.

Category 5: Job Growth and Levels of Income

Strong job growth is vital in any area targeted for investment. It is a simple equation: Jobs attract people, and when people need housing, the real estate market grows. A good source for information on job growth is the U.S. Bureau of Labor Statistics (**www.bls.gov**). This agency not only tracks job statistics on a national level but also on state and local levels. This, however, is only a starting point. Examine the statistics to get a realistic view of the local situation. For example, is the job growth in your area characterized by good-paying jobs or by minimum-wage jobs? This is important to know because minimum-wage workers are unlikely to be in the market to buy a home.

Also, has the area attracted diverse companies, offering a variety of jobs? The more diverse the economy, the less likely it is that an economic downturn will damage or devastate the real estate market. Detroit and Seattle are two examples of local economies relying too strongly on only a few manufacturers. As go the auto and airplane markets, so go Detroit and Seattle. Always seek diversity.

An investor also must consider the types of industries within the targeted investment area and their prospects for growth. Historically speaking, the farming sector is slow growing as are small retail businesses. Real estate values will grow slowly as well. On the other hand, if you target an area with such high-growth industries as technology companies, then real estate values will grow at a faster pace. For example, if you plan to build retail office space, you will need an area with professionals like businesspeople, lawyers, and doctors who would be interested in your property. In addition, such amenities as restaurants, shops, and entertainment venues should be easily accessible.

Without a thriving job market, your investment will stagnate or actually lose value. Look for companies paying stable or increasing wages, indicating that there is a market for their goods or services. It may also indicate that the company does not plan to outsource jobs soon. Check the region's unemployment levels. Have they been rising or declining?

Naturally, it is best when unemployment is low. Finally, look for employment fields like education, government, and medical services that are somewhat resistant to market downturns.

THE LOCAL AREA

After researching the demographics, turn your information to the targeted areas to make sure all the factors are in place to ensure your success. Avoid declining areas, overbuilt areas, and areas where demand is weak. At the same time, avoid locales where properties are expensive or overpriced. These properties offer little opportunity for the appreciation that would make the investment worthwhile. Expensive properties also can be difficult to sell. Look for properties between the two extremes. They are easier to buy, easier to sell, and overall demand is greater.

The basic laws of supply and demand apply in your local community just as they do on the regional or national levels. Strong demand and limited supply combine to create shortages and opportunities for you. The following factors indicate that supply is greater than demand:

- Large number of building permits

- Weak absorption or rental of new properties

- Excess of income property listings

The result of excess supply is low occupancy, low rents, and rental concessions. This situation ends up costing the investor in terms of lower cash flow and smaller appreciation potential. Of course, if you have the following indicators, then you are in a good position to invest:

- Few vacancies

- Strong absorption or rental of new properties

- Few income property listings

Specific indicators should be considered to evaluate the "investment worthiness" of a local area.

Building Permits

When trying to determine the investment potential of a particular area or neighborhood, the number of building permits that have been issued is a clear indicator of the future real estate supply. If a great many permits have been granted over a long period of time, future appreciation will be negligible because the market will have an oversupply of properties. On the other hand, if few permits have been issued, it may indicate that interest rates are too high or that the market is saturated. Evaluate these influences to make sure the area is a good environment for your investment. Positive absorption, mentioned earlier in the book, is a situation in which the demand for space is greater than the supply, which is a good measure of the health of the real estate market. If available new properties are rented within months, it is a robust and thriving market. Absorption is measured differently in residential and commercial markets. Residential properties are measured in housing units, while commercial properties are measured in square footage. Negative absorption describes markets in which real estate properties are built at a rate greater than the demand for them.

Local planning or building departments can supply information on building permits. Absorption numbers are more difficult to find, but you can get them from local real estate appraisers and brokers, especially brokers holding Certified Commercial Investment Member (CCIM) certification. These brokers specialize in the sale of income properties and track absorption statistics.

Keep in mind that both building permits and absorption are specific to different types of properties. In other words, industrial property will not have an influence on commercial or retail property unless the use of a property is changed.

Cost of Renting Versus Cost of Buying

Supply and demand also is affected by the numbers of renters versus buyers. For example, if the cost of buying a home is low compared to the cost of renting, then renters will buy homes, simultaneously increasing home sales and lowering demand for rentals. Property listings often will reflect this trend when they increase in number. Such upswings can indicate the market is saturated with listings, suggesting that it is time for investors to move elsewhere. Too many listings give buyers the opportunity to be extremely selective. The result is that prices move downward, making investment opportunities much less attractive for investors. To avoid this situation, look for a decrease in property listings, which indicates that demand is greater than supply. In this case, renters stay put, and the sales relative to listings drop. Prices will move upward as will the opportunity for appreciation.

Levels of Occupancy

Another method of measuring supply and demand is the

market occupancy rate. The market occupancy rate is defined as the percentage of that type of property available for occupancy that is currently rented. If there is an area with 3,000 total rental units in apartment buildings and there's a 95 percent occupancy rate, then 2,850 units are occupied. This means that 5 percent, or 150, of the units are vacant. When dealing with commercial, industrial, or retail space, occupancy level is measured in terms of square footage rather than units.

Market occupancy rate is important because it tells the potential of a particular property. Look for low vacancy rates (and a lower number of building permits). This combination suggests that real estate prices will appreciate. When low vacancy rates occur, it is a landlord's market. The low rates create higher demand for the existing units which, in turn, keeps market prices higher. Avoid high vacancy rates, which imply an oversupply of real estate. This situation pressures rental rates downward because competition is so great among landlords for tenants. Concessions may also signal a weakness in the rental market. Concessions are items like free rent, upgrades, and special deals designed to attract renters. If too many concessions are offered, then the rental market may indeed be weak. However, be aware that in some areas concessions are offered as a matter of course and may not be an indicator of market strength or weakness.

Where do you find information about occupancy rates? It can be as simple as doing a walk-through of a commercial, industrial, or retail property. In cases in which the rates are obvious (apartments, for example), consult trade organizations and industry service providers like the National Apartment Association (**www.naahq.org**) or the Building Owners and Managers Association (**www.boma.org**). These organizations have local affiliates who can provide you with the data you need to make informed decisions.

Rental Rates

Rental rates, or rent levels, also provide good indicators of the supply and demand situation for income properties. When real estate demand keeps up with the supply of housing and when the local economy is growing, rents generally increase, meaning real estate prices will continue to appreciate.

Information is not always easy to get from owners and property managers, however. They are reluctant to divulge information, especially in soft markets because they do not want present tenants learning that new tenants get a lower rent. Nevertheless, you must be competitive, so you must find and calculate the effective rental rate. If a rental property is available for $1,500 a month, but the owner is offering a concession of one month's free rent on a yearly lease, then the effective rent is really $1,375 per month. When you compare rates, be sure to include concessions as well.

The Path of Progress

Earlier in this book, the path of progress was explained, but it is worth mentioning again here. It pays to buy properties in developing areas with potential for several reasons:

- It is easier to find and keep good tenants.

- It is easier to achieve high occupancy.

- The turnover rate is lower.

- Appreciation rates are higher.

In most major cities, new construction and growth are ongoing. Inevitably, certain areas gain "cachet," becoming areas where people really want to live. Through word-of-mouth referrals, advertising, and other means, these areas become "the place to be." This demand increases both prices and appreciation. So how do you determine where the path of progress is headed? First, look for major retailers. Such companies as Best Buy, Lowes, Costco, and The Home Depot do an exhaustive amount of research before they select a site. If they have a location in your area, then they see potential there. Second, look for where new highways are planned. That information tells you where properties likely will be available for development. Third, look for cities or neighborhoods in which revitalization efforts are taking place. Many times, cities with blighted areas form redevelopment districts and offer incentives to attract investors. This can be a great opportunity; however, be sure that the local leaders and agencies have a clear and definite plan for redevelopment along with the revenues to support that plan and the political clout to implement it.

The Benefit of Problems

Problems have benefits? Yes, here's an example: There is an area of a city in which there are apartment buildings, but the neighborhood opposes building more such properties because of environmental concerns, negative impacts upon property values, or any one of a number of other factors. If you own existing apartments in this area or purchase or invest in these buildings, your competition is severely restricted or even eliminated.

Often, environmental issues are at the heart of real estate development projects these days. Everyone wants clean air, clean water, and the best possible quality of living. Everyone wants to live in a beautiful area, free of eyesores, contaminants, and massive amounts of concrete. This desire often creates a shortage of buildable land in certain areas. Land is set aside for conservation and preservation, generating a limited supply of available properties and an increase in demand — a great situation for any investor.

The trend toward decentralization in cities can also be a "positive" problem. As more authority is put into the hands of local and neighborhood planning boards, opposition to growth because of increased traffic congestion, overcrowded schools, and so on increases. They often object to the building of low-income properties. This increase creates an opportunity for investors because it results in higher prices and greater appreciation.

The Governmental Climate

Needless to say, taxation, incentives, and other governmental factors have a huge influence on your investment. Look for a business-friendly environment. The state, regional, and local governments in your targeted investments area should be committed to economic growth, welcoming investment. Second, check to see if the area offers economic development incentives. Many cities compete aggressively for new businesses with inexpensive land and low property taxation, low income taxation, or combinations of the two. Third, check your targeted area's reputation for its commitment to job growth and its efforts to attract great employers. If the area has an excellent reputation in these areas, then it is committed to long-term growth. Contact the local chamber of commerce, tourism board, city hall, or other agency responsible for economic development to determine the local government's level of support. Finally, learn the property tax structure. In particular, check for special assessments levied to pay for schools, parks, fire, and police services. These make for attractive investment areas, but weigh the extra costs against the income you will receive from properties in an assessment district.

NEIGHBORHOOD COMPARISONS

Now is a good time to review the components to consider when choosing a neighborhood for investment. Avoid stagnant or deteriorating neighborhoods, and invest in those with good reputations and potential for growth.

- **Take your time.** The first rule to remember is to take your time and be as objective as possible. Investing in a property—especially if you plan to live in it—can be an exciting experience, making you want to buy quickly. Be patient, always keeping in mind that once you buy the property, you may have to live with it for quite a while.

- **Search many neighborhoods.** Choose neighborhoods you would like to live in and be sure to see the full range of properties in those areas. Often, you can find bargains. For example, many properties are listed for more than they are worth in the current market because the seller is simply hoping to get that price. Actually they will sell for less, so a great investment may be within your budget.

- **Research, research, research.** You may find a great property in a neighborhood you like, but do your research on the following areas:

— **Schools.** All parents want the best education for their children, so choose neighborhoods where schools have good reputations. If you plan to live in a property for a while and if you have children, visit the schools and talk to the teachers. Also talk to parents to see how they feel about the school's quality. Even if you do not have kids, you should still care about the quality of the education system because that quality affects the value of your property.

— **Amenities.** Check out parks, recreational facilities, and so on. After all, everyone wants to enjoy themselves so they will want nice facilities in which to play and relax.

— **Property taxes.** Check with the community's assessment office to find out the amount of property taxes you will pay.

— **Crime.** High crime rates can have a devastating effect on income properties of all kinds. Families obviously do not want to expose themselves and their children to burglaries, muggings, or worse. Commercial tenants definitely do not want to expose themselves or their customers to the same dangers. And you, as an investor, obviously do not want to expose your investments to declining value. Check out crime statistics by calling the local police department. Other good sources are the library, local newspapers, and the Internet (including sex offender registries).

— **Future development.** What kind of plans does the community have for future development? Is the development going to affect the property you want to buy? Call the community-planning department to find out about these plans.

— **Natural risks.** Some communities are prone to natural disasters (floods, fires, mudslides, earthquakes). Investigate the history of the community for these risks before you invest in a property because you will need to have insurance coverage to protect yourself financially against such disasters (if you are living in the home). Possible sources of information are the U.S. Geological Survey (for earthquakes) and the Federal Emergency Management Agency (FEMA) for flood, hurricane, and tornado information. Insurance companies and agents also can provide you with this information.

Visual appeal is another issue to consider when comparing neighborhoods. Visit neighborhoods to see if lawns or grounds are well-kept. Are the streets free of litter? Are the houses well-painted and in good repair? Are there gardens that enhance the beauty of homes and businesses? All this adds up to "curb appeal" and is a sign that both residents and commercial owners and managers are committed to keeping their properties in top condition. This commitment increases property values, rental rates, and occupancy—all signs that an investment in the neighborhood will be reasonably secure and profitable. Obviously, avoid blighted neighborhoods with unkempt lawns, junk-filled vacant lots, and so on.

Evaluate the potential of a neighborhood from the viewpoints of an appraiser and of a tenant looking for a place to live. These perspectives will provide both an objective and a subjective view of the area and its properties. Use a property knowledge sheet for each of the rental property locations you are considering. A property knowledge sheet is simply a listing of all the basic information about a rental property, including the following:

- Size

- Type (residential, multi-unit, etc.)

- Age

- Type of construction

Such sheets give a snapshot of a property and can help you make an informed decision about investing in a particular property. On page 135 is an example of such a sheet. You can use standardized forms or create one to fit your particular needs.

If you are interested in commercial real estate investments rather than residential, then you can use a variant of the property knowledge sheet to judge the viability of a business property. Of course, the key factor in any commercial or industrial business is location. Look for areas where successful retailers congregate. The initial success of an anchor, or primary, tenant brings about further success. Avoid retail centers and strip malls in which there are empty spaces and "For Lease" signs in the windows, signaling that trouble exists in the management or in the neighborhood. Most investors begin locally because they are familiar with the properties, but more distant properties also can be good investments, providing you have thoroughly researched the area.

THE REAL ESTATE MARKET— TO TIME OR NOT TO TIME

Real estate investment is cyclical, and the cycle boils down into two markets: a buyer's market or a seller's market. A **buyer's market** happens when property owners cannot sell their properties quickly, meaning they must be more flexible on the price and the terms, which results in a great opportunity to seek seller financing. A **seller's market** means many buyers are in search of a limited supply of properties. It's a seller's market when properties sell for more than the asking price. The cycle works this way: A high demand for real estate creates a shortage of properties, higher rents, and increased property appreciation. So to meet the demand, more properties are built. Then overbuilding occurs, and rents and property valuation declines. Then the cycle begins again. Of course, national or international economic factors also have an influence on the cycle, but this influence can often have an uneven effect on real estate properties, depending on which region of the country you are in. California may have high rents and property values, while at the same time Michigan's investment potential might be dismal.

It is important to remember that although the real estate investment market does have its ups and downs, it does not move as rapidly as the stock market does. This is an advantage of real estate over equities. Real estate investment allows you to look long-term and keep an eye out for an up cycle or a down cycle.

In terms of timing, experts disagree. Some believe in holding properties long-term regardless of cycles because real estate almost always appreciates over time. They believe if you invest soundly, then there is no reason to jump in and out of the market. This is a distant investment horizon; that is, the belief that patience and time will pay increased income and appreciation. Other experts believe in finding markets with great economic fundamentals. These markets have prices that have remained low over time and, thus, provide excellent value. Gary Keller in his book, *The Millionaire Real Estate Investor*, takes another view of timing, which has nothing to do with the markets whatsoever. To Keller, timing is finding the best time to buy or sell—period. It is not a passive approach in which you react to the cycles. Rather, you have to be active all the time in searching for deals that meet your criteria. His rule is this: "Any time an opportunity meets your strict criteria, act. If you do, you will have timed the market successfully." Keller reinforces the thought with this rule: Timing isn't about being in the right place at the right time. It's about being in the right place all the time.

In the end, you will have to adapt a strategy that fits your needs and style. Through experience, you will gain the knowledge you need to operate successfully within your chosen arena of investment. No matter which strategy you choose, practice due diligence—research, research, research, and follow the fundamentals of economic analysis.

Property Knowledge Sheet

Information on Property

Rental address_____Unit#_____ City/State _____ ZIP _____

Office hours (if any) _____ Unit(s) square footage: _____

Unit mix: Studios_____ 1 Bedroom_____ 2 Bedroom/1 Bath_____2 Bedroom/2 Bath _____

Rent: 1 Bedroom_____ 2 Bedroom/1 Bath_____ 2 Bedroom/2 Bath_____ Other_____

Application fee: _____ Security deposit:_____ Concessions: _____

Rental age: _____ Construction type: _____ Parking: _____

Recreational facilities_____ Laundry_____ Pets _____

Storage_____ Utilities (who pays)_____ A/C/Heat _____

Appliances_____ Floor coverings _____

Special features/comments_____

_____

Community Information

School district_____ Elem. school_____ Middle school_____

High school_____ Jr. College_____ College_____

Trade school_____ Preschool(s)_____

Childcare_____ Places of worship_____

Police/Fire stations/Ambulance service_____

Electric_____ Natural gas_____ Telephone_____ Cable _____

Water_____ Sewer_____ Library_____ Post Office _____

Hospital/Pharmacies/Vet/Medical facilities _____

_____

Nearby employment centers _____

Transportation availability _____

Groceries/Shopping _____

Local services _____

Restaurants _____

Notes _____

_____

_____

Rental Market Information

Rental competitors/rental rates/concessions _____

_____

_____

My competitive advantages _____

_____

_____

My competitive disadvantages _____

_____

_____

UNDERSTANDING LEASES AND VALUE

U nderstanding leases is fundamental to your success as a real estate investor. In legal terms, a lease is a contractual obligation between a lessor (landlord) and a lessee (tenant) to transfer the right of exclusive possession and the use of real estate for a defined period for an agreed-upon consideration (money). The language of the lease makes an enormous difference in the income stream the property generates. A poorly written lease can result in a property that produces little income or appreciation. When the lease is written fairly, then both landlord and tenant should benefit from the transaction. In order to legally enforce the lease, always get the lease in writing. Oral agreements can be enforceable, but such contracts are much harder to enforce and prove. Spell out every detail. Written leases and contracts are the foundation of good business practices.

- They are clear.

- They define the rights and responsibilities of both the landlord and the tenant.

- They can be interpreted and enforced by a third party.

- They provide consequences for violating the terms.

- They provide a prescribed manner of dispute resolution.

Get everything in writing. When offered a lease, obtain the complete lease and read every word. Do not accept the first page or two or a summary of the main points. If you want to add modifications or addendums, make sure those are in writing as well. Always have your legal advisor review any lease before you sign.

TRANSFERABILITY OF LEASES

In most cases, existing leases transfer with the property upon change of ownership. This means they are enforceable, and as a new owner you cannot simply renegotiate or void an existing lease. A buyer is legally obligated for all the terms and conditions of current leases. You must fully understand every aspect of the lease before signing it. A flawed lease can be detrimental to your investment. Vague or faulty terms can decrease a property's current and future value. Watch for the following warning signs:

- **Boilerplate (generic) forms.** A lease should be tailored to a specific property and the tenant-landlord agreement. Boilerplate forms may neither comply with laws in your area nor be relevant to your agreement.

- **Vague or undefined charges and fees.** If fees and charges for such items as late payments and returned checks are not clearly defined, then you may be unable to enforce them. The same is true of the property's rules and regulations. If they are unclear, they may not be enforceable.

- **Vague rent escalation clause.** A vague clause (or worse, none at all) can result in loss of income if you cannot raise the rent as the market dictates.

Although most sellers are honest and disclose all facts about properties they are selling, many states do not have the same written disclosure requirements mandated for residential transactions. So you and everyone in your team (broker, agent, advisor, etc.) must analyze the lease closely to make sure the terms are reasonable and fair. Look at the expiration date of any lease you examine. Evaluate them against current market conditions and consider the expense of any concessions you may have to make in a renewal of a residential lease. If it is a commercial lease, see what tenant improvements or rent concessions may have to be made, and weigh them against the income and appreciation you'll receive from the property. Generally speaking, it is less costly to renew a tenant than to lose one and have to negotiate a new lease.

RESIDENTIAL AND COMMERCIAL LEASES

Residential leases are much clearer and less complex than commercial leases. All the same, you still need to perform due diligence in examining a residential lease. Examine every lease carefully and have it reviewed by the appropriate member of your team. Watch out for leases loaded with rent concessions in exchange for upfront higher rents. These concessions can include free rent, limited rent increases, promises of new carpets or fixtures, and any number of other costly upgrades. This tactic is designed to make the seller's financial statement look better than it really is, and it can be misleading because it is not the net effective rent. If you sign this type of lease, you lose money in the form of free rent, carpet replacement, and the like.

Commercial leases are distinctly different from residential leases. You must have a thorough understanding in these leases because they are much more complex than residential leases. Fortunately, that is where lease abstraction comes in to play. **Lease abstraction** puts all the "legalese" into plain English so that you can understand all the legal clauses within the lease. A lease abstract describes in detail the following items:

- Issues and calculations affecting the lease (rent, square footage, length of lease, renewal date, options, signage, rights of expansion/contraction, and leasing restrictions).

- The dates, rights, and options available to each party that affect the lease.

- Legal clauses that specifically inhibit or enable you to perform in a certain manner.

Either landlords or tenants can have abstracts prepared by the appropriate legal members of their teams. Another option is to hire a Lease Abstractor who combines both the legal and accounting professions. An attorney may struggle with the financial and business aspects of leases, and an accountant may struggle with the legal implications, but a Lease Abstractor can handle both sides of the equation. In any case, be sure to get a lease abstraction for every commercial lease you consider.

When considering commercial property financing, expect a lender to require a certificate or signed rent roll with a written lease abstract for each tenant. Lenders want to make sure you can meet their debt service obligations; in plain language, they want to know that you can make payments as promised. For this reason, lenders do their own income projections based on information they require you to obtain from the tenants. Here is the information they will require.

- **Lease estoppel.** In technical terms, these are documents used in commercial mortgage transactions in which the lender is secured by property that is leased to tenants. They are also called **tenant estoppel letters** or **tenant acceptance** letters. American Banker Online **www. americanbanker.com**) defines lease estoppels this way:

  > Lease estoppels are *"written admissions that are obtained by the lender prior to funding to create estoppel. In an estoppel letter, the tenants attest that they believe the lease to be valid and enforceable, that they are making lease payments as agreed, that the landlord is not in default of any lease provisions requiring landlord performance and that no rent has been prepaid. The estoppel letter gives the lender more rights and more flexibility for disposing of the property in the event that the borrower defaults."*

  Keep in mind that lease estoppels benefit the buyer as well as the lender. To make sure you are aware of all contingencies, you should require lease estoppels from all tenants when you buy a commercial property.

- **Financial statement.** Any lease should require a financial statement from the commercial tenant. The rent in the lease may be stipulated, but can the tenant actually pay it? If not, you are losing money. Requiring financial statements on a regular basis ensures that the tenant is making a profit and is able to pay rent.

- **Current sales information.** Be sure to review any current sales information. In general, retail leases have provisions for percentage rents. This means the tenant pays a base rent plus additional rent based on a percentage of sales. Often, a sliding scale applies. In this case, the percentage paid by the tenant increases as sales increase.

THE PRINCIPLES OF REAL ESTATE VALUATION

Seven economic principles underlie valuation of real estate. The first four form the basis of an understanding of the current value and future potential of real estate, but you also need knowledge of the remaining three (regression, progression, and conformity) because they can affect value now and in the future.

1. **Demand.** Do people want or need to own or possess a property and do they have the money to satisfy that need?

2. **Utility.** Can the property fulfill its intended purpose? An example of an unfilled purpose would be a trendy retail property located in a remote area that customers cannot easily find.

3. **Scarcity.** The theory of substitution holds that the value of a property replaceable in the market tends to be set by

the cost of acquiring an equally desirable "substitute" property. In other words, value is set by comparing similar properties.

4. **Transferability.** This simply refers to the ease with which ownership rights are transferred from one owner to the next.

5. **Regression.** Regression occurs when a property's value is negatively affected by surrounding properties that are of lower value, inferior in construction, or in worse condition. Buying the best property in a bad neighborhood is simply throwing your money away.

6. **Progression.** The opposite of regression. A property's value is positively affected by surrounding properties that are of better quality, are in excellent condition, and have a higher value. This means you can buy a property that is essentially sound but neglected in a good neighborhood. By bringing the property up to neighborhood standards through repairs, maintenance, and upgrades, you stand to gain great value at a lower cost.

7. **Conformity.** This simply means that property values are maximized when a property conforms to the surrounding properties. The opposite is also true. If a property is "out of synch" with surrounding structures, its value decreases. If you buy a distressed property, you want to renovate it to conform to neighborhood standards — but do not over-improve it. Over-improvement can push a home or property into a higher cost bracket and limit prospects for selling or renting it.

THE HIGHEST AND BEST-USE CONCEPT

"Highest and best use" is a basic concept of real estate. In a legal sense, it's the use of a property that makes it the most valuable to a buyer or to the market. In a business sense, it means one single use will result in maximum profitability through the best and most efficient use of the property. All the principles previously described are based on this premise. Of course, many variables can affect the highest and best use of a property, so it does not remain constant over time. Zoning can change the use of a property. The path of progress can alter the value of a property, which often happens with agricultural land. Financially speaking, agriculture acreage does not have the best and highest use, but when it is bought because it is in the path of progress, suddenly it has that best and highest use because of the development possibilities.

FAIR MARKET VALUE VERSUS INVESTMENT VALUE

What is the difference between fair market value and investment value? The Internal Revenue Service defines it this way: "The **fair market value** is the price at which the property would change hands between a willing buyer and a willing seller, neither being under any compulsion to buy or to sell and both having reasonable knowledge of relevant facts." Of course, this definition refers to any property of any type, so here is a more precise definition for real estate: Fair market value is the price a buyer is willing to pay and the seller is willing to accept at a given point in time. **Investment value,** on the other hand, is the value to you, as an investor, based on your investment goals and requirements (tax rate, cost of capital, etc.). That value can vary according to competing investors' goals. Competitors may be willing to pay more for a particular property than you are because they are looking to maintain Tax-Deferred 1031 Exchange status. You will recall from an earlier chapter that this tax law allows investors to sell one property and buy another without incurring capital gains taxes. Investors simply have to reinvest all their profits into the next property (or properties) within a specific timeline. The point to remember is that investment value may be higher or lower than fair market value; avoid being drawn into bidding wars if the investment value doesn't meet your goals.

Three main sources decide the value of a particular property:

1. **Brokers and agents.** These individuals have Competitive Market Analyses (CMAs) done to estimate the values of properties in their area. A typical CMA is completed by reviewing all recent property sales in an area and determining what a house is selling for given such items as square footage, number of bedrooms, amount of land, and other factors. Brokers and agents offer this information with the goal of getting listings on the properties, so keep that in mind when studying CMAs.

2. **Professional appraisers.** These individuals are specialists in the valuation of properties. They are hired by owners or lenders to establish a property value. They are not often used by sellers unless legal complexities like probate, litigation, or government entities are involved.

3. **Sellers.** They often do their own research on an informal basis. They collect information about recent sales of properties in their targeted area. Because their research

is informal and not exhaustive, variations in valuations occur.

Of course, you cannot rely on these sources alone to value properties. Much more formal research is required. Consider hiring a professional appraiser to get in-depth information. Another option is to become a professional appraiser yourself by earning the professional appraiser certification. Not only do you get a better understanding of the complexities of appraisals, but you also may qualify for favorable tax status. A good source for information on certification is The Appraisal Foundation (**http://appraisalfoundation.org**), a non-profit educational organization dedicated to fostering professionalism by "establishing educational and experience qualification criteria for the licensing, certification and recertification of appraisers." Whichever method you choose, be familiar with the standard value benchmarks used in real estate investing.

STANDARD VALUE GUIDELINES

Over the years, the real estate industry has used several standard formulas as a point of reference for setting prices and evaluating possible purchases. These include:

- Gross Rent Multiplier (GRM)

- Gross Income Multiplier (GIM)

- Price per unit and square foot

- Replacement cost

These formulas are easy to calculate and easy to understand. However, they are only guidelines. There are much more accurate formulas to be applied including Net Operating Income (NOI), which will be covered later in this book. Also, recognize that GRM, GIM, price per unit and square foot, and replacement cost are not universally approved practices of either professional appraisers or federal lenders.

Gross Rent Multiplier and Gross Income Multiplier

The GRM is most often used for residential income properties because almost all of the income is from tenant rent payments. These properties include single-family rental homes, small apartment buildings, and the like. The GRM is a ratio used to estimate the value of income-producing properties, giving you an approximate estimate of value. The ratio uses two pieces of financial information: the sales price and the total gross rents possible. This information is gathered for multiple sales of similar types of income properties in a particular area. It can then be used to estimate the market value of other similar properties in that area. The GRM can be used on a monthly basis or a yearly basis.

The monthly GRM formula is this:

**Sales Price of a Property ÷ Potential Monthly Gross Income =
Monthly GRM**

The yearly GRM formula is this:

Sales Price ÷ Yearly Potential Gross Income = Yearly GRM

Here is an example: If the sales price for a property is $200,000 and the monthly potential gross rental income for a property is $2,500, the GRM is equal to 80.

$200,000 + $2,500 = 80

Monthly potential gross income is equal to the full occupancy monthly rental amount which assumes all available rental units are occupied. In general, properties in prime locations have higher GRMs than properties in less desirable locations. When comparing similar properties in the same area or location, the lower the GRM, the more profitable the property, assuming that operating expenses are proportionate for the properties compared. Keep in mind that because the GRM calculation does not include operating expenses, this statement might not hold true for similar properties in which one of the properties has significantly higher operating expenses.

Use the same information to calculate gross income. To apply the GIM formula, assume you are looking at an area with several similar properties that have sold recently with an average monthly GRM of 80. This information can be used to estimate the value of comparable properties for sale. If the monthly potential gross income for a property is $3,000, estimate its value in the following way:

GRM x Potential Gross Income = Estimated Market Value
80 x $3,000 = $240,000

Using these formulas, you can get an approximate estimate of value when consistent and accurate financial information is available for sales of similar types of properties in a particular market place. Remember, they do have limitations. Operating expenses, debt service, and tax consequences aren't included in the GRM calculation. You could have a situation where two properties have about the same potential gross income, but one property has significantly higher operating expenses. So the GRM might not give you an accurate estimation of the market value for these properties. Also, since the GRM formula uses the monthly potential gross income and doesn't account for a vacancy factor, this can also affect the accuracy of the property value estimates. This is why it's so important for you to perform due diligence and have accurate and detailed financial information for comparable sales beyond the GRM or GIM.

Price per Unit and Price per Square Foot

If you are interested in investing in multi-unit properties and want a general sense of the value of apartments, you can calculate by price per unit. This is a simple formula:

Number of Units ÷ Asking Price = Price per Unit

So a ten-unit building priced at $250,000 would be valued this way:

10 Units ÷ $250,000 = $25,000 per Unit

Again, this formula has limitations. It does not take into account important factors affecting the value of the property — location, age, size, condition, etc. Use the formula only to get a quick idea of the relative values when comparing other properties in the same market.

In the commercial, industrial, and retail markets, the formula most often used to calculate value is price per square foot. Here's the formula:

Asking Price ÷ Square Footage = Price per Square Foot

For a building with 7,000 square feet and an asking price of $300,000, calculate price per square foot as follows:

$300,000 ÷ 7,000 = $42.86 per Square Foot

The formula gives you an approximation of the value of the property under consideration. However, again, it does not take into account such important factors location, quality of construction, parking, occupancy level, and so on. Inexpensive square footage in a crime-ridden neighborhood is no bargain at all.

REPLACEMENT COST

Replacement cost is the current cost to construct a similar property that serves the same purpose as the original property. Calculate the replacement cost by comparing the price per square foot to an estimate of the cost per square foot, to build a similar new property, including the cost of land.

CHAPTER

ENSURING A RETURN ON YOUR INVESTMENT

This chapter is all about number-crunching, an activity that is vital in achieving the best possible return on your investment (ROI). ROI is determined by four important elements.

1. **Net cash flow.** This is the money produced by the property after deducting all costs and debt service from the income.

2. **Depreciation tax benefits.** One of the great benefits of real estate investment is the tax benefits derived from depreciation.

3. **Equity buildup.** Many properties are acquired through loans. Equity grows as the debt is paid down over time.

4. **Appreciation.** Appreciation is the result of buying property and selling it for a higher price at a later date, often many years later.

The standard for creating a profitable real estate portfolio is straightforward: Buy properties with the potential for high occupancy and growth in income while keeping turnover and expenses to a minimum.

Number-crunching will not only help you make decisions based on fact, but it will also prevent you from making an emotional decision about a property that would drain your resources. The formulas described below produce reliable results.

NET OPERATING INCOME

Always start with this formula. This simple calculation is the most critical element in determining the potential for return on your real estate investment. Net operating income (NOI) is equal to a property's yearly gross income less operating expenses, or:

Income − Expenses = NOI

Gross income includes both rental income and other income such as parking fees, laundry, and vending receipts. In other words, gross income is all income associated with a property. **Operating expenses** are costs incurred during the operation and maintenance of a property. They include repairs and maintenance, insurance, management fees, utilities, supplies, and property taxes. Not included are principal and interest, capital expenditures, depreciation, income taxes, and amortization of loan points. To follow is an example of how to calculate NOI:

Income	
Gross Rents Possible	$100,000
Other Income	$3,000
Potential Gross Income	$103,000
Less Vacancy Amount	($2,000)
Effective Gross Income	$101,000
Less Operating Expenses	($31,000)
Net Operating Income	$70,000

On the more technical side, NOI is used in two important real estate ratios. It is not likely that you will use them in your financial analysis of properties, but you should be aware that lenders use them. NOI is an essential part of the **Capitalization Rate** (Cap Rate). This is a calculation used to estimate the value of income-producing properties. For example, assume you have a market capitalization rate of 10 for the type of property you are considering purchasing. A market cap rate is calculated by evaluating the financial data from current sales of comparable income-producing properties in a given marketplace. You are evaluating a similar income property that is currently for sale with a net operating income of $50,000. To estimate the value of this property:

$$\text{Estimated Value} = \frac{\text{Net Operating Income}}{\text{Capitalization Rate}} = \frac{\$50,000}{.10} = \$500,000$$

Another ratio used to evaluate income-producing properties is the **Debt Coverage Ratio** (DCR). The NOI is also an important part of this ratio. Lenders and investors use the DCR to measure a property's ability to pay its operating expenses and mortgage payments. A debt coverage ratio of 1 is breakeven. Most lenders require a minimum of 1.1 to 1.3 to be considered for a commercial loan. The larger the debt coverage ratio, the better the risk from both the lender's and the investor's point of view. Debt coverage ratio is figured like this:

$$\textbf{Debt Coverage Ratio} = \frac{\textbf{Net Operating Income}}{\textbf{Debt Service}} = \frac{\$50,000}{\$40,000} = 1.25$$

Debt service is the total of all interest and principal paid in a given year. It is equal to the mortgage payment multiplied by 12 or the mortgage payments times 12, if there is more than one loan on a property.

When considering properties, it is necessary to value them based on the projected NOI for a minimum of the next year. It is best, however, to project over several years. A seller can provide a current NOI, but verify the numbers. Some sellers, brokers, and agents will give you a generic NOI that projects higher rents and lower expenses based on the assumption that you, as the new owner, will raise the rents to market level and lower the costs of operating the property. However, a well-managed property will already have below-market rents, and if the property is professionally managed, expenses are most likely already low.

Remember to take NOI projections with a grain of salt, particularly from sellers, brokers, or agents who tell you that the sky is the limit and that your NOI will continue to grow far into the future. As discussed earlier, real estate has its cycles and is affected by the law of supply and demand. Spend time carefully analyzing any figures you receive on a particular property.

GET REAL NUMBERS

By their nature, estimates do not produce exact figures, which means you have to find out what a property can produce in terms of projected rent and income for you, should you invest in it. You can start this process with a *zero-based* budget. Essentially, you start from scratch with paper (or a computer program) and write down or enter the rents for each tenant in the property and the projected income. Evaluate the strength of each tenant in a commercial, industrial, or retail property. Make sure they can truly meet their rent obligations; otherwise, your investment will suffer. Likewise, you want to make sure the tenants increase your income over the years. Ask the seller for a list of tenants to use as a starting point for this formula.

Beyond this basic due diligence, look at the income and expense reports and know the terminology. Here are two basic formulas you should know well:

- **Gross Potential Income (GPI).** This is the maximum gross income that would be generated from the rent if a property were at 100 percent occupancy and all money owed were collected in full.

- **Effective Gross Income (EGI).** EGI estimates the total income of the property while taking vacancy loss and other (non-rent) revenues into account. More specifically, EGI is calculated by taking the EGI and then subtracting the collection losses, concessions, delinquencies, and vacancies, and then adding the other income from late charges, returned checks, and other related sources.

Now take a closer look at the elements you need to consider when evaluating the real potential of a property.

Vacancies

Vacancy rates will give you an idea of the strength or weakness of the real estate investment market. Brokers, agents, and lenders often have a vacancy percentage at hand, but that percentage may have nothing to do with real market conditions. Check more closely into the market to determine the actual vacancy rate. This is particularly important if you are an investor wanting to move from the single-family home market to multi-unit properties. Apartments and the like are a different animal from the residential market. If you do not check vacancy rates along with property taxes, utilities, and so on, you can underestimate the amount of income, which can be risky if your cash reserve is too small to cover unexpected expenses. You must expect to lose income one way or another during the year and plan to cover that loss by figuring a vacancy rate that fits your situation. For example, you might figure that you will lose 1 month's income for every 12-month period. This translates into an 8.3 vacancy rate ($1 \div 12 = 8.3$).

Concessions

Concessions are designed to attract and keep tenants. Most commonly, they include free or reduced rent, ceiling fans, microwaves, new carpet or carpet cleaning, and so on. Concessions, however, take money out of your pocket. Consider a month's free rent. Assume the property charges $1,000 for monthly rent. Over a 12-month period, that's $12,000. However, one month's free rent drops that amount to $11,000. So the effective rental rate is only $916.17 ($11,000 $\div$ 12).

Delinquencies and Collection Losses

Collection losses are rent or other charges that the landlord must write off as uncollectible. A general rule is that it is one-half of one percent of rental income. However, like all general rules, it may not apply to your situation. That is why you must do your own analysis of actual collection loss, based on tenant strength, the strength or weakness of the local job market, security deposits held, tenant and landlord laws, and other factors.

Additional Income Streams

Rental properties have the capability of producing additional income through secondary items. For residential properties, these items can include laundry, vending, parking, storage, Internet service, garages, and so forth. Commercial properties can include all of those as well as such items as common area maintenance fees, security requirements, telecommunications, heating and ventilation, and so on.

OPERATING EXPENSES

It is going to cost to operate any property. Obviously, you want to keep expenses to a minimum so it is wise to review both past and projected expenses. The current landlord may overpay for some services or offer other services that you plan to take care of yourself. As always, it is prudent not to accept expense information offered by owners or real estate agents at face value. They want the property to look as attractive as possible so they may underestimate the operating expenses. To get the real figures, ask the seller to provide a copy of his or her federal tax return Schedule E for each year of ownership.

Utilities

Utility expenses are typically one of the larger property operating costs and can increase rapidly due to natural disasters. Check with the local service providers for current and projected rates for electricity, natural gas, water and sewer, telephone, cable, and waste removal. Many of these utilities are state or locally regulated so they are required to file projected rate increases well ahead of implementation.

In addition, you can take action to lower utility expenses. Simple improvements can reduce utility usage significantly. Consider energy-efficient light bulbs, low-flow toilets and shower heads, insulation, automated sprinkler systems, and other improvements that make sense.

The simplest way to cut utility costs is to require tenants to pay for them. This action can have a dramatic impact on your NOI.

Management Fees

Remember that you will invest time as well as money into property and that you should be compensated for that time, especially if you personally manage the property. If in the future you decide to concentrate on the further acquisition of real estate, you can hire a property manager, and you will have his or her future services accounted for with your management fee.

Insurance

To be fully covered and protected in the property-casualty area, work with insurance agencies to determine the best protection at the lowest price. Some insurers offer a package or volume program.

Additional Operating Costs

There are a number of service and maintenance costs that can exhaust your income—landscaping, pest control, cleaning, janitorial—if you do not track them carefully. Do not simply accept the historical figures of the property owner or agent. Talk with each service firm for its current pricing. Solicit bids if you believe the charges are too high.

CASH FLOW

Cash flow is the NOI minus debt service and capital expenditures.

SAMPLE INVESTMENT PROPERTY CASH FLOW

Annual gross potential rental income	$1,000,000
+ Other income	$30,000
+ Common Area Maintenance (CAM) reimbursement	$20,000
– Vacancy and collection loss	($40,000)
Effective Gross Income	$1,010,000
– Operating Expenses	($300,000)
Annual Net Operating Income	$710,000
– Annual debt service	($500,000)
– Capital improvements	($50,000)
Annual Cash Flow Before Taxes	$160,000

Once you have your NOI, you can project your annual cash flow. Here's the formula:

NOI – Debt Service – Capital Improvements = Pre-Tax Cash Flow

Debt Servicing

Make sure that debt-service projections are based on a solid financing commitment. Do not rely on the figures shown in sales flyers or broker information sheets. For most conventionally financed properties, the debt service will be 80 to 90 percent of the NOI. Fixed-rate financing is easy to figure, so if you have that type of financing, you can simply plug it into your income and expense statement.

Capital Improvements

Capital improvements refer to the replacement of such major building elements as a roof, driveway, windows, appliances, and floor coverings — anything that involves a relatively large expense. Account for capital improvements to a property. Do not underestimate the expenses that will be incurred. If you are interested in investing in multi-unit properties, remember that items will get broken, and you will have to replace them. Set aside a reserve fund every year so you are not caught short when things break or deteriorate. Capital improvements in a neglected property can increase its value and appreciation. In any case, to get full knowledge of a property's good and bad points, do a thorough inspection with a qualified contractor or appraiser, looking particularly for health or safety concerns. Also consider including a leasing broker on your team. He or she can prioritize needed work and recommend inexpensive upgrades that will re-position the property to produce higher income and appreciation. All information should be documented in written summaries and be specific to a suite or unit number. It should also include an evaluation of all common areas.

Once you have compiled all the information, it is time to contact contractors and suppliers to get estimates. Depending on the property, estimates will vary due to age, location, and overall property condition. To keep a balance in terms of capital improvements, make needed repairs and upgrades to keep the property in top shape. Deferred maintenance costs money in the long run. On the other hand, avoid making improvements that cost more than they are worth in terms of improving the quality of the property. That money could be saved or better spent elsewhere.

COMMERCIAL PROPERTY LEASE OPTIONS

There are three basic forms of commercial property leases:

1. **Gross lease.** The tenant pays a set amount of rent while the landlord is responsible for payment of taxes, insurance, and other property-associated costs.

2. **Net lease.** The tenant pays the rent plus a portion of the maintenance fees, insurance premiums, and other operating expenses.

3. **Triple-net lease.** This type of lease is typically associated with a freestanding facility. The tenant pays for all fees and operating expenses associated with the space.

When the tenant is responsible for the costs of maintenance and janitorial services, then the costs of those services should not be included as a property expense. In general, commercial property leases can be gross leases, modified gross leases, or net leases; however, residential properties are almost always leased on a gross basis, except for utilities.

Common Area Maintenance Charges

Common area maintenance (CAM) charges are costs passed on to tenants in multi-tenant commercial buildings. They can include security, maintenance, snow removal, utilities, and other services necessary to keep the property in good shape. Typically, they are assessed on a proportional basis to the tenants. These charges can be due in advance or paid in arrears. The CAM charges are usually listed in the cash flow as "Common Area Maintenance reimbursement" or "CAM reimbursement." This is an income item, but it is offset against the corresponding items listed in the operating expenses for the property.

To get a basis for the monthly CAM charge collection, develop an estimated annual budget for the property. Then, on an annual or other basis, calculate and reconcile the actual expenses incurred for the items against the total of the estimates paid during that time period. Once that is done, you can collect a shortfall or refund any excess to the tenant.

If you decide to buy a commercial property, pay close attention to the language of the lease and determine what operating expenses, if any, are paid by the tenants. It is important to understand whether the property is using gross or net leases. If you are not clear on this, you may be misled as to what the actual NOI and cash flow are that you will receive for the property. Rent will be lower for commercial properties with net leases. With net leases, the tenants are directly responsible for their own maintenance and for making property tax and insurance payments. However, with a gross lease on a similar property, you may receive higher rent, part of which will go toward those same expenses and costs. In that case, the end result will be about the same.

Which Type of Lease Is Best?

Opinions differ on which type of lease is best. Many investors prefer net leases because management of the property is reduced. However, the investor still must ensure that the tenant does not skimp on maintenance. A **modified gross lease** is the preference of other investors. With this lease, tenants pay for expenses they can control. Apartment buildings are a good example of the use of the modified gross lease. In this arrangement, the landlord is responsible for all property maintenance, repairs, and upgrades inside and outside of the building. He or she is also responsible for property taxes, insurance coverage, and other associated items. At the same time, the tenants are responsible for water, sewer, heat, and electricity. Because utilities are a considerable and ongoing expense, it would be prudent to invest only in multi-unit residential properties and commercial properties with separate meters for those services.

THE THREE BASIC METHODS OF DETERMINING REAL ESTATE VALUE

Typically, professional appraisers consider real estate value from three points of view:

1. The comparable sales method

2. The income approach

3. The cost approach

Each of these methods produces a slightly different estimate of value, so the appraiser weighs, or reconciles, the three valuation methods against one another to produce an estimate of value.

Comparable Sales (Market Data) Method

The comparable sales method is simple. It determines an approximate property value based upon sales of similar properties within a reasonable recent period of time. Similarities include type of property, age, location, and size. In practice, appraisers usually look for at least three similar properties in close proximity to the subject property. Because every property has advantages and disadvantages, appraisers make positive or negative value adjustments based on those qualities relative to the subject property. For example, if a sold property is in better condition, or newer, than the subject property, then an adjustment is made to lower the sold property's actual value to make it more comparable to the property under consideration.

The Income Approach

Most often used for larger income-producing properties, this approach determines an estimate of total real estate value based upon the rate of return from potential net operating income from the property (assuming it was leased to a third party). In this method, an appraiser estimates an annual income rate for the property based upon similar rates for similar users. For example, the appraiser might determine that a retail space might rent for a rate of $10 per square foot per year. This rate should be comparable to other retail spaces in the vicinity.

Once this lease rate is determined, the property's value is estimated using a type of multiplier known as a capitalization rate, or cap rate. Historically, cap rates are subject to several factors including the strength of the type of tenant, the level of landlord involvement, the local economic conditions, and the type of industry. For example, a property with a good tenant in a choice location might command a cap rate of 12 percent in a strong market.

The value of the real estate is determined by multiplying the net rental rate by the reciprocal of the cap rate. To continue our example, the value would be calculated by multiplying $10 per square foot by 8.3 (100 percent divided by a 12 percent cap rate). This would mean that the investment value of the real estate would be equal to $83 per square foot. These figures are often further adjusted to take into account other variables, including vacancy rates, property management costs, and other investor-related factors.

The Cost Approach

This approach evaluates the replacement value of the property by analyzing the cost components of the specific land and building. It is commonly used for new properties, proposed construction, or non-income producing properties like schools, hospitals, churches, public buildings, among others. The variables involved in estimating value are contingent upon location, geographic region of the country, labor, and material costs. Factors considered are costs for land acquisitions, site preparation, utilities, types of building materials, tenant improvements, and so-called "soft" costs like architectural and engineering costs along with legal and brokerage fees. This method is often useful for estimating replacement cost. Here are the steps appraisers typically use in the cost approach:

1. Estimate the value of the land if it were vacant and if it were used in its highest and best use.

2. Estimate the current cost to reproduce the building as new (before depreciation).

3. Estimate all forms of accrued depreciation.* Subtract that amount from Step 2. Arrive at an approximate cost to reproduce the building in its current condition.

   *Accrued depreciation has three sources. First is normal wear and tear (**physical depreciation**). Next, there is **functional obsolescence** due to a decline in the usefulness of a property because of changes in consumer preferences. Finally, there is **external obsolescence**, which is a loss in value resulting from such external forces such as a major employer closing or moving to a different location.*

4. Combine the value of the land and the value of the depreciated improvements to arrive at the total value of the property.

Here is an example of how the cost approach works: Assume you are looking at a duplex that is ten years old. The cost of a comparable lot would be $50,000. After checking with local builders, you find that the cost to build a new property would be $75 per square foot. However, because the duplex is not new, you estimate the cost to rebuild the property in its present depreciated shape is $65 per square foot. If the property total square footage is 3,000, then the total value of depreciated improvements is $195,000. By adding the land value of $50,000 to this figure, it gives you an overall property value of $245,000.

Reconciliation

To arrive at a single estimate of the market value of a property at a specific time, professional appraisers take the figures from all three approaches and reconcile them. They do not simply average them because all three methods are equally valid and reliable. Instead, an appraiser matches the approach to the type of property considered and gives more weight to the appropriate method. For example, when considering income-producing real estate, appraisers generally rely on the income method because the property will be an investment.

Assume the three methods have been applied to an income-producing property, arriving at the following figures:

- Sales method: $300,000

- Cost method: $320,000

- Income method: $298,000

In this case, the most credence would be given to the income method. The cost method does not carry as much authority because it tends to be used for new construction, and the building under consideration already exists. Now you can compare the sales-method figure ($300,000) with the income-method figure ($298,000) and assume that the second amount is the right amount for an offer.

If the asking price for the property is $300,000, the seller may or may not accept your $298,000 offer. If he or she does not accept the offer, remember that you are looking for below-market opportunities and move on. Do not pay retail; rather, continue looking for opportunities to increase income and add value.

Although appraisals tend to be more of an art than an exact science, it is important to understand the three basic methods of valuation. That understanding will help you avoid overpaying for properties. In addition, lenders will require an appraisal to determine how much you may borrow. Finally, these appraisal methods can help determine an appropriate asking price when it is time to sell your real estate investment.

Advanced Valuation Techniques

Professional real estate brokers and investors go beyond the three valuation techniques to analyze cash flow over a period of several years in order to arrive at an estimate of the valuation. Although you will not use these methods if you are new to real estate investing, be aware of them and the way they work. If you are daunted by the mathematics, investigate some of the software applications that expedite the calculations. A Google search on your computer will provide plenty of possible applications.

- **Discounted Cash Flow (DC)** — The discounted cash flow calculation, which is suited to an income-producing property, would included the following elements:

  — The initial investment amount.

  — A series of estimated yearly future after-tax cash flows.

  — The after-tax sales proceeds in a given year.

  — A discount rate determined by you, the investor.

  The discount rate you use reflects the investment risk and anticipated return required to take that risk. In other words, you enter the rate of return that you would like to make on the investment. With a negative discounted cash flow/net present value, this indicates the investment does not meet your expectations. The larger the net present value, the better the investment is for you.

- **Net Present Value (NPV)** — This method of evaluating a property considers the time value of money. In effect, it allows you to find the present value in "today's dollars" of the future net cash flow of a property. Using this method, you can then compare that amount with the amount of money needed to acquire the property. If the NPV is greater than the cost, the project will be profitable for you. If the NPV is less than the cost, then the property will fall short of the target yield.

- **Internal Rate of Return (IRR)** – This method of analyzing a major purchase or project allows you to find the interest rate equivalent to the dollar returns you expect from a property. Once you know the rate, you can compare it to the rates you could earn by investing your money in other properties or investments, including stocks, bonds, and money market accounts, to determine the best value for your money. This is the most popular of the sophisticated valuation techniques and is often used and quoted by real estate brokers who specialize in the marketing of investment properties.

ALL THE RESEARCH IS DONE—NOW WHAT?

Once you have done the research, it is time to decide if a property is a good opportunity or not. The property should produce future increases in NOI and cash flow, meaning you should consider a property in which the income can be increased or the expenses reduced. It also means you should have good knowledge of the valuation techniques covered in this chapter because sellers are using the same techniques to get the maximum price from buyers. If you do not understand the techniques, sellers can manipulate the facts to put the best possible face on their properties. Nearly every seller of an investment property will tell you that his rents are below market, saying, "Once you buy this building, you can raise rents and get that cash flow going!" Your immediate thought should be, *If that's true, why doesn't the present owner increase the rents and sell for a much higher price?* Actually, sellers often do raise the rents just before putting the property on the market, leaving a buyer little room for maneuvering after purchasing the building.

Deceit also can occur with regard to expenses. Sometimes, sellers trim their spending to show artificially low expenses. They may even claim that you can cut expenses through energy conservation. Ask yourself, *If that's true, why haven't they implemented an energy-conservation program?*

Of course, not all sellers resort to these kinds of shenanigans, but it pays to question claims and numbers that sound too good to be true. Especially watch for pro-forma estimates of the NOI, which can result in an above-market asking price that is unrealistic. Keep in mind that pro-forma estimates are just that — estimates.

So how do you find worthwhile properties that will produce future increases in NOI and cash flow? As stated previously, look for properties that show a reasonable potential for increased income or for reducing expenses. These can be properties with no vacancies and a waiting list or properties that have low turnover and many applicants for the few vacancies that occur. Another opportunity occurs when investment properties are priced below market for various legitimate reasons (illness, divorce, financial difficulties, etc.). Other sellers simply do not like the bargaining process and price below market to make the sale done quickly. In a few cases, you will find sellers who simply do not know the true market value of their property.

In general, look for older sellers with no mortgage who have taken advantage of all the tax depreciation deductions associated with their property. Also, look for value-added properties, which allow you to either increase the NOI or decrease the rate, thus increasing value. Apartment buildings often provide simple ways to increase value. Typically, the apartments have nearly the same floor plans. However, some units face quiet areas or swimming pools while others face noisy streets. Because those quieter units are more desirable to tenants, you can charge a higher rent for the prime locations within the building.

Sherrye Coggiola
Phone: 864-699-1480
Fax: 864-596-0641
1874 East Main Street
Spartanburg, SC 29307

Prior to beginning my real estate investment career, I worked as a residential agent for five years. From there, I went on to work in television sales for a decade. After two corporate takeovers, I decided enough was enough. It was time to drop out of that world. With the financial and spiritual support of my mom, I began a new career in real estate investing.

One of the first things I learned is there are no mistakes in investing; there are only expensive lessons. In addition, many people have a hard time getting financing to purchase investment properties. However, I used several investment strategies that led to my success, including:

1.   Buying right. You want to make money on your purchase.

2.   Never over-finance your properties.

3.   Have a three-month financial reserve for all property mortgage payments.

4.   You must be willing to be creative on the sale end.

I mainly purchase foreclosures, and I have a mixed portfolio of both short-term and long-term investments. In fact, I'm always willing to entertain best use options for each property.

Handling taxes on rental properties can be a challenge – I've been through three accountants in three years. I read a lot and know when an accountant has missed something. However, it's not a good use of my time to fill out lengthy tax forms.

The reality is real estate investing is hard work, and it can be very stressful. However, there are plenty of advantages to investing. As an investor, you are in control. You can make changes as quickly as the market changes, and you have plenty of options.

10

NEGOTIATIONS

Knowledge is power in any business transaction. Superior knowledge is definitely superior power when it comes to negotiating for investment properties. Combine that knowledge with effective negotiation strategies, and you have a winning combination.

In this case, knowledge refers not only to mastery of the information covered in previous chapters but also to in-depth knowledge of your target market. For example, imagine that by keeping your finger on the pulse of local developments, you have discovered that a major employer will move into an undeveloped or distressed area. This great opportunity is a reward for all your research. You can buy property in the affected area or, if you already own it, you can renovate or upgrade it, reaping the benefits of increased income and higher appreciation.

COMMON SENSE GUIDELINES FOR NEGOTIATION

You will find the following guidelines mentioned by many real estate gurus in their publications. However, these guidelines are not effective if you do not back them up with personal integrity. In the relatively closed world of real estate, your reputation is everything, and it should be one of honesty, sincerity, and a genuine desire to create a win-win situation for everyone involved in the negotiation process. If you get a reputation for being unfair or difficult, then your leads and even your career may wither.

Guideline 1: Prepare for Negotiations

Prepare yourself thoroughly for the negotiation process. Find out what the local chamber of commerce has in terms of information. Check with the local economic development agency to discover potential opportunities. Often the most powerful source of leads is knowledge of the right people. If you are new to real estate investment, it will take time to learn who the right people are, but it is time well-spent. Here are some ways to develop a network of friends, mentors, and lead-providers.

- **Become visible.** Join local associations to get your name into circulation among decision-makers. Start with a real estate association, a charity organization, Toastmasters, or any other organization to which real estate power brokers belong.

- **Find a mentor.** Within the above organizations, there are always a few people who love to teach and share information. Seek them out, but be prepared to offer knowledge and leads in return. Mentoring is a two-way street. The object is for both of you to grow in knowledge, expertise, and wealth.

- **Market yourself.** Once you have some experience, write articles for the local influential papers. If you do not have writing skills, find a ghost writer. Once your name appears in print, you will have some credibility, which can lead to radio and television interviews. Before you undertake these marketing activities, be knowledgeable about your subject and be prepared to speak in a professional manner. You can improve speaking skills through Toastmasters, which is a non-profit organization devoted to helping people develop public-speaking and leadership skills through practice and feedback in local clubs. Its vision statement states the goal of the entrepreneur:

"Toastmasters International empowers people to achieve their full potential and realize their dreams. Through our member clubs, people throughout the world can improve their communication and leadership skills, and find the courage to change."

- **Give back to your community.** Share your good fortune with citizens of your area and give in terms of time and money. Not only is this the right thing to do, but it also is a good investment for your career. Your generosity will repay you in terms of visibility and influence.

Of course, these are long-range, on-going activities. In the short term, there are more immediate and practical tasks to prepare for negotiations. Again, this is where research and intuition are crucial. Keep an eye out for opportunities similar to the following:

- A major employer is seeking land in a run-down area.

- Local companies have started hiring many new workers, indicating rapid growth.

- There are signs of a housing shortage developing.

- Transit authorities plan to extend light rail service through a neglected area.

With any of these opportunities, look for the best property at the best price. If you do not do your homework, you will end up paying too much.

Part of research means determining the market climate. Is it a seller's market or a buyer's market? If it's a seller's market, will it be wise to buy a property for more than replacement cost? It probably will not, especially if you plan to hold it for only a short period of time.

Whether it is a buyer's market or a seller's market, you need to know as much about the property as possible before considering a purchase.

Guideline 2: Determine the Seller's Motivations

It is important to determine why a seller wants to sell. Ask:

- How long has this property been on the market?

- What problems, if any, does this property have?

Of course, you will likely deal with a listing agent who may or may not be willing to share information with you. After all, they are maneuvering for the best price, just as you are. Aim to get as much useful information as possible from the agent or seller without revealing your goals for the property; it will help you structure the offer. If you have trouble getting useful information or encounter unwarranted delays, be suspicious. The seller may be simply testing the waters to see what price buyers will bite. Or, he may be trolling to find a buyer who is willing to pay well over market price.

In general, release as little information as possible both to keep your negotiating position as strong and to give the seller as little leverage as possible.

Guideline 3: Bring the Power of Facts to the Negotiation Process

The research you have done is one of the strongest weapons you can bring to the bargaining table. The seller and agent want the best price they can get, which can lead to some "creative" asking prices. Those prices have nothing to do with the reality of the market. Put your current market data on the table and point out that the figures do not support their offer. The seller and agent will soon realize that you have done your research and will settle down to serious negotiations. If the property needs repairs, the seller and agent may offer to provide estimated costs for the items that need to be fixed. Get your own bids from licensed professional contractors and use them as a check against the seller's bids.

Guideline 4: Be Patient and Objective

No matter how attractive a property may seem, do not let your heart rule your head. Stay patient and take time to consider the seller's offer as objectively as possible. Rely on your research to keep yourself grounded.

Guideline 5: Create a Win-Win Atmosphere

Both parties should walk away from the negotiating table feeling good about the process. Again, think long-term. More than likely, you will work with the same people again over the years, so it does not pay to create enemies for a short-term gain. Avoid both the "my way or the highway" style of negotiation, as well as the practice of "lowballing" or making a ridiculously low offer. If you adopt those tactics, few people will want to negotiate with you, and your real estate investment career may end up as a short one.

PUTTING TOGETHER AN OFFER

Your knowledge of a property will help you create an attractive offer. For example, suppose you are considering a property and have the following information:

- It is a residential property with four bedrooms and three baths.

- It is located close to a major redevelopment area and close to a school that has hired a principal with a reputation for bringing academic excellence to the education process.

- The demand for rental properties is strong.

- The seller wants $250,000 for the home, which is near the market value (not including deferred maintenance).

- You estimate the home will rent for $2,000 a month.

Although the property is realistically priced and looks like a good investment, the key question is, "What is the deferred maintenance going to cost?" Assume this property needs a new furnace, a new roof, and various other maintenance items like repainting and landscaping. Your bids show that these expenses will cost about $20,000. Your immediate response may be to make an offer of $230,000. Although that is a good first step, you must remember that your time (and willingness to take a risk) must be considered as well. In addition, there are always surprises during any repair process, and you need to plan for those contingencies as well. Add as much as 50 percent to account for those costs. So if you factor in 50 percent of the $20,000 estimate, you could adjust your offer down to $220,000.

Another strategy to pursue lies in the area of concessions. That is, you can offer to meet the full price of the seller while asking him or her to make repairs or improvements. Naturally, you should always ask the seller to correct any health and safety issues before agreeing to a purchase. Beyond that, however, you can also ask the seller to provide a credit in escrow for the replacement of specified items.

Do not forget the option of seeking seller financing. If the seller will not budge from his selling price, then ask him to lend you money at a below-market interest rate. Over a number of years, that can save a considerable amount of money in interest charges.

CONTRACT BASICS

An understanding of the basic elements of a real estate contract is essential so that you know what you are signing. In addition, you should always have your attorney review a contract before you sign. Once you sign a contract, you are legally bound to meet its terms.

In real estate circles, a sales contract is referred to as a **purchase agreement**. It sets the ground rules and spells out each party's expectations. There are two basic forms of real estate contracts.

1. **Bilateral contracts.** Most real estate contracts take this form. In a bilateral contract, each party promises to provide consideration (something of value) in exchange for the other party's promise to perform. In the usual real estate contract, the buyer and seller exchange reciprocal promises respectively to buy and to sell the property. Often, for example, the seller will give the buyer title to the property in exchange for cash and/or a promissory note. If one party refuses to honor their promise and the other party is ready to perform, the non-performing party is said to be in default.

2. **Unilateral contracts.** This is a one-sided contract in which one party makes a promise so as to induce a second party to do something. The second party is not legally bound to perform; however, if the second party complies, the first party is obligated to keep the promise. An **option agreement** is an example of this type of contract. In this situation, the seller (the optionor) gives a potential buyer (the optionee) an unconditional purchase option for a certain period of time. The option is enforceable only by the optionee. If the option isn't exercised within the stated period of time, both the optionor's obligation and the optionee's rights expire.

Real estate contracts are based on common law principles. Essentially, these are offer, counteroffer, and agreement. There are standardized contracts used by real estate agents and attorneys in most states. The contract is generally drafted in the form of an offer. The offer is usually signed by the buyer (the offeror). The contract is not binding until the seller accepts, creating "mutual assent" or a "meeting of the minds." If the offeree (the seller, in this case) agrees to the exact terms of the offer, then an acceptance is made. If, however, the seller answers, "I will accept your offer if you agree to close in 30 days or sooner," then there is no binding contract, but rather a counteroffer. If that counteroffer is not met within the time frame, then there is no contract. In order for a contract to be valid, it must contain the following elements (beyond the offer and counteroffer already described):

- **Legal capacity.** Both parties to the contract must be of legal age (usually 18 in most states) and have the mental ability to understand the results of their actions. This may rule out certain convicted criminals, mentally ill individuals, or elderly people who have trouble communicating or understanding the nature of the transaction.

- **Identification of the parties.** The contract must identify the parties. Although not legally required, a contract often sets forth full names and middle initials. This helps the title company in its preparation of the title commitment. If one of the parties is a corporation, it should so state (for example, "American Land Acquisitions, Inc., a California Corporation").

- **Acceptance.** This is a written "yes" in a timely manner to the terms of an offer. The buyer must be given legal notice of the acceptance. Most often, the seller will not accept the offer as presented, but will suggest changes in the terms of conditions—the counteroffer described earlier.

- **Consideration.** This is the payment of money or something else of value or the agreement not to do something. Typically, it is offered by the buyer to the seller so that the seller will enter into the contract for purchase of real estate. The contract is not binding if each of the parties doesn't offer at least some consideration to the other party.

- **A unique property.** The property under consideration needs to be clearly and exactly described so there is no doubt about which property is being sold and transferred to the buyer. Most often, a legal description of the property is provided.

- **Contingencies.** A real estate contract contains three major contingencies: financing, inspection, and attorney approval. Most purchasers buy property with the aid of a loan on which they give a mortgage to the lending institution. Therefore, many contracts give the buyer a deadline by which to prove to the seller that he or she has qualified for a loan and can bring enough money to closing to buy the property. Most buyers also want an opportunity to inspect the property before they commit to purchase it. So the contract will provide for a number of days (usually around five to seven days) during which the purchaser must arrange for an inspection to determine if there are any defects in the property that need correcting. Finally, because most real estate contracts are prepared originally without the aid of an attorney, there is a short period during which each party has their attorney review the contract, recommending changes.

- **Prorations.** Many of the taxes and other expenses

associated with owning property are paid in arrears. This means it is necessary to provide a means for the seller to pay for his fair share of the taxes and costs accrued while he had possession of the property. This amount is determined on a pro-rata basis "in proportion," known as "prorations." Here is an example: Assume that real estate taxes are paid one year in arrears in your state. So if a contract closes on June 30, 2006, the seller will be responsible for all of the property taxes for 2005 and for half of the taxes due for 2006. However, because the parties will not learn the amount of taxes due for 2005 until 2006, the seller gives the purchaser a credit, or set off, so that the purchaser can pay the taxes when they become due. Depending on your state, it may be customary to estimate the next year's taxes as 105 percent to 110 percent of the previous year's amount. Be sure there is a provision in the contract setting the rules for calculating the prorations and describing which expenses are to be calculated on this basis.

- **A written contract.** With few exceptions, a contract for purchase and sale of real estate must be in writing to be enforceable. Be sure to get the contract in writing because if you make an offer in writing and the seller accepts orally and then backs out, you have no recourse. In short, never make an oral agreement. Get everything in writing so there is no confusion as to what is included in the contract. This can prevent a lot of heartbreak and bitterness between parties.

- **Purchase price.** The contract must state the purchase price of the property or a reasonably ascertainable figure (for example, "appraised value as determined by Universal

Appraisal Associates"). This is the gross amount for which the buyer is offering to purchase the property and the seller is willing to sell. If there are setoffs, credits, and so on, the cost of these items will be deducted from the gross amount.

- **Closing and possession.** This provision describes when and where closing will take place. Often, this takes place at the office of the title insurance company. The title company may also send a "closer" to the office of an attorney or real estate agent if that is more convenient. The date is important because it is normally the date on which the purchaser can take possession of the property, and he or she can begin to exercise control and use of the property. As of that date, they are also responsible for insuring the property against casualty loss and third-person injuries.

- **Signatures.** A contract must be signed to be enforceable. The party signing must be of legal age and sound mind. A notary's signature or witness is not required. A facsimile signature is usually acceptable as long as the contract states that facsimile signatures are valid.

If the contract fails to include or meet all of these essential elements, then the contract may be declared void. That means it has no legal standing or effect and would be unenforceable in a court of law. A voidable real estate contract is one considered legally unenforceable.

All in all, keep in mind that once you sign a contract, you and the other party are bound by its terms. If there is a breach of contract on either part, then you or the other party are either entitled to or liable for damages.

The Purchase Agreement

As stated previously, the purchase agreement is the legal document outlining the specifics for the purchase of the subject property. Different states have different terms for the purchase agreement: sales contract, offer to purchase, a contract of purchase and sale, an earnest money agreement, deposit receipt, among others. No matter what it is called, it is the most important document in the sale of real estate because it includes the following:

- How much you pay

- When you pay

- The terms and conditions for closing the transaction

- Cancellation terms

A real estate agent may tell you that you must use a certain purchase agreement form. There are many available, but which form you use is up to you. The sensible thing to do is choose one written in clear and simple terms. That way, you will know exactly what terms and conditions you are agreeing to, and you will not get lost in confusing—and potentially expensive—language. You can get these forms from local title and escrow companies, the local Realtor association, or from stationery or office supply firms that stock such forms.

Examine the form with your broker or agent and with your attorney. Read each clause carefully. If you do not understand a term or condition, then ask for an explanation. Strike any clauses that do not apply or that you do not accept. Initial any changes you make. Keep in mind that there may local standards regarding such conditions as the amount of earnest money or length of contingency periods. Your real estate broker or agent should be able to provide you with information on those items.

There are other important provisions you must understand before you sign any purchase agreement.

- **Earnest money.** The purpose of earnest money is to show the buyer's good faith and intention to follow through on the purchase agreement. Of course, the more you offer, the more "earnest" you become. If you offer little earnest money or none at all, you are not likely to be considered a serious buyer. The earnest money deposit is normally fully refundable within a set time period. The deposit should be held in trust either by the seller's agent or by a title or escrow company. Do not ever pay it directly to the seller. The amount of earnest money paid varies from area to area because of local custom and other considerations. Depending on state law, the deposit also may or not pay interest. If you are a buyer, make sure the deposit is placed in an insured, interest-bearing trust account and that the purchase agreement includes a provision that you will be credited with all interest earned. Keep in mind that if you are a buyer and you do not either live up to the agreement or cancel it within the designated time frames, the deposit is forfeited to the seller. This is called **liquidated damages**. In essence, it is payment for any and all damages incurred by the seller as the result of the buyer not meeting the terms of the proposed purchase agreement. Follow these guidelines when dealing with earnest money:

  — Know the exact date on which your earnest money becomes non-refundable.

— Give yourself time to cancel the purchase agreement. Do not wait until the last moment.

— If you decide you cannot complete the purchase agreement as proposed, send a written cancellation and try to negotiate for more time.

— Get any changes in writing.

- **Assignment.** This is the transfer of rights or duties under a real estate contract by the buyer to a third party. In other words, if you are a buyer, you can assign your interests to another party. This is an extremely important provision for you as a buyer because it gives you more maneuverability in terms of what to do with the property once you have bought it, so be sure to include the phrase "or assignee" after your name or after the name of the legal entity acting as purchaser. This provision allows you to use the "buy and flip" strategy if you choose to do so. With this strategy, you can assign or transfer the purchase agreement to another investor, making a profit without closing on the deal yourself. Essentially, you are simply selling a contractual position. This can be a good strategy in a robust housing market, but it can also be risky because it is a form of speculation. You are betting that you can buy up property and that it will appreciate. If it does not, you are left with a fistful of purchase agreements and the obligations to meet their terms.

- **The closing date.** The proposed closing date determines the expected escrow periods. (**Escrow** is the method of finalizing a real estate transaction. It is a process wherein a disinterested third party acts as the intermediary to coordinate the closing formalities.) The length of the escrow period is normally negotiated by the buyer and seller. These negotiations usually consider the length of time needed to obtain financing as well as the amount and complexity of due diligence required to complete the sale. In other words, if it is a simple sale, the escrow period is likely to be short. If it is a complicated sale involving issues such as zoning changes and environmental issues, then the period will be longer.

MORE ON CONTINGENCIES

As stated previously, a contingency is a condition or event that must be fulfilled before the contract is binding. Either the seller or the buyer can include contingencies. Buyers often have contingencies for physical inspections, financing, or other items. Sellers may require that the sale be approved by a court if probate is involved. The reason contingencies exist is that they provide protection against potential or hidden problems for both buyers and sellers. Contingencies are a way for buyers to make sure everything is in place before making an offer. The same is true for sellers. They want to qualify buyers who are serious about the purchase of the property and can meet all necessary obligations. So before a contract is signed, both parties must agree on all contingencies. Generally speaking, there are three outcomes following initial negotiations:

1. **The contingencies are met.** If all contingencies are agreed upon, the sale is a go; it is no longer subject to cancellation or modification of those items.

2. **The contingency is waived or removed.** These two actions can be done by either the buyer or the seller, depending on the beneficiary. An example might involve a 1031 tax-deferred exchange contingency by a seller. Originally, he might have indicated the property would be identified as a replacement one, but later decided not to do an exchange. So the seller notifies the buyer that he is waiving that particular contingency.

3. **The contingency is rejected or fails.** An example might be a property in which an appraisal turns up the fact that there is serious damage to the foundation. The buyer sees the report and decides he or she is no longer interested in the property because of the extensive costs of repair. The buyer can receive the earnest money back because of failure of this contingency.

What contingency clauses should be included in any agreement? Contingencies vary with the type, size, and location of the property, but here are some important ones to include:

- **Appraisal.** Require that a licensed independent professional conduct an appraisal of the property. The appraisal should show that the property is at a value equal to or greater than the proposed purchase price. This helps prevent you from overpaying for the property.

- **Books and records inspection.** This contingency is especially important for multi-unit, commercial, and industrial properties. As a buyer, you need to know the income and expense statements as well as the nature of the lease. To make sure the seller is giving you real numbers, request their IRS Schedule E statement. The seller may refuse to give it to you, but you are putting him or her on notice that the figures had better be accurate. If problems were to occur after the purchase, the records could be subpoenaed for purposes of proving any fraud or misrepresentation.

- **Contracts.** If you are the buyer, be sure you receive copies of all current service agreements and contracts associated with the property. Unless they are especially attractive to you, you may request that the seller cancel or end all non-essential contracts at the end of escrow, giving you the option of bringing in your own vendors.

- **Financing.** The specific terms of the loan should be outlined — type of loan, maximum interest rate, and so on. If you intend to assume existing financing, get copies of the current loan documents and the most recent loan statement.

- **Marketable title.** If you are the buyer, get a preliminary title report. It should have copies of every exception. Have your attorney review these documents carefully.

- **Physical inspection.** As a buyer, you definitely need to have a physical inspection of the property done. Your team of property inspectors — roofing, plumbing, electrical specialists — should have unlimited access to the interior and exterior. They should conduct a complete inspection so you can use this information to negotiate with the buyer to do one of three things: make necessary repairs, adjust the purchase price, or terminate the purchase agreement.

- **Property survey.** Often required by lenders, an ALTA (American Land Title Association) property survey shows all the boundaries of the property as well as the site plan for existing improvements. In addition, it should include any easements and restrictions.

Beyond the above clauses, if you are a buyer, you may want to negotiate a separate clause to give yourself the right to extend the closing date under certain conditions. This is a good idea because unexpected delays can occur. For example, a lender may require an environmental report on a commercial or industrial property. If the report indicates that further investigation is warranted, the lender will require time for that action to be completed before committing to any loan. Or it could be a situation in which a current occupant refuses entry to the property and time is needed to get legal compliance. To avoid disputes, insist that the extension is agreed to in writing before the closing date shown in the purchase agreement.

If you are a buyer, make sure the purchase agreement spells out what personal property will be included in the sale. This is particularly important for multi-unit buildings (apartment buildings) because personal property can include appliances, window coverings, common area furnishings, fixtures, and so on.

As a buyer, you may also want to include a clause in the purchase agreement specifying that the property be conveyed with or without tenants. For example, you could have a situation in which you could increase property value by renovating and gaining new tenants at higher rental rates. In that case, you could require the seller to deliver the property as vacant and in good shape at the end of escrow. (Of course, this cannot be done if the tenants are on long-term leases.) If the seller occupies the property, you could also require them to vacate or, if you would like them to stay, negotiate a lease for continued tenancy at mutually agreeable terms.

PRESENTING THE PURCHASE AGREEMENT IN AN EFFECTIVE MANNER

Once the purchase agreement is completed, have the offer presented in person by your agent. Electronic transactions may be easier, but you and your agent cannot get a clear idea of the other party's personality or negotiating style in cyberspace. When you make the offer, be sure to include a set time for response. Typically, it is in the 24- to 72-hour range, unless it is an extremely complicated transaction. Within that time period, a seller can accept an offer "as is," return with a counteroffer, or reject the offer completely. If the offer is accepted, then you move to the next stages — escrow, due diligence, property inspections, and closing.

CHAPTER 11

ESCROW, DUE DILIGENCE, AND OTHER VITAL MATTERS

A fter your offer is accepted, you must begin the process of verifying that the property is what the seller says it is. You will be working in the four areas of escrow, formal due diligence, property inspection, and closing.

ESCROW

As mentioned earlier, escrow is the method of finalizing a real estate transaction. It is a process wherein a disinterested third party acts as the intermediary to coordinate the closing formalities. Escrow begins after the buyer and seller sign the purchase agreement. At that time, earnest money is deposited with the escrow holder, and an escrow account is opened in the buyer's name. The escrow holder—the neutral third party—handles most of the details of the transaction. Most often, an officer at the title company will handle escrow proceedings. However, it is also possible that an attorney may handle this task, depending on the area of the country.

Whether it is an attorney or an escrow officer, he or she will prepare the instructions that set the rules for the transaction between you and the seller. Those instructions have a direct link to the purchase agreement terms and to any other written documents you have agreed upon with the other party. As you might expect, you need to pay close attention to the escrow instructions. The escrow holder will rely on them if a dispute arises, and the holder cannot make any changes to the instructions unless both you and the seller agree to them in writing. In other words, you are bound to honor the instructions, so they must be correct right from the start.

Once you have signed the escrow instructions, the title copy will send you a copy of the **preliminary title report** (or prelim). This report contains vital information on the current legal owner of the property as well as the following information:

- Liens (unpaid mortgage, property tax, or judgment liens)

- Unpaid income

- Easements, restrictions, or third-party interests that limit the use of the property

Have your attorney review this document carefully, clearly explaining the terms so you know exactly what the situation is regarding the property. If there are encumbrances, obtain detailed information on them. Remember that the preliminary title report is, in effect, a contingency. If the report contains items you cannot accept, you have the right to cancel the purchase or renegotiate the terms. The other party also has this right.

During escrow, the escrow officer will keep track of contingencies as part of the process. As stated earlier, three things can happen with contingencies:

- The contingencies are met.

- The contingency is waived or removed.

- The contingency is rejected or fails.

It's the officer's task to get instructions on contingencies from the buyer and seller and to follow those instructions. Often, deadlines are included in the contingencies; that is, a certain action must be completed with a specified amount of time. If you are the holder of a contingency, you have to notify the escrow officer immediately if it is rejected or fails. He or she will notify the other party. However, it is not the escrow officer's job to negotiate or to find a resolution for rejected contingencies. That job is left to the buyer and the seller.

Setting a **closing date** for the transaction can be frustrating. Closing takes place after all the particulars — appraisal, financing, and contingencies — of escrow have been satisfied. Nevertheless, the estimated closing date does not always take place as scheduled because of complications that can occur. For example, appraisers are not always available immediately. Sometimes, lender bureaucracy can slow down the process. Because there inevitably will be delays, a good strategy is to bargain for the right to extend the escrow process when the delays are beyond your control.

FORMAL DUE DILIGENCE

What is the difference between the due diligence talked about earlier and formal due diligence? **Formal due diligence** is the span of time between the acceptance of the offer and the close of escrow or completion of the sale. This is the time when you look deeply at the property to make sure both that you are getting what you are paying for and that you are not going to end up with hidden problems that could cost you money, time, and aggravation. Once the contract is signed, you are legally bound to abide by it. Talk to everyone connected to the property and its owner — the tenants, neighbors, contractors, suppliers — to get a complete picture of the situation.

Review Books and Records

Before you close on the property, make sure you see the seller's books and records, closely reviewing the following items:

- **The seller's income and expense statement.** Request a copy of the statement for the past 12 months in the form of Schedule E. This schedule should give an accurate picture of the financial state of the property since the seller is unlikely to misrepresent his or her figures to the Internal Revenue Service. Look for any "red flags," such as problems in collections. From an accounting point of view, you or your accountant should verify and determine the following:

  - The mathematical accuracy of the balance sheet. All asset and liability amounts should be traced to such supporting documentation as bank account reconciliations, ledgers, and trial balances.

— Verification of the accounts receivable from the balance sheet and/or the delinquent rent report. You need to know what collection efforts have been made for past due receivable amounts.

— Confirmation that statements of accounts payable and accounts receivable have been included in the monthly reporting package.

— Verification of the accounts payable from the balance sheet to the accounts payable ledger.

— Confirmation of the security deposits from the asset and liability on the balance sheet to the rent roll, the security deposit register or the detailed rent roll, as well as the bank account reconciliation.

— Determination of the amount spent for capital expenditures and identification of individual capital expenditures over the agreed threshold limit, verifying that the owner authorized them.

— Verification of the mathematical accuracy of the income and expense statement.

— Comparison of the actual income and expenses from the income and expense statements to budgeted income and expenses on the annual cash budget. If there are significant variations from the budget, ask for an explanation of those variances.

— Verification of the mathematical accuracy of the cash receipts and disbursements records and the schedules of accounts payable and accounts receivable.

- **Rent rolls/receipts.** A list of all rental units as well as the tenant names, move-in dates, lease expiration dates, current and market rents, and security deposits should be provided. More specifically, you and your accountant should take the following actions:

  - Find out if the number of units on the rent roll and the detailed rent roll agrees with the number of units in the building.

  - Verify that the number of vacant and occupied units on the detailed rent roll provided by the agent agrees with the latest rent roll sent by the owner.

  - Verify that the unit number, tenant, rent amount, lease term, and security deposit amount as reported on the rent roll agrees with the leases.

  - Find out if the leases are properly signed and executed and conform to the owner's requirements.

  - Determine if new tenants have signed leases at rental rates approved by the owner.

  - Trace receipts from the rent roll and detailed rent roll to the income and expense statement, to the deposit register, and to the bank statement to ensure that all funds are accounted for and properly classified.

  - If security deposit is not returned to the former tenant, determine the justification for keeping the deposit or documentation that the former tenant waived the return of the security deposit.

— Confirm that the agent is collecting full months' rent, recording uncollected rent as a receivable, properly accounting for prepaid rents, and making efforts to collect delinquent rents.

— Determine if there are any rental concessions and whether or not they conform to the management and marketing plan.

- **Service agreements/contracts.** Typically, an owner will have agreements or contracts with providers of maintenance, landscaping, pest control, HVAC, snowplowing, and other services. Carefully review copies of these documents. You may want to keep some or all of them, or you may want to terminate the services in order to get better terms. If the latter is the case, ask the owner to send a conditional termination notice to the providers stating that the services will not be needed as of the close of escrow.

- **Licenses and permits.** A rental property owner may be required to have a business license or permit, so make sure you receive all copies of these items. When licenses or permits are involved, notify the appropriate government agency of the change in ownership and billing address (if different). It is important to do this because a penalty or fine may be levied for noncompliance with regulations.

- **Personal property list.** As stated previously, personal property can include appliances, equipment, and supplies. Be sure to get a complete list of these items. All personal property should be listed in writing; otherwise, it may not be included in the sale.

- **Utility billings.** Utilities may include gas, electric, water and sewer, garbage collection, telephone, cable, and Internet access. Obtain the latest billings on each of these services. If they are unusually high, check the historical record of billings to see if they are consistently high or if the latest rates are a one-time variation. If they are historically high, consider weatherizing expenses such as insulation. Before escrow is closed, contact each utility and arrange for the transfer of services or for a change in billing responsibility as of the estimated closing date of escrow.

- **Insurance coverage.** Ask for a copy of the seller's insurance policy. Although it cannot protect you, it will give a history that can be useful to your insurance broker or agent. From that information, they can calculate the correct coverage for your needs. Insurance is one of the most vital elements of your purchase of a property, so make sure you have policies in place by the time you are the new owner. It is not only the smart thing to do to protect your investment, but also many lenders will not give you a loan until you provide proof that the property is insured with policy limits in excess of their loan amount.

In general, review all records for accuracy and get everything in writing. An oral agreement can be difficult to prove and lead to misunderstandings between you and the seller.

PROPERTY INSPECTIONS

Always conduct a thorough physical inspection of any property you are considering. It is important to review all the documents and records mentioned, but you need to walk the property to see what you really have. Repairs are costly, so it is wise to pay for a professional inspection. If an inspector finds problems, you can require that the seller correct those problems or reduce the price. There are two general categories of defects an inspector can find. The first category is **obvious** defects, including peeling paint, broken windows, and leaking plumbing. The second category is **hidden** defects, which includes corroded pipes in the walls, roof or window leaks, and dry rot. The purchase contract should provide for cancellation without penalty or loss of earnest money if the physical condition of the property is not up to standard.

Many states require a seller to provide a **disclosure statement**. This applies to a residential rental property with four or fewer units. Generally speaking, sellers are responsible for disclosing only information within their personal knowledge. However, some states specify certain problems that are the seller's responsibility to search for, whether or not they see indications of the problem. In these cases, or when a seller turns a blind eye to a defect, you can take him or her to court for compensation. Within the United States, California provides an example of a state with extremely comprehensive disclosure requirements. Its disclosure form requires a seller to list such items as:

- Leaky roofs

- Deaths that occurred on the property within the past three years

- Neighborhood nuisances such as a dog that barks every night

In addition, California requires that potential hazards from floods, earthquakes, fires, and so on, be disclosed in a **Natural Hazard Disclosure Statement**. The state also obligates that sellers alert buyers to the availability of a database maintained by law enforcement authorities on the location of registered sex offenders.

This legislative protection often does not apply either to residential investment properties with five or more units or to any type of commercial property. It is assumed that buyers and sellers will perform the due diligence necessary to protect their interests. However, even if a **transfer disclosure statement (TDS)** is not required, many states stipulate that a seller has a legal obligation to disclose any and all facts that could affect the value or intended use of a property. For example, if a seller had a foundation repaired by a professional, he or she should disclose this fact and provide a copy of the invoice of the work done and the name of the person or business that made the repairs.

A few sellers may offer their properties on an "as is" basis, thinking they are neither required to correct any defects before the sale nor legally responsible for any problems that arise after the sale. In most cases, they are wrong. They may be liable for misrepresentation, fraud, or negligence. In any case, avoid "as is" properties. The seller may be naïve, dishonest, or receiving bad advice from an agent. Be honest and aboveboard in terms of disclosures. It is the best choice not only because it is the right thing to do, but also because it will enhance your reputation within the real estate community. Think of it as a long-term investment in your future.

Different Forms of Inspection

Property inspections can take different forms. First of all, you should do your own physical inspection. Although you may not be a professional inspector, many defects are obvious, even to the untrained eye. If this is the case, then you have saved time and avoided the expense of hiring an inspector. The seller should allow you complete access to the property with no time limits. If he or she tries to restrict access or specifies only certain hours, be suspicious and demand complete access. If the seller refuses this request, then walk away from the deal.

The professional forms of inspection include the following:

- **The physical or structural inspection.** As a buyer, you want to ensure the building is structurally sound, and you need to hire a professional inspector for this task. If you are considering large multi-unit residential or commercial properties, the lender may require a separate inspection by a company of its choice. You may also want to consider the services of an architect if you plan to change the use of the building or renovate or remodel it. The inspector can tell you if the plans are feasible or not worth the investment. When you hire a professional inspector, he or she will ask the following general questions:

  — What needs to be repaired at the property?

  — What is unsafe or causing rapid, costly damage?

  — What are the priorities of repair?

  — How should repair priorities be adjusted for your circumstances?

  — What repairs may involve significant costs?

— Which repairs are minor or are nonessential improvements that might be deferred?

— What are the biggest risks of hidden damage?

— What are the repair alternatives? Who should perform them?

— What further investigations are most appropriate?

More specifically, he or she will examine the following areas:

— Overall structural integrity

— Property drainage/landscaping

— Walks and drives

— Foundation, footings, crawl space, basements, sub-flooring, decks

— Exterior walls, siding, trim

— Windows, doors, cabinets, counters

— Gutters, downspouts

— Roof, shingles, chimneys, attic

— Floor, wall, ceiling, roof structures

— Interior floors, walls, ceilings

— Heating and cooling systems

— Plumbing systems (fixtures, supply lines, drains, water heating devices, etc.)

— Electrical system wiring, service panel, devices, and service capacity

— Energy conservation/safety items

— Insulation and ventilation

— Moisture intrusion and mold

Warning signs of damage can sometimes be obvious even to the untrained eye. Be alert to the following:

— Cracks can occur around the foundation, walls, ceilings, windows and door frames, chimneys and retaining walls. Sometimes a seller will tell you that these are naturally occurring subsidence cracks. This may or may not be true, so let a professional inspector uncover the facts. In general, if a crack is wide enough to stick a pencil into it, then it is not subsidence.

— Slanting/sloping floors can be a sign of serious problems with the foundation or the quality of construction. Also, look for soft spots on upper floors, indicating structural damage.

— Buy a laser level and walk through the property looking for floors, walls, and ceilings that are not in plumb. Open and close doors and windows as well.

— Look for evidence of poor drainage or excess groundwater. These can be clues to soil issues that can be expensive to fix. Make sure all drains are correctly installed and maintained.

— Discoloration and stains on ceilings and walls as well

as around windows and door frames are indications that rain or snow has penetrated the structure or that leakage has occurred. If there is a smell of mold, check it carefully. It may simply be lack of ventilation, but if not, it could indicate a serious health issue for future occupants. Look for sump pumps. If you find them, have the inspectors check the property in detail because these pumps are specifically designed to handle flooding in lower levels.

- A plumbing contractor should check for all sources of leaks or moisture. He or she should check sinks, faucet lines, toilets, dishwashers, washing machines, and sprinklers. Avoid any property with polybutylene domestic water-supply systems. These have been the subject of class-action lawsuits over the years because of their tendency to gradually deteriorate through interaction with chlorine and other chemicals in drinking water. Even though the plumbing might not be disturbed, the gradual hardening of the fittings or pipe can cause a leak years after installation. It is used for both hot and cold plumbing. In terms of overall plumbing, it may well be worth your while to replace all dated water-supply lines with modern, steel braided lines. These can prevent leaks that could cause serious damage to the property.

- Several types of insects can cause serious damage to a property. These include termites, carpenter ants, powder post beetles, and any other bug that likes to eat wood. Beyond insects, however, there are other destructive beasts like fungi (dry rot). A pest-control inspector should be able to identify these problems. He or she will inspect the property and provide you with a diagram that indicates the locations of any problems. Serious problems, including any infestations that affect structural elements, must be dealt with immediately. Typically, the seller pays for this work. A lender will not fund the property until problems are taken care of by a professional pest-control operator or a licensed contractor. Even if the pest or fungus problem is not serious, you still must require that the seller take care of it before completing the purchase. A pest-control operator will typically do the following tasks to eliminate a pest problem:

— Spray or dust chemical solutions, powders, or gases into rooms, furnishings or wood, and over marshlands, ditches, and catch-basins.

— Set mechanical traps and place poisonous paste or bait in sewers, burrows, and ditches.

— Inspect premises to identify the infestation source and extent of damage to the property, wall, and roof porosity, and access to infested locations.

— Cut or bore openings in the building or surrounding concrete, access infested areas, insert nozzle, and inject pesticide to impregnate the ground.

— Study preliminary reports and diagrams of infested areas and determine treatment type required to eliminate and prevent recurrence of infestation.

— Direct and assist other workers in treatment and extermination processes to eliminate and control rodents, insects, and weeds.

– Measure area dimensions requiring treatment and calculate fumigant requirements.

– Clean and remove blockages from infested areas to facilitate spraying procedure and provide drainage.

– Position and fasten edges of tarpaulins over building and tape vents to ensure airtight environment and check for leaks.

– Post warning signs and lock building doors to secure area to be fumigated.

• If you are considering commercial or residential investment properties with five or more units, it is likely that your lender will require a Phase I Environmental Report. This report reviews the historical use of the building through property records, including all prior uses and aerial photographs. Also known as a Due Diligence Report, it will typically include the following items.

– Identification of past and present ownership and uses.

– Inspection of the entire site and any structures for the presence of potentially hazardous building materials, including asbestos, lead paint, or PCBs.

– Description of site environmental characteristics, including the size, layout, extent of development, and natural features.

- An assessment of hazardous material or waste storage, handling, or disposal practices.

- An assessment of nearby properties whose activities may have an environmental impact on the subject property.

- Conclusions regarding potential problems and recommendations for further action.

In general, most properties do not have serious problems in the environmental area, and only a Phase 1 report will be required. However, avoid any type of property where there is the potential for expensive cleanup. This usually includes tenants using chemicals in one form or another — dry-cleaning solvents, petroleum solvents, gasoline, oil, or any other chemical that can raise health or environmental issues. It can cost a lot of money and time to fix these problems. Remember, also, that the federal government does not care if the violations occurred before your ownership. Lenders shy away from any property with environmental hazards, and, if they do lend the money, they will most likely require you to be responsible for any clean-up costs. In addition, you are still responsible even if it is a nonrecourse loan — a loan in which the lender can only foreclose on the underlying property in the event of a default. Also known as "carve outs," these loans stipulate that fraud, material misrepresentation, and environmental matters are all personal obligations of the buyer. In essence, an environmental carve out protects the lender from owners who may want to dump a contaminated property into someone else's lap.

Getting a Qualified Inspector

It is wise to interview a minimum of two or three inspectors before choosing one. They should all be full-time professionals conducting a minimum of 50 to more than 100 inspections a year, depending on the area, and they should carry "errors and omissions" insurance. The American Society of Home Inspectors (**www.ashi.org**) was founded in 1976 and is "North America's oldest and largest professional society of home inspectors." On page 231 is the ASHI Code of Ethics. It is a good idea to hire an inspector who adheres to this code because there is no national government licensing and fewer than half the states license or certify home inspectors. In other words, anybody can print a business card and call himself an inspector. Ask inspectors for copies of their recent written inspection reports. If they refuse to show them to you, do not hire them. Any professional should be willing to show you samples of their work. Also ask for a minimum of three references or clients who have used the inspector's services within the past six months. Contact those clients and get their opinions on the inspector's work and behavior. A true professional will be happy to give you references since it is proof of his or her abilities and leads to more business. Once you make your choice, go along with the inspector on a tour of the property. It is not only an opportunity to see how this person works, but it is also a chance to learn the specifics of inspection. Then use this information in the future to eliminate any unscrupulous contractors who may tell you that you need a new roof or new plumbing when you need nothing of the kind.

Credit Negotiation

One of the areas in which inspections can pay off is in the discovery of deficiencies that need to be corrected — property damage, pest control problems, and so on. There are two choices for handling deficiencies. The first is to require the seller to fix all the problems at his expense. If he complains, show photographic evidence from the inspection and refer him to the warranty of condition clause in the purchase agreement. The second choice is to negotiate monetary credits through escrow. In this case, you get a reduction in price while taking care of the repairs on your own. You might want this option if you have personal preferences for carpet, drapes, and so on. Sellers may appreciate this approach as well. The cost should be equal to or less than what they would spend, and they do not have go to the trouble of finding workers to do the job. Be aware that credit negotiation can be difficult. If you are a seller, watch out for buyers who try renegotiating the entire purchase agreement by using an overly long inspection period to find absolutely every tiny flaw in a property. They are trying to get you to lower the price dramatically by tying up the property in escrow. It is unprofessional conduct, and you will not want to work with this individual in the future. Finally, do not get overly excited about repairs and make them before the close of escrow. It is always possible that the sale of the property can fall through, and in that case, you have spent money to upgrade the seller's property, having no way to get it back. Be sure to get all bids and proposals set during the escrow period so you are ready to go as soon it closes. A good way to handle work contracts is to include a contingency saying that the proposal is void if the property transaction does not go through.

THE TITLE HOLDING

There are several ways to hold the title to a property. Each has its advantages and disadvantages, so you must decide which is right for you. The best way to do that is to consult with your real estate team.

Sole Proprietorship

This is most common form of ownership. All that is needed is a title of the property vested in your name (or other designated person). Its advantages include:

- It's the easiest and least expensive form of ownership.

- You have complete control and decision-making power.

- Sale or transfer can take place at your discretion.

- There are no corporate tax payments.

- There are minimal legal costs to form a sole proprietorship.

- There are few formal business requirements.

Its disadvantages include:

- You can be held personally liable for the debts and obligations of the business; you have no protection against lawsuits or other claims.

- All responsibilities and business decisions fall on your shoulders.

- A sole proprietorship holds no significant tax advantages. All your income and expenses are reported directly on your personal tax return. You do not get any favorable tax treatment or avoidance of probate in the case of your death.

Joint Tenancy

This is a form of ownership by two or more individuals

together. It differs from other types of co-ownership in that the surviving joint tenant immediately becomes the owner of the whole property upon the death of the other joint tenant. This is called "right of survivorship." A joint tenancy between a husband and wife is known as a **tenancy by the entirety**. This form has some characteristics different than other joint tenancies, such as the inability of one joint tenant to sever the ownership and differences in tax treatment. A joint tenancy requires a unity of time, title, interest, and possession. "Unity of time" means that all the joint tenants must take title by the same deed at the same time. Each tenant must own an equal interest or percentage of the property. So if you have two joint tenants, they each own 50 percent; three joint tenants 33-1/3 percent; and so forth. If the percentage or interest is unequal, then it is not a joint tenancy. By law, each joint tenant is entitled to the right of possession and cannot be excluded by the others. A judgment lien or bankruptcy can terminate a joint tenancy. A new joint tenant can be added by executing a new deed. Here are the advantages of joint tenancy:

- You get a stepped-up basis on your deceased joint tenant's portion of the property. This means that the taxable basis is increased for the portion of the property owned by the deceased joint tenant to the current market value at the time of death. This may allow surviving joint tenants to sell the property with much lower taxes.

- Married couples often hold title to investment properties in a joint tenancy. If one spouse died, this can result in a step up in basis to the fair market value at the time of death, rather than just a step up for the portion owned by the deceased joint tenant. Laws on this subject vary from state to state and may include additional options.

Some of the disadvantages of joint tenancy include the following:

- A constant in joint tenancy arrangements is that the co-owners may disagree or quarrel. If the co-owners do disagree, a costly and time-consuming lawsuit may be required for the original owner to exercise his or her intentions for the asset.

- If an asset is owned before marriage, the original owner may lose part of the asset in a divorce.

- A jointly owned asset will be subject to judgments against every owner and may be lost in the bankruptcy of any owner.

- The financial management advantages of trusts are eliminated, especially when aged parents or minor children are involved, as are the possible tax-savings features of trusts and estates.

- Assets may not be available to the executor of a deceased joint owner's estate. In such a situation, it may then be necessary to sell other assets, possibly at a sacrifice, in order to meet tax payments or other cash needs to settle the affairs of the deceased.

- The one who originally owned property, and subsequently places it in a joint tenancy, is no longer the sole owner.

- If the original owner later desires to dispose of the property, in many cases he can sell only his interest unless the other joint tenants agree and cooperate.

- If both joint owners die in a common accident or disaster, and it cannot be determined who died first, serious legal problems and an increase in the cost of probate may result.

- If a conservator is appointed for the original owner, the probate court's authority may be required to use the asset for that owner, increasing the cost of the conservatorship.

- If minors or legally disabled adults are involved, costly and cumbersome conservatorship proceedings may be necessary.

Tenancy in Common

This is a situation in which several owners each own a stated portion or share of the property. This form of ownership has the following advantages:

- Each owner can own a different percentage, can take title at any time, and can sell his or her interest at any time.

- If you are an owner, you also have complete control over your part of the property and may sell, bequeath, or mortgage your interest as you decide without any need for permission of the others.

- Upon your death, your share becomes part of your estate, and you can will it as you see fit.

Tenancy in common has the following disadvantages, most of them related to the actions of other owners:

- If another owner dies, you may find that he has left his interest to someone you dislike.

- Another owner can sell or borrow against his property, which can create conflicts.

- Financial difficulties of another owner can negatively affect your interest in the property. If an owner had a judgment leveled against him, it could lead to foreclosure on his interest in the property. A bankruptcy proceeding could order the forced sale of the property to satisfy creditors—unless you and the other owners are willing to pay off the creditors and buy out the owner in question.

- Different owners may have different plans for the property, creating strife among the tenants in common. For instance, some may want borrow money using the property as collateral, while others may want to sell the property. If no one can agree, a business feud can erupt into legal action that results in acrimony and expense.

Partnerships

As the name suggests, partnerships consist of two or more partners who join together to acquire, operate, and hold real estate. It is an effective way of pooling capital and talent. A key feature of a real estate partnership is that the investors do not actually have the title or ownership directly in acquired properties. Instead, they own a partnership interest. Partnerships usually take one of two forms.

- **General partnerships.** In this setup, each partner possesses the right to fully participate in property management and operations. Advantages of a general partnership include the following:

— They are easy to establish and maintain. You do not have to register with the state or pay fees, as you do to establish a corporation or limited liability company.

— You can file income tax returns with relative ease because a general partnership is normally a "pass through" tax entity. This means the partners, not the partnership, are taxed.

— Unlike a regular corporation, there is no need to file separate tax returns for the corporate entity and its owners.

— They offer flexibility. Partners are able to set their responsibilities and benefits as they see fit or as the needs of the business dictate. The flexibility extends to distribution of profits and losses. For example, an individual partner can reap higher profits for taking on more financial risk.

— A partnership is considered a discrete asset. It can be transferred to other people, heirs, or estates, unlike a sole proprietorship. Transference is usually limited by the terms of the partnership agreement.

Of course, partnerships also have disadvantages. They include the following:

• One business-related act of a partner can make all partners legally liable for that act. So it is important that you enter into partnerships only with people you trust. Back up that trust with a written partnership agreement that establishes each partner's share of profits or losses, day-to-day duties, and what happens if one partner dies or retires.

- **Limited partnership.** This ownership form differs from a general partnership in the role and responsibilities of the partners. It consists of one or more general partners and one or more limited partners. Typically, the general partners run the operations of the business, and the limited partners provide capital and help arrange financing. They do not take an active role in running the business. In return for their investment, they receive a share of the profits. Statutes regarding limited partnerships vary by state so check with the appropriate government agency for a definition of the obligations and responsibilities of partners in this type of business arrangement. The partnership is required to file with the secretary of state, and it must also file various reports. A key feature of a limited partnership agreement lies in the area of liability, which falls on the general partners, and typically not on the limited partners. For this reason individuals are reluctant to be general partners. The general partner of a limited partnership can itself be a corporation or LLC to mitigate liability issues. However, this does not mean that a limited partner cannot be part of, or have a vote in, major decisions that affect the partnership. The advantages of a limited partnership include:

  — As a limited partner, you can invest even though you do not have expertise or the time to devote to being a hands-on part of the business.

  — You can take on the financial risk but not the liability risk, which is also more attractive to a limited partner.

— Partners are able to allocate profits, losses, and gains as they see fit, regardless of the equity interest of a specific partner, subject to compliance with tax laws. The general partners prepare an IRS Form 1065 for the partnership. Each partner then prepares his or her own tax form listing all profits, losses, and depreciations.

— It is a pass-through operation with profits passing through to the partners who then include their allocated income on their personal tax returns.

— It is much easier to attract investors as limited partners.

— It allows general partners to use their expertise, make key decisions, and manage the business.

— Limited partners can leave the business or be replaced without the need for the limited partnership to be dissolved.

A limited partnership has the following disadvantages:

— Filings, formalities, and state requirements.

— If you are a general partner, you assume personal liability.

Limited Liability Companies

This is hybrid form of ownership that combines the properties of a corporation and partnership. It has many advantages including:

- It provides the flexibility and tax advantages of a partnership while maintaining the limited-liability benefits of a corporation. Like a corporation, an LLC is a separate legal entity that limits the liability of its members. However, it has the tax benefits of a partnership.

- LLCs are also free of many of the legal requirements that govern corporations (including annual reports, director meetings, and shareholder requirements).

- LLCs are a pass-through tax entity, which means company profits and losses are passed through the business and taxed solely on the members' individual tax returns.

- Members can hire a management group to run the LLC. This group can consist of members, nonmembers, or a combination.

- Members can split profits and losses any way they wish.

- Dividend distribution is nontaxable; unlike an S corporation, in which dividends are taxable.

- An unlimited number of members may join a single LLC, and most states allow single-member LLCs.

- An LLC may affiliate with other businesses; unlike an S corporation, in which that ability is limited.

Disadvantages of LLCs include the following:

- Costs can be greater. Some states impose income or franchise taxes on LLCs or require LLCs to pay annual fees to operate in that state.

- Lack of legal precedent. Because LLCs have existed as legal business entities only since 1996, there is little legal precedent available to help owners predict how legal disputes may affect their businesses.

Every state has its own requirements, so check with an attorney who specializes in LLCs before deciding to form or join a limited liability corporation.

Corporations

A **corporation** is a legal entity owned by one or more shareholders. It can be public like Ford, Microsoft, or Federal Express, among others. As a real estate investor, you can create your own private or closely held corporation by filing articles of incorporation and bylaws with the appropriate state agency. Requirements for incorporation vary from state to state, so consult the appropriate members of your team before pursing this form of ownership. The great advantage of incorporation is the owners of a corporation actually own stock and not the real estate; the most shareholders can lose is their equity investment.

The disadvantage of incorporation is it costs money to have an attorney draw up the organizational documents. There are also costs to cover extensive reporting requirements at state and federal levels for maintaining corporate status. If these requirements are not met or if there is lack of capitalization, then creditors or a lien holder can seek personal liability for individual shareholders.

There are two types of corporations available to you:

- **C corporations.** These have the advantage of continuity (they continue in the event a shareholder dies). The major disadvantage of a C corporation, however, is that it is taxed twice: once when the business makes a profit and then a second time when those profits are distributed to shareholders. Another disadvantage is that if the corporation has losses, it has to carry them over to the next tax year because the shareholders cannot use C corporation losses on personal returns.

• **S corporations.** A major advantage of the S corporation is that it avoids double taxation by passing on all tax liabilities to shareholders. As such, S corporations are only taxed once. However, they are seldom used in real estate ownership because their primary disadvanage is that the liquidation of an S corporation is a taxable event. This means that even if the shareholders agree to an equitable distribution of assets, the Internal Revenue Service will consider the liquidation as taxable. The shareholders will then be forced to pay capital gains taxes and possibly sell some of the assets. In addition, there is the issue of **material participation**. This is an IRS term that indicates whether an investor worked and was involved in a business activity on a regular basis. There is a series of tests to determine material participation, which affects the tax benefits you may or may not receive.

In general, incorporation is an expensive choice for holding real estate assets if you are an average real estate investor. You must be willing to pay for the professional, legal, and accounting advice not only at the beginning but also on a continual basis. You also have to deal with the hassle of ongoing technical requirements and the possible expensive possibility of double taxation.

CLOSING ESCROW

After all the negotiations and inspections, it is time to close
the transaction. This occurs only when all the terms of the
funding, the escrow instructions, and the purchase agreement
have been met. Because real estate transactions have so many
facets to them, many details need attention as part of the closing
process. How a closing is handled depends upon the part of the
country in which you live. In some states, all parties are brought
together and the escrow officer coordinates all necessary
activities. In others, an attorney performs similar functions.
What matters most at this time is that your team members have
done their jobs well so there are not any surprises. Pay close
attention to the documents. Errors or omissions can creep in
without anyone noticing. Also, stay in close touch with your
lender, making it less likely that you will be surprised with
last-minute requests. Finally, resign yourself to the fact that it
may take some work to get all parties together for the closing.
Holidays, vacations, long weekends—all can delay the closing
meeting. In addition, documents can be lost or misplaced,
messages missed, and so on. Patience is definitely a virtue when
it comes to closing a transaction.

Before the expected date for escrow closing, you and the other
party should receive a copy of the estimated closing statement.
The sample Estimated Closing Statement at the end of this
chapter shows the types of fees listed. Expect the fees to change
a bit by the time of closing. An escrow officer may estimate
the expenses slightly higher to prevent any shortage of funds,
which can prevent escrow from closing. Any overages can be
credited or refunded to you or to the other party. If you are the
buyer, pay close attention to the statement because it shows
the monies expected to be received from the lender or credited

to the seller when there is seller financing. It also shows the amount of additional cash funds the buyer needs to deposit in the form of a cashier's check, wire transfer, or other certified method of payment. If you are a buyer, remember to provide funds well ahead of time for the escrow to close.

Title insurance is another necessity in the closing process. This type of insurance insures that the title of the property transferred is legally valid and clear. It provides protection against title defects that were unknown to you at the time you purchased the policy. The term "title" refers to the cumulative ownership records of the property. This includes the transfer of any property rights and any loans using the property as collateral. A clear line of title is important because it makes you less susceptible to ownership claims from other parties and to outstanding debts of previous property owners. Before it writes a policy, a title company checks for defects in a title by examining public records, including the following:

- Deeds

- Mortgages

- Wills

- Divorce decrees

- Court judgments

- Tax records

- Liens

- Encumbrances

- Maps

If any claims to the property are made, the company defends you in court, subject to certain limitations. If the company loses, it pays you for covered losses up to the amount of your policy. Two types of title insurance policies are issued in most instances:

- A lender's title insurance policy does not protect the buyer's interest, but the buyer can get title insurance for his or her own protection. Often, buyers purchase a policy to protect themselves against any claims that the property purchase was not a clear and marketable title. However, title insurance for the buyer can be paid for by either the buyer or the seller. Local custom may dictate who pays. The cost is based on the purchase price. The higher the price, the higher the title insurance premium. Although this type of insurance is optional, it is a good idea to have to guard against unexpected claims.

- The second kind of title insurance is required by mortgage lenders because they want to protect against another person claiming legal title to your property. In the event property ownership changes, their money would not be protected if a claim of improper transfer of title is made, which is why they require title insurance.

Because title companies are regulated by most state insurance departments, they are generally reliable. However, it never hurts to check with the appropriate state office to get the rating and background on a title company. These firms are also rated by insurance-rating companies, so you can request copies of the most recent report from the insurer. Remember that you can shop around for the best offers from title companies. You do not have to rely on the firms recommended by a real estate agent or a lender. Ask for an itemization of all expenses since seemingly minor (but expensive) fees can be hidden in the information provided. Low-fee title companies sometimes make up for those less expensive fees by charging more for such items as document preparation, and mailing costs.

Property insurance is another necessity. It protects against physical loss or damage by theft, fire, or other means. You will need to have a certificate of insurance to close a transaction and take over the property. Such insurance can be costly, so plan for this expense while you are still in the due diligence phase. You may want the insurance agent to examine the property before he gives you a quote. He may be able to alert you to potentially expensive problems that need correction. If such corrections are needed, you can negotiate those costs with the seller.

Closing Statement

This is an accounting of funds made at the end of the real estate transaction. Usually, it is provided to the buyer and seller separately by the escrow officer. By law, it is required to be made at the completion of the deal. A closing statement itemizes all funds received from or credited to and all payments made or debited to the party for whom the statement is prepared. Typically, the items listed on a closing statement include the broker's commission, escrow fees, recording fees, selling price, and so on. Usually, the escrow officer or other closing agent handles the mandatory reporting of the real estate transaction to the IRS and state tax department. However, if he does not file the required 1099-S form, then the brokers or the buyer or seller may be required to handle this reporting function. The information includes property identity, sales price, social security number of buyer and seller, and so on. Be sure to keep a copy of the closing statement so it is available for future transactions. For example, if you decide to sell the property, then it can help you establish the initial cost basis and determine capital gain. Also, some escrow expenses may be deductible on your tax return.

Recording of the Deed

This is the final, critical step in the process. Until this step is taken, you are not the owner of the property. Deed-recording procedures vary by state so you will need to use the appropriate agency. Often, deeds are handled by the office of the county clerk and recorder. Many of these offices have entered the digital age and offer electronic document processing, improving the speed and efficiency. Once the deed has been recorded, you are officially the owner and can begin the takeover procedures, include the following:

- Conducting a final walk-through to check for any damage.

- Verifying that all personal property is present.

- Ensuring that all keys were received; you may want to change locks.

- Personally meet with tenants to let them know you are interested in them and are a responsible property owner.

The entire process is done, and you are now the owner of the property, ready to move to the next step — managing the property for maximum value, down the landlord path.

SAMPLE OF GOOD FAITH ESTIMATE

Source: www.hud.gov/offices/hsg/sfh/res/resappc.cfm

[Name of Lender][1]

The information provided below reflects estimates of the charges which you are likely to incur at the settlement of your loan. The fees listed are estimates — the actual charges may be more or less. Your transaction may not involve a fee for every item listed.

The numbers listed beside the estimates generally correspond to the numbered lines contained in the HUD - 1 or HUD - 1A settlement statement that you will be receiving at settlement. The HUD - 1 or HUD - 1A settlement statement will show you the actual cost for items paid at settlement.

Item[2]	HUD - 1 or HUD - 1A	Amount or range
Loan origination fee	801	$XXXX
Loan discount fee	802	$XXXX
Appraisal fee	803	$XXXX
Credit report	804	$XXXX
Inspection fee	805	$XXXX
Mortgage broker fee	[Use blank line in 800 Section]	$XXXX

---

[1] The name of the lender shall be placed at the top of the form. Additional information identifying the loan application and property may appear at the bottom of the form or on a separate page. Exception: If the disclosure is being made by a mortgage broker who is not an exclusive agent of the lender, the lender's name will not appear at the top of the form, but the following legend must appear:
This Good Faith Estimate is being provided by XXXXXXXX, a mortgage broker, and no lender has yet been obtained.

2 Items for which there is estimated to be no charge to the borrower are not required to be listed. Any additional items for which there is estimated to be a charge to the borrower shall be listed if required on the HUD - 1.

(April 1, 1993; amended February 10, 1994)

CLO access fee	[Use blank line in 800 Section]	$XXXX
Tax related service fee	[Use blank line in 800 Section]	$XXXX
Interest for [X] days at $XXXX per day	901	$XXXX
Mortgage insurance premium	902	$XXXX
Hazard insurance premiums	903	$XXXX
Reserves	1000 - 1005	$XXXX
Settlement fee	1101	$XXXX
Abstract or title search	1102	$XXXX
Title examination	1103	$XXXX
Document preparation fee	1105	$XXXX
Attorney's fee	1107	$XXXX
Title insurance	1108	$XXXX
Recording fees	1201	$XXXX
City/County tax stamps	1202	$XXXX
State tax	1203	$XXXX
Survey	1301	$XXXX
Pest inspection	1302	$XXXX
[Other fees – list here]		$XXXX

Applicant
Date
Authorized Official

These estimates are provided pursuant to the Real Estate Settlement Procedures Act of 1974, as amended (RESPA). Additional information can be found in the HUD Special Information Booklet, which is to be provided to you by your mortgage broker or lender, if your application is to purchase residential real property and the Lender will take a first lien on the property.

ASHI CODE OF ETHICS

1. Inspectors shall avoid conflicts of interest or activities that compromise, or appear to compromise, professional independence, objectivity, or inspection integrity.

   A. Inspectors shall not inspect properties for compensation in which they have, or expect to have, a financial interest.

   B. Inspectors shall not inspect properties under contingent arrangements whereby any compensation or future referrals are dependent on reported findings or on the sale of a property.

   C. Inspectors shall not directly or indirectly compensate realty agents, or other parties having a financial interest in closing or settlement of real estate transactions, for the referral of inspections or for inclusion on a list of recommended inspectors, preferred providers, or similar arrangements.

   D. Inspectors shall not receive compensation for an inspection from more than one party unless agreed to by the client(s).

   E. Inspectors shall not accept compensation, directly or indirectly, for recommending contractors, services, or products to inspection clients or other parties having an interest in inspected properties.

   F. Inspectors shall not repair, replace, or upgrade, for compensation, systems or components covered by ASHI Standards of Practice, for one year after the inspection.

2. Inspectors shall act in good faith toward each client and other interested parties.

   A. Inspectors shall perform services and express opinions based on genuine conviction and only within their areas of education, training, or experience.

   B. Inspectors shall be objective in their reporting and not knowingly understate or overstate the significance of reported conditions.

   C. Inspectors shall not disclose inspection results or client information without client approval. Inspectors, at their discretion, may disclose observed immediate safety hazards to occupants exposed to such hazards, when feasible.

3. Inspectors shall avoid activities that may harm the public, discredit themselves, or reduce public confidence in the profession.

A. Advertising, marketing, and promotion of inspectors' services or qualifications shall not be fraudulent, false, deceptive, or misleading.

B. Inspectors shall report substantve and willful violations of this Code to the Society.

THE LANDLORD PATH

12

CHOOSING THE RIGHT LANDLORD PATH

O nce you own a property, you have a decision to make: manage the property yourself or hire a property manager. The decision depends on your personality and your investment objectives. If you want to be a landlord, then the following statements must be true:

- **You enjoy people.** You enjoy being around people and listening to them.

- **You enjoy solving problems.** A landlord is, above all, a solver of people problems. You must be able to handle complaints and service issues smoothly, fairly, and positively.

- **You love numbers.** As a landlord, you have to have basic accounting skills and an affinity for paperwork—lots of it (although software has made this part of the job much easier.)

- **You love fixing and maintaining things.** You can save a lot of money by being able to make minor repairs like fixing leaky faucets yourself. For major jobs, an added bonus is the ability to find qualified contractors who do good work at reasonable prices.

- **You are flexible and available at all hours.** As a landlord, you will have to handle calls in the evenings and on the weekends. Pipes burst, people get locked out—all these problems fall on the shoulders of the landlord.

- **You can commit time and effort.** Landlording takes time and work beyond tenant and physical plant issues. You must know property management laws, be able to calculate rates, keep abreast of market trends, and many other things as well.

- **You have to be a combination of salesperson and negotiator.** Whether it is a multi-unit residential property or a commercial or industrial property, you have to sell prospective tenants on occupying your space.

If you possess all of these qualities, you will be a great landlord, saving on property-management fees and maintenance costs. If not, then you need a property manager. Another consideration is your long-range goals. Do you want to concentrate time and effort on acquiring properties to build wealth through real estate investment? If so, then your time is better spent on investment than on property management because you are a "big picture" wealth-builder. If, on the other hand, you enjoy people and the duties of the landlord, then you should concentrate on acquiring properties you can manage effectively yourself. Of course, there is nothing wrong with starting out as a landlord, and then, as your success grows, transitioning out of the property management side of the business into the investment side.

THE PROFESSIONAL MANAGEMENT OPTION

As stated by the U.S. Bureau of Labor Statistics, "property and real estate managers oversee the performance of income-producing commercial or residential properties and ensure that real estate investments achieve their expected revenues." Choosing professional management for your properties is extremely important. After all, you invested to generate a source of income and profits, and you want a management firm to maintain and increase the value of your real estate investments. Generally speaking, property management firms handle the financial operations of the property. This means they ensure that rent is collected and that mortgages, taxes, insurance premiums, payroll, and maintenance bills are paid on time. Some property managers, called **asset property managers**, "supervise the preparation of financial statements and periodically report to the owners on the status of the property, occupancy rates, expiration dates of leases, and other matters." As shown on page 239, the Bureau of Labor Statistics provides a good description of a property manager's duties.

Of course, it is the execution of the duties that counts. A good management firm will increase your profits and maintain the integrity of the property. A poor one will cost you money, not only in profits, but also in maintenance of the property. If the buildings and the grounds are neglected or leased to unsuitable tenants, you can lose on many fronts. The best way to avoid this situation is, of course, to research several property management firms before choosing one. Use the following guidelines:

- **Interview several property managers.** Make sure they are true property managers and not real estate office property managers who specialize in selling property, not managing it.

- **Check references** by making the necessary phone calls.

- **Review the company's track record** for management of properties. Ask for a list of clients, and contact the rental owners for information.

- **Ask for proof of licensing.** Depending on the state, a property manager should have a real estate license, a property manager's license, or both. Also, ask for professional accreditation from the Institute of Real Estate Management (IREM). This is an organization of professionals providing designation in three areas:

  - CPM—Certified Property Manager

  - ARM—Accredited Residential Manager

  - AMO—Accredited Management Organization

- **Require proof of insurance.** Any property management company you hire should carry insurance for general liability, automobile liability, workers' compensation, and professional "errors and omissions" insurance. Also make sure they have a substantial fidelity bond. This is your protection should an employee mishandle or embezzle your money.

PROPERTY MANAGER DUTIES

Source: Bureau of Labor Statistics (www.bls.gov/oco/ocos022.htm)

…Often, property managers negotiate contracts for janitorial, security, groundskeeping, trash removal, and other services. When contracts are awarded competitively, managers solicit bids from several contractors and advise the owners on which bid to accept. They monitor the performance of contractors and investigate and resolve complaints from residents and tenants when services are not properly provided. Managers also purchase supplies and equipment for the property and make arrangements with specialists for repairs that cannot be handled by regular property maintenance staff… *Onsite property managers* are responsible for the day-to-day operations of a single property, such as an office building, a shopping center, a community association, or an apartment complex. To ensure that the property is safe and properly maintained, onsite managers routinely inspect the grounds, facilities, and equipment to determine whether repairs or maintenance is needed. In handling requests for repairs or trying to resolve complaints they meet not only with current residents, but also with prospective residents or tenants to show vacant apartments or office space. Onsite managers also are responsible for enforcing the terms of rental or lease agreements, such as rent collection, parking and pet restrictions, and termination-of-lease procedures. Other important duties of onsite managers include keeping accurate, up-to-date records of income and expenditures from property operations and submitting regular expense reports to the asset property manager or owners. Property managers who do [work offsite] act as a liaison between the onsite manager and the owner. They also market vacant space to prospective tenants through the use of a leasing agent or by advertising or other means, and they establish rental rates in accordance with prevailing local economic conditions. Some property and real estate managers, often called *real estate asset managers*, act as the property owners' agent and adviser for the property. They plan and direct the purchase, development, and disposition of real estate on behalf of the business and investors. These managers focus on long-term strategic financial planning, rather than on day-to-day operations of the property…

- **Separate accounting.** The management firm should have separate accounting for each of its managed properties instead of a master trust account in which funds from several clients are mixed together, leading to financial complications and creative accounting that can cost you money.

In any contract you sign, the property management firm will be granted the right and ability to make emergency repairs without advance notice from you — up to a specified limit, of course. If you own a larger property, that limit might be $2,000 to $3,000. If you own a smaller one, the limit might be, say, $300 to $500. This limit is negotiable with the property management firm. Whatever limit is chosen, make it clear that you want the company to keep up to date on any expenses incurred. When you hire a firm, you must monitor its activities and expenses closely, particularly in the beginning. This will prevent the firm from making the unnecessary repairs sometimes ordered by property management companies bent on making money at your expense.

In general, management firms are paid in one of two ways: In exchange for their services, they may receive a percentage of the collected income, or they may charge a flat fee on a monthly basis or a dollar amount per unit per month for the entire property. The better option is the first one — a percentage. It provides an incentive for the company to keep rents at market value as well as to enforce rent collection. If you have invested in single-family homes, condos, or small rental properties, you will find the fees run around 8 to 10 percent. With medium-sized properties, it will have a range of 6 to 8 percent. Management fees for large residential properties will fall in the 3 to 5 percent range. Expect additional fees in the leasing of vacant commercial, industrial, or retail space. This is because it takes considerable time and effort to find and qualify new tenants when an old tenant leaves. The property manager has to get the space ready and show it to prospective clients. In this case, the leasing commission is usually a percentage of the gross rent. It is often based on a sliding scale; the longer the lease, the lower the percentage in later years. In the case of residential rentals, the charge may either be a flat fee or a percentage of the monthly rental rate.

THE LANDLORDING OPTION

A landlord is a person who buys and maintains one or more properties in order to create a steady cash flow through rent. A smart and ambitious landlord can create considerable wealth over a number of years!

A good income is obviously one of the advantages of being a landlord, but there are other benefits as well. An important advantage is that you do not need a great deal of money to get started in the field. It is one of the few businesses in which you can buy the product—a house, for example—below market value, increase your net worth at the same time, and have a regular cash flow. Another advantage is that to be a landlord, you do not need a lot of education. If you are dedicated and doggedly persistent, you can succeed in real estate!

Of course, every occupation has its disadvantages, and landlording is no different. You have to deal with tenants and expenses from unexpected repairs. In addition you must keep vacancy rates low to maintain cash flow and deal with governmental regulations and paperwork.

A more subtle disadvantage is the unfair image of the landlord as a money-grubbing Scrooge who is out to pinch every penny he can find at the expense of his tenants. Most landlords are honest people who have simply chosen a career they like and make a good living at it. You can fight this unfair image by being ethical and fair in all dealings with your tenants. They will respect you for your honesty, and that honesty will pay off in the best advertising possible—good word-of-mouth. Word-of-mouth advertising will keep vacancy rates low and increase your cash flow. Integrity pays in both reputation and income. Now that you know the advantages and disadvantages of being a landlord, look at the product you sell—housing.

TYPES OF HOUSING

As a landlord, you need to know what types of housing are available in your particular market. You also need to know the upsides and downsides of owning, renting, and maintaining these properties. In addition, as stated earlier in the book, you should be aware that the value of any property depends upon the neighborhood in which it is located. Check the area thoroughly before you buy any property. Contact every source you can. Talk to police officers about the crime rate. Talk with other landlords in the neighborhood. Walk the streets and see how clean or dirty the houses and yards are kept. If possible, speak with homeowners and renters to get their take on the area. Definitely check out the reputation of the school system. A great indicator of a good neighborhood is the quality of the schools, because an excellent education system attracts excellent homeowners and renters.

There are eight common types of housing that are usually available in markets. As an investor, you may not be interested in all of these types, but you should be aware of the potential of each.

1. **Single-room occupancies like hotels, motels, and converted houses.** Single-room occupancies are older motels, hotels, and converted houses. They are low-cost properties in which people rent a room by the night or week. Single-room occupancies (often called SROs) work this way as a landlord: Assume you buy one of these properties for $65,000 or $70,000. It is a ten-room house, which you have the option of renting for $800 a month. Or, you can rent each of the ten rooms in the same house for $200 a week, making your weekly income $2,000, and the monthly income $8,000. SROs have their disadvantages, of course. They are often located in low-income areas, which means they often do not hold their value over time. In the short term, it means you are constantly collecting rent. More than likely, it also means that you will have to deal with crime, vandalism, and difficult tenants.

2. **Mobile home parks.** The biggest advange to mobile homes or trailer parks is usually cash flow. Assume you have bought a low-end mobile home park. To set it up, you paid anywhere from $1,500 to $3,500 for each trailer. Now you charge from $500 to $700 a month to rent each mobile home, which means you are getting the same amount of rent as you would be able to charge for a $60,000 house or a $75,000 duplex. So you are earning a high cash flow from your investment.

   The disadvantages of owning a trailer park are the amount of managing and maintenance required. If you have a property with 100 trailers, you will have a lot more responsibility than you would with the occupants of a single-family home or a duplex.

Furnaces quit, air conditioners give out, and plumbing springs leaks, and as the owner of a mobile home property, you have to be prepared to deal with these problems on a larger scale.

3. **Low-end houses and duplexes.** Prices of low-end houses and duplexes will vary according to region, but may range from $5,000 to $20,000. They may rent in the $300 to $500 range on a monthly basis. The great advantage of owning property in this category is that your cash flow is about the same as for medium-income houses and duplexes, but your return on investment is much higher because you have paid so much less for your properties. Duplexes are an especially great property to own. Instead of one tenant paying $500 a month, you have two tenants paying you a total of $1,000 on a monthly basis.

   The disadvantages of the low-end category can be crime, property damage, and challenging tenants, but you have control over these disadvantages if you knew the area well before you invested in any property. Contact the sources mentioned earlier to find out about the quality of the neighborhood. Talk to police officers, other landlords, homeowners, and renters. If you do your homework, then you can choose wise investments in this category of housing.

4. **Apartment buildings.** Apartment building are often found in low- to moderate-income as well as high-end areas of town. The advantage of apartment buildings is cash flow, of course. A 100-unit building at $500 a month brings in $50,000 a month. There are disadvantages to owning an apartment complex, however. First of all,

it calls for a considerable investment of your money upfront. You are putting all of your financial eggs in one basket. If the neighborhood changes for the worse or if the city builds an incinerator next to the building, you may be stuck with a devalued investment. A second disadvantage is high turnover rates among tenants. People move to take new jobs, buy a house, or lease a different apartment in another part of town, which means you lose income and have to find new tenants. Consider all these factors before investing in this type of property.

5. **Town houses and condominiums.** Town houses and condos tend to draw tenants with stable incomes. There are fewer of them to deal with as well, which means lower maintenance costs. However, you will have to be able to deal with a certain amount of friction among people. This is because there is usually a governing association in the town house and condominium category. The association lays down the rules on such items as parking and lawn maintenance. If a tenant disobeys these rules, conflicts can arise that the landlord must settle.

6. **Single-family homes and duplexes.** This is the "American dream" category. Everybody wants a single-family home with a big yard and a two-car garage in a wonderfully safe neighborhood. Owning these properties has advantages for you as a landlord. First of all, tenants will tend to be more stable, meaning turnover will be low and income will be steady. Second, you can distribute your financial risk by buying properties in different neighborhoods. If homes in one area start to decline in value, you have properties in a different neighborhood

that are appreciating in value. One disadvantage of renting single-family homes and duplexes is a lower cash flow than with other properties because you have to invest more money upfront to buy a single-family home. Another disadvantage is the great cost when tenants move. You often have to do a makeover of a home before a new tenant moves in because expectations are higher. Paint, wallpaper, plumbing fixtures, and other maintenance items can all be big expenses for a landlord. A third disadvantage is the fact that you need a lot of money to cover your mortgage when a property goes 30 days or more without generating any rent.

7. **Commercial properties.** Commercial property is an area in which a landlord can make a lot of money, and it has two other advantages as well. The first is that commercial tenants have a considerable investment of their own at stake so they tend to be highly responsible with your property. A second advantage is that typically you rent the building to such tenants, but you are not responsible for property maintenance. Because commercial property can be so valuable, it creates disadvantages as well as advantages. Such properties can be much harder to finance and call for a considerably larger investment upfront. Commercial property is tied to the economy. If the economy cools, then you may have one or more buildings empty for months or several years, and you still have to pay the mortgage on those buildings. In such cases, you also have to find new tenants, and that process can cost thousands of dollars. Plus, once you do find a new tenant, you may have to renovate to suit its particular needs. For example, if the previous tenant had an auto parts business and the new tenant wants to open

a restaurant in the space, then you are definitely going to have some renovation expenses.

8. **Upper-income homes.** Luxury homes can bring the most income, but they can also be the riskiest investment. If the economy takes a tumble, luxury-home tenants often cannot afford the rent and move to lower-income homes or apartments.

So on which of these eight properties should you concentrate? It depends upon your objectives, but, in general, commercial properties and upper-income homes should not be your first choice. As mentioned before, commercial property and upper-income homes are tied closely to the economy and you can be seriously affected if the economy weakens. If you are new to investing, a better choice would be the low-end house and duplex category. Why this recommendation when the return can be higher in the more expensive housing areas? It is simple: You are always going to be able to rent low-end houses and duplexes no matter what the state of the economy. People have to live somewhere, even when times are tough.

You will have to deal with the disadvantages in difficult economic times, of course. Vacancies will be longer, and security deposits will not be as large. You may have to offer incentives to attract and keep tenants. You will probably have to spend more time collecting rent from slow payers. But, overall, the advantages outweigh the disadvantages. It is much easier dealing with minor hassles when you have a steady income from low-income houses and duplexes in a weak economy.

Assume you have chosen your area of investment. What are the duties and responsibilities of a landlord? They can be divided into two broad areas: finding and keeping tenants and maintenance and repairs. A great deal goes into each of these areas, but you do not make any money without tenants, of course, so that is the area to look at first.

ADVERTISING FOR TENANTS

As a landlord, the first order of business is to attract tenants. Before advertising for occupants, your property must be in good condition, clean, and attractive. Your properties need to look as good as or better than competitors' properties in the same category.

Once you have your properties in shape for occupancy, it is time to attract renters through advertising. When advertising, avoid a "shotgun" approach, trying to appeal to everyone in the market. Instead, target your advertising toward the kind of renters you want in your properties. For example, if you are looking for steady, reliable renters who tend to stay in one place and treat property with respect, then target older people.

An important point to remember about advertising is that housing laws do not allow you to discriminate against renters on the basis of creed, color, disability, race, or religion. However, you can certainly target certain age group or occupations. For example, if there are a fair number of schools and universities in your area, you can shape your advertising toward attracting teachers and professors. Or, if a particular company has a large number of employees, you can focus your advertising in that direction. Be sure to check out the neighborhood for these kinds of opportunities ahead of time.

Ways You Can Advertise Your Property

The first, simplest, and often most effective method of

advertising is signage. That's right—a simple "For Rent" sign placed in the yard. According to the National Association of Realtors, nearly 88 percent of all homes are sold to drive-by customers. Put up a sign immediately when you open up the property and, after that, whenever you have a vacancy. Make sure the sign is attractive. If it is cheap and crudely made, it says to the public that your property is not a first-class operation and that you are probably more interested in money than in taking care of renters. On the other hand, if it is clean, colorful, and appropriate to the exterior of the building, it says you take care of your properties and the people who rent from you. The best course is to hire a professional sign maker to make signs for you.

Signage is inexpensive and offers an instant visual message on the street. The downside of signage is that it can be damaged or stolen and invites vandalism to the property. Its effectiveness is also dependent upon the amount of traffic on the street. A second form of advertising is classified advertisements. This includes not only the daily newspaper but also community newspapers and free "shoppers." Before you pay for this type of advertising, make sure your potential renters are people who read these materials! In other words, select newspapers and shopping guides that appeal to your renters.

The key to writing an ad is to make it short and attractive. Use appealing words like "beautiful," "cozy," "roomy," and other adjectives to conjure up a positive picture in the reader's mind. A simple, effective ad might read:

CLOSE TO CAMPUS 4 BEDROOM!
Carpeted, stove, refrigerator, cable, garage.
$650. 555-4321

At the same time, be sure to put enough information in the ad so that you do not have to spend all your time explaining what is provided with the property. It is tedious to repeat the same information over and over to prospective renters and is not an effective use of your resources. Make sure your ad is readable by avoiding too many abbreviations. It can look like alphabet soup to a casual reader, and readers don't always know what the abbreviations mean or appreciate having to decode them. Perhaps the best way to create a good ad is to review competitors' advertisements and discover for yourself which ones are most attractive and effective.

A good way to avoid repetition of information over the phone is to have a pre-recorded phone message describing the property for rent. This method cuts out casual "lookers" and gets your message to serious prospects. That message might sound something like this:

" We're glad that you called! We have an exciting opportunity available in a three-bedroom home! Find yourself a pencil and a piece of paper and write down this address: 1234 Elm Street. That's 1234 Elm Street. This three-bedroom home with two bathrooms and detached garage is located two blocks east of Elm Elementary School. To get there, take the I-00 exit and go west five blocks. Take a left on Maple. The home is three blocks down on the right."

Classified ads have the advantage of reaching a large readership. They are also simple to compose, saving time. If the population in your area is large enough, then investigate advertising in rental guides. These guides, which tend to be published in lower-income, urban areas, contain a convenient, thorough listing, which is usually more up to date and detailed than newspaper ads. The advantage of this form of advertising is that it is free to landlords because the guide is paid for by the advertising of other businesses. Rental guides also allow you to get more information in your listing, helping to "sell" the property to a renter more effectively.

One disadvantage of rental guides is that customers have to buy them, which can limit your potential pool of renters. Unethical competitors may also offer deceptive listings in which they promise luxury accommodations at bargain rates. When customers contact this person, they find out these "special" properties have already been rented, but other regular apartments are available. This kind of deception can cause customers to associate you with disreputable firms even though you have no connection with them whatsoever. Always review a rental guide ahead of time before listing your properties.

A simple, time-honored method of advertising is the handbill or flyer. The advantages of this method are obvious. It is quick and inexpensive. With today's computers, you can create handbills with ease. The disadvantage of handbills is that you have to distribute them, which can be time-consuming. However, you can limit distribution time and increase effectiveness by targeting your market. Ask reputable local merchants to display them, and put them on bulletin boards where such handbills are allowed. Remember to keep track of the locations where they are posted so you can take them down as necessary.

One last method of advertising is the Internet. At present, there are two basic ways of advertising on the Internet:

1. Create and maintain your own Web site, which allows you to customize the site to your own needs. You can provide photographs, floor plans, and maps to direct

renters to the properties. It is also inexpensive. The disadvantage is that you have to learn HTML and how to set up a Web site. However, this is extremely easy now with such Web-authoring software as Front Page and DreamWeaver. These applications provide templates that make it simple for you to create your site. Often, software companies will let you download a trial version so you can get an idea of how the software works. Whichever software you choose, the key to success with a Web site is the same as with other forms of advertising — target your audience, which means getting it indexed on the major search engines so potential customers can find your site. When you log onto the computer, enter "search engine optimization" in the Internet search window, which will lead you to information about optimization.

2. The second method of using the Web is to list vacancies on a site devoted to classified advertising in your area. To find these sites, run Internet searches on "classifieds [your town]" and "apartments (or houses) for rent [your town]." Check each site. Avoid those with little or no classified advertising. With this method, you can also cast a wider net with such nationwide services as ForRent.com (**www.forrent.com**) or Rent.com.

In general, remember: Keep your properties constantly before the public eye. Advertising is not a one-shot deal. If you have vacancies now or upcoming, then they are going to remain vacant if nobody knows about them. In addition, retaining vacancies costs a great deal more money than the amount you would spend on advertising. It is just good business to advertise on a consistent basis.

Now for the most important part of landlording—the people who generate income for you—the tenants!

FINDING GOOD TENANTS

Every landlord wants the perfect tenant—a person who pays on time, never moves, and treats the property with respect. However, you are seldom going to find the perfect renter for your properties. Be prepared to deal with different likes, dislikes, needs, and temperaments. However, you can reduce difficulties with renters by planning ahead and establishing ground rules for the customers you will accept within the housing law guidelines.

First of all, qualify your applicants by asking good questions and using your intuition. What are good questions to ask? Here is a suggested list to which you can add your own questions:

- Where are you living now?

- How long have you lived there?

- Why do you want to move from there?

- Do you have enough money for the deposit?

- Do you have good credit?

- Have you ever been evicted or asked to move out?

- Do you smoke?

- Do you have pets?

Of course, people can and do lie when answering these questions, which is where the intuition comes in to play. Through experience, you will develop a sense for when a person is telling the truth and when they are lying to you. At this point, you may think that some of these questions are too direct or blunt. If asking such questions makes you uncomfortable, remember that you want the best possible tenants occupying your properties. They are your source of income. Undesirable tenants end up causing you grief and costing you money.

Assuming you get the answers you want to those initial questions, take the next step and inform the person that you would like to do a credit check, which requires their authorization. Ask them first what their credit rating is. Some may not know what it is, which is fine, because what you are looking for is honesty. If a potential tenant lies and tells you he has excellent credit, and one of the credit reporting agencies sends you a report with a low credit score, then you know this person is not a tenant for you.

Depending upon the area in which your properties are located, you may also want to do a criminal background check. This also requires written authorization by the prospective tenant. If the person hangs up on you or leaves your office quickly, then you have just screened out an undesirable tenant.

Before calling previous landlords for a recommendation on the people applying for your property, it never hurts to ask what they think that former landlord will say about them. Their response can tell you volumes about their suitability as tenants.

The next step is to show the property. Explain where the property is and, if they are driving separately, give clear directions. Then, show the property by highlighting its good features while being honest about the neighborhood and any problems. If you have done your job by asking the prospective renters about their likes and dislikes and have selected the property to meet their needs, this should not be a problem. Simply remember that it is a waste of your time and their time to try to shove a property on them that you know they are going to reject.

A more efficient method of showing a property is to hold an open house. Showing the property to several people at once has great benefits for you. It saves time and money and, at the same time, it creates a buyer's atmosphere. It is human nature for interest to rise when several people attend an open house. They get competitive, which puts you in the driver's seat in terms of the amount of rent you can charge.

Whether you hold an open house or an individual showing, this is an opportunity for you to judge the prospects as potential renters. The remarks they make, the way they treat the property, the way they treat you — these are all clues as to how they will behave as tenants. Be sure to offer applications to all who attend a showing, and be sure to tell them that you will review all applications. This demonstrates that you are methodical and non-discriminatory in your application process.

Your next step is to review the applications. Application forms do not need to be complicated affairs, but they should ask for certain basic information, including the following:

- Name, address, and telephone number

- Date of birth

- Driver's license number

- Social Security number

- Current and past tenancies

- Current and past job history

- Financial status

- Number of occupants to be in your property

- Pets

Along with the application, provide instructions on how to fill it out. Do not forget to ask each person to fill out an application if there will be more than one occupant. For example, if a husband and wife are applicants or there are two roommates, each should fill out an application. This creates more paperwork, but it also protects you against discrimination while, at the same time, giving you information to use in case a renter decides to leave without paying rent.

Review each application and use common sense. If applicants have not provided you with previous addresses or if job histories are sketchy, then a red flag should go up in your mind. You do not want to rent a valuable piece of property to people hiding their backgrounds. Plus, unwittingly, these individuals have done you a favor, eliminating themselves at minimum time and cost to you.

Once you review the applicants and find the tenants you want, check their references. If they are legitimate and the applicants are given a good rating, act quickly. Remember, you are in competition with other landlords for good tenants, so there is no time to waste in nailing down a rental agreement. Make a signing appointment. When applicants arrive for the meeting, explain the agreement to them point by point, making it clear from the start what is expected of them as renters and of you as a landlord. This can prevent misunderstandings down the road. During the explanation process, do not be afraid to ask the applicants for their understanding of such points as deposits, vacating notices, and other major items. First of all, this is a great method of checking to make sure they do actually understand. If they do not, then explain the point again. Second, it is a good way of firmly planting the conversation in your memory and in their memories, so if disputes arise later, you can remind them that those specific points were discussed during the meeting.

After a thorough explanation of the rental agreement, have the applicants sign the form. Then request a deposit and a minimum of the first month's rent.

MOVING IN YOUR TENANTS

When tenants move, it is a great time to establish a good relationship with them. They are your customers, after all, and you want them to be steady, rent-paying tenants for years, if possible. To establish a good relationship, take the following steps.

First, inspect the property thoroughly before the tenants move in. Fix what needs to be fixed and have the place as clean and sparkling as possible, creating a good impression of the property, and of you as well. Second, when the tenants move in, go through the property thoroughly with them with your manager's checklist. The checklist should note all the items in the property and the condition of those items. This procedure is important because it allows you to deal with any problems immediately and prevents them from turning into sources of complaint later. It also prevents disagreements about the condition of the place at the end of the leasing term. As you go through the list, ask the tenants to initial the items and sign the form. Most important, if something needs to be replaced or repaired and you promise to do it, follow through on that promise and fix it as quickly as possible. That demonstrates to the tenants that you keep your word and want them to have the best experience possible. They will then tell their friends about your honesty and commitment, and word-of-mouth will bring you more business.

During the move-in, remember to mention your inspection procedures. Tell tenants that you will check back with them on a scheduled basis (say, once a month) to make sure they are satisfied with the property and to fix any problems. This shows that you care and will not be an absentee landlord. It also allows you to check the condition of the property and to spot any problems that might have cropped up in the meantime. After all, you do not want unsavory renters damaging the property and offending other renters or neighbors.

One last note for this section: At the time of move-in, recommend to tenants that they purchase renter's insurance so they are covered in case of fire, theft, and other damages. It is inexpensive insurance and worth every penny in terms of protecting assets.

RETAINING GOOD TENANTS

Think of good tenants as an investment in your future. They are a steady source of income and can help you reach your financial goals, so treat them well. When tenants leave, you have vacancies, which cost money, time, and trouble. Retention of good tenants should be one of your primary goals as a landlord. Right from the start, write out a tenant-retention program with that goal in mind. Here are a few suggestions that are low cost or even free and will encourage your tenants both to appreciate you and to want to continue to live in your properties.

- **Memorize names.** This is the most basic way to keep good tenants, and it is free. Good tenants expect you to know their names. If you do not take the time to learn their names, they may feel you do not have time for them at all. If you do not show any commitment to them, they will not feel any commitment to you.

- **Listen, listen, listen!** This is another free and basic skill, but it is important. Everyone likes to feel that his or her concerns and problems are heard. Try to make your tenants feel as if you know them individually. Look them in the eye when they are talking to you and give them your full attention. Avoid doing other things at the same time. Second, nod during the conversation and say phrases like "I see… I understand… Is that right?" This tells them that you are listening. Third, prove that you have been listening by summarizing what they said. Of course, any property is going to have its share of bores with frivolous complaints as well as tenants with legitimate concerns. Through practice, you will learn to keep them happy and satisfied while limiting conversation with them.

- **Hire tenants.** This is a good idea if you have handyman-type tenants. They appreciate the money (or deduction from the rent), enjoy the work, and take more pride in the building and the grounds because they now have a personal investment.

- **Redecorate for good, long-term tenants.** Keep track of the condition of apartments or houses for your good tenants. You want these properties to be as attractive as possible to retain these tenants. Offer to redecorate the place if it has not been done for a while. They may be perfectly happy with the current condition of the place, but they will definitely appreciate the offer.

- **Move-in gifts.** These are items that brighten up a living space and show the new tenants that they are welcomed and that their business is appreciated. Such gifts can include thank-you baskets, flowers, memo pads with pens and pencils, and other inexpensive items.

- **Holiday/birthday cards.** Send your tenants cards for holidays and birthdays.

- **Lease renewal gifts.** Remind tenants that you still appreciate their business and enjoy having them in your property. Gifts can include ceiling fans, new blinds, and other such items. This is a win-win gift. The tenants appreciate the improvements, and, at the same time, it increases the value of the property.

- **Incentive programs.** Offer a long-term tenant $50 or $100 off the first month's rent after the lease is renewed.

- **Referral bonus.** This is a low-cost prospecting tool. Offer a $25 or $50 referral bonus to a good tenant. Word-of-mouth referrals are especially powerful coming from long-term tenants.

There will come a time when a good tenant needs to leave. After all, circumstances change. A new job, a marriage, more children—these are all facts of life that cause tenants to seek new housing. Be sure to ask specifically why a tenant is leaving, and make sure it is not because of some problem with the property. If there is a problem, you may be able to take care of it and not lose a tenant.

Whatever the cause, if the tenant has definitely decided to leave, then be sure to talk to him personally and wish him well. Remember, they will tell others how you treated them, so it is good business sense to treat them with respect. In fact, use the situation as an opportunity to ask them if they know of anyone who would like the vacated space. They may have friends or relatives who are looking for a place.

With good tenants, another issue you will have to deal with is rent increases. No one likes rent increases, of course, but you especially do not want good tenants upset at paying more money on a weekly or monthly basis. This situation calls for a personalized letter from you. Explain why the rent is being increased. Rent increases are usually the result of higher energy costs, taxes, or inflation. Go a step further than explaining the rent increase. Tell the client, "We are going to clean the carpet and put in new blinds as a small measure of our thanks for your continued patronage." Rewards like that take some of the sting out of the rent increase.

You also can reduce complaints from good tenants by keeping their rents slightly below those you charge for new tenants. This tactic shows that you are giving them special consideration, and they will appreciate the gesture. You can further reduce the complaints about rent increases by preparing all tenants for the increase ahead of time. Simply let it be known that your costs have risen, too, because of economic conditions and you will have to raise the rent at some point. Next, let tenants know exactly when the rent will increase so they can adjust to the idea. Give tenants at least 30 days' notice of a rent increase. Sixty days is even better because it gives more time for the idea to be accepted. If possible, attach the rent increase to some improvement to your properties. Maybe you plan to have the exterior painted, the swimming pool refurbished, or the grounds improved. If so, time the rent increase so it occurs with those improvements. That gives tenants visible proof that their rent increase is actually providing a benefit.

COLLECTING RENT

As a landlord, you must be consistent and have a reliable system set up to collect rent so that tenants know exactly when their rent is due. The best way is to use a computerized rental tracking system. You can find this software on the Internet by doing a search. Possibilities include RentTracker at **www. renttracker.com/about.htm** or Rental Property Tracker Plus **http://productivity-software.com/rental**. Or you can set up your own system using readily available financial management software like QuickBooks at **http://quickbooks.intuit.com**. Review each software package to find out which one best meets your needs. The goal of your rent collection system is simple: At any given time, you should be able to tell what percentage of your rent has been collected as of that date. That way, you can tell who the late payers are and you can target your rent-collection efforts.

You will need to be persistent and firm with those tenants who do pay late. They signed an agreement and are occupying your valuable property. It is their responsibility to pay on time! If a tenant is late, contact them and remind them of the agreement and, at the same time, explain your collection procedures. For example, assume you collect rent on the first of the month. You might tell the offending tenant that rent is considered late if it is not paid by the fifth of the month, and that you will be paying them a visit by the sixth if the money and the late-penalty fee are not forthcoming.

Of course, you should have a standard collection procedure in place when you start your business. It can help reduce the number of late payers because they understand your policy from the moment they sign an agreement. Your policy should include the following items:

- A standard collection procedure

- Specified form of payment

- Written receipts

- A set rental due date

- A set late-payment date

- Late-payment penalty

Customize these forms to fit your particular situation.

You will need to adapt collection procedures as well because every landlord's situation is different. Tenants may come to your office or to a manager's office to drop off their rent checks. Or, you may collect by mail or have a drop box. Of course, you can always collect the rent in person, but this is probably the least efficient method. Depending on number of properties or apartment units, it consumes valuable time. The upside to this method, however, is that it both establishes your presence to the renters and allows you to make sure the property is in good shape.

When collecting late rents, consider the people from whom you are collecting. If tenants have been good payers and are suddenly late, it may be simply because they forgot, were sick, or had a death in the family. Such tenants deserve your patience and understanding.

On the other hand, chronically late-paying tenants deserve nothing but firmness on your part. They are costing you money and not living up to their legal agreement. Visit them personally and be blunt. Tell them that they need to pay on time, all the time, or you will have to terminate the agreement and put the apartment up for rent. This kind of firmness is important, not only for the individual tenant concerned, but also because it sets an example for other tenants who might be inclined to pay late.

An alternative to collecting late rent payments is to use collection attorneys. The advantage of this approach is that it takes collection procedures out of your hand and puts it in the hands of professionals. The disadvantage is that the attorneys may charge up to a third of what they collect as well as court fees.

A better approach may be to recommend a list of social, religious, and governmental agencies who are dedicated to helping out individuals who are short on income. This approach creates a better image for you than using collection attorneys. Use your judgment in this area. If the tenants are honest, hard-working people who are simply in a bad situation, then recommend the "helping-hand" agencies. If the tenants simply make it a habit to avoid payment, then choose the collection agency route, which brings us to the least pleasant aspect of being a landlord—evictions.

EVICTION PROCEDURES

Eviction is a legal procedure that must be followed to the letter. The only person who can actually move a person out of a property is a sheriff or other duly-appointed officer of the law. Remember also that legally you cannot do the following:

- Turn off the gas, electricity, or water to get a tenant to move.

- Confiscate belongings.

- Harass.

- Threaten bodily harm.

Ethically, you should not be doing this in the first place, no matter how obnoxious the tenant has been. On the practical side, you are setting yourself up for lawsuits and fines that can cost you much more than the rent lost to a bad tenant. For more information on the subject, check out Fairhousing.org at **www. fairhousinglaw.org/fair_housing_laws**. Or go straight to the Housing and Urban Development (HUD) site at **www.hud.gov/ offices/fheo/FHLaws/index.cfm**.

Hopefully, you will not have to do many evictions, but, if you do, you have two choices in eviction proceedings: You can do it yourself or you can hire a specialist, an eviction/collection attorney, to do it. Doing it yourself is less expensive and faster. Hiring an attorney protects you against lawsuits. Eviction laws are different in every state so the attorney will be aware of the technicalities. However, an attorney is more expensive, and the process will take longer.

The first step in eviction proceedings is to serve a **notice of eviction**. To meet legal requirements, it must be properly filled out and properly served. The notice should state the following information:

- The number of days tenants have in which to comply with the order.

- The names of all the tenants in the property.

- The address of the rental dwelling.

- The amount of rent due (in cases of non-payment of rent).

- The period for which rent is due.

- Date of the notice.

- Your signature.

It is better to serve the notice in person rather than mail it because longer waiting periods may apply for mailed notices. You can serve it yourself if you feel up to handling an emotional situation, or you can hire someone. If you hire someone, make sure they understand the legal aspects of eviction. Eviction procedures vary from state to state, so know those procedures well before you perform any evictions.

MAINTENANCE AND REPAIR

For a landlord, the downside of maintenance and repair is that the costs can cut into your profits and cause considerable exasperation. The upside is that it is an opportunity to show good tenants that you are committed to giving them a good rental experience and are paying attention to their needs. Remember, a good tenant experience creates good word-of-mouth, and that, in turn, brings more business. So look on the positive side and attempt to keep maintenance and repair costs to a minimum.

Appliances — refrigerators, stoves, and air conditioners — are a major source of expense. In the first place, they cost a lot to replace, usually $500 or more. In the second place, they are expensive to repair. You must either build the cost of these appliances into your rent, or encourage tenants to bring their own appliances.

Repair costs for other items can be high as well. Carpets need replacing, faucets leak, and plumbing bursts in cold weather. The best way to keep these costs to a minimum is to do preventive maintenance. Check the condition of fixtures, furnaces, and other items before a move-in and regularly thereafter with all tenants. Depending on the number of properties you own, you can do repairs yourself or, if you have a manager, you can have him or her fix items.

Speaking of repairpeople, consider offering a deduction in rent to tenants who are good at repairs. Establish a maximum amount for minor repairs, say $100 or $200, and offer them $10 or more off the rent in exchange for their services.

A three- to five-day policy is recommended for maintenance and repairs. This tells tenants that you are a responsible landlord, who intends to meet their needs in a timely fashion.

In a related topic, damage to your property can occur either intentionally or unintentionally. The tenant is responsible for this damage and should pay for it. Make tenants aware of this policy at the time of the rental agreement signing. If need be, remind the tenant of this fact when damage occurs; this will undercut the argument that the landlord should pay. Damage, especially to several properties, adds up to a lot of money over time.

PROTECTING YOUR INVESTMENTS

The importance of protecting your investments with the proper insurance cannot be stressed enough. If being a landlord is your entire livelihood, you cannot withstand catastrophic losses resulting from fire, bad weather, or liability suits. Compared to those major expenses, insurance costs are a bargain. Here are the types of insurance to consider:

- **Title insurance.** This makes clear who owns the title and prevents you from throwing away money on a property that might legally belong to someone else.

- **Fire insurance.** Do not skimp on protection in this area. Insure your properties for top value, or the insurance company may discount their payment.

- **Liability insurance.** Be sure to have this, and be sure to note any exclusions. You may want to spend extra money to have any exceptions included in the insurance. You may also want to get a separate contractor's insurance policy if you do any building, remodeling, or painting.

- **Extended coverage.** This is also called "comprehensive" coverage or a "package policy." It is often offered along with the standard fire insurance policy, and it is protection well worth buying. This coverage can protect you from damage caused by hail, windstorms, smoke, rioting, falling trees, vandalism, freezing temperatures, landslides, and accidental water discharge from burst pipes. Fit the coverage to your particular geographic area.

- **Earthquake coverage.** This is always a separate policy. If you live in an earthquake-prone area, you should definitely have this policy.

- **Flood insurance.** Insurers consider flood damage different from water damage caused by burst pipes and such. If your property is in a flood-prone area, be sure to have this coverage.

- **Vandalism/Malicious mischief.** This is inexpensive insurance worth the price. It can pay for repairs caused by vandals who may damage or destroy property.

- **Property-improvements insurance.** A standard building policy will not cover damage to such items as swimming pools, fences, signs, parking lots, and other areas. Because weather can badly damage these items, it pays to have them insured as well.

- **Business-interruption insurance.** This is "loss of rent" coverage. For example, if a fire damages one of your properties and becomes unlivable for a while, then you will lose rent until it is repaired. Meanwhile, fixed expenses keep accumulating. With business-interruption insurance, the insurance company compensates you for loss of rental income over a specified period.

- **Mortgage insurance.** The purpose of this insurance is to pay off the balance of your outstanding mortgage if you die or become otherwise incapacitated. It is well worth the price. Check with a lender for the type you need.

- **Boiler/Machinery insurance.** Boiler and other machinery explosions can have horrible results. The insurance company will inspect the equipment on a regular basis and, in effect, becomes your partner in maintenance and safety.

You may want to consider other insurance policies as well, depending on your situation. If you manage properties, get **management insurance** so the insurance company handles any lawsuits instead of you. Another possibility is an **umbrella policy**. It is called umbrella insurance because it is designed to give added liability protection beyond the limits of other insurance policies. In other words, it begins when the liability on other polices has been exhausted. With an umbrella policy, depending on the insurance company, you can get an additional $1 to $5 million in liability protection. **Workers' compensation insurance** is also a good idea if you have employees or contractors working for you. When accidents are concerned, it is better to be safe than sorry. Such protection defends you against frivolous lawsuits.

Of course, it never hurts to have legal protection available to help you. Find a good lawyer. If the expense is too much, use pre-paid legal services. Such plans are inexpensive, and they charge you a monthly fee in the range of $10 to $30 a month. Check with the American Prepaid Legal Services Institute online at **www.aplsi.org** for a partial listing of plans and services. Or try Pre-Paid Legal Services, Inc. at **www.prepaidlegal.com**. This service covers civil cases or work-related criminal cases.

Finally, don't forget your will. In the event of your death, you want to make sure your investment goes to your relatives or designated beneficiaries and not to the government. Without a will, the government takes charge and may take a third of your assets before the estate is settled.

LANDLORD FORMS

In this section, you will find a sample of typical landlord forms on various topics — greetings, dwelling checklists, rent, among others. The number of forms you require will depend upon the size and number of properties you own or manage. Here are some additional sources for these forms and others you may need:

- On the Internet, order forms from Landlord.com at **www. landlord.com/landforms_main_general_forms.htm** or at MRLANDLORD.COM at **www.mrlandlord.com**. To find sites that are state-specific, use a search engine. Review the sites and select the one that best matches your needs.

- In print, there are two good sources of information as well as forms. One is *Secrets of a Millionaire Landlord* by Robert Shemin. It is easy to read and is a good primer on landlording. A more comprehensive book is Leigh Robinson's *Landlording*. This book covers the topic in great detail and has extensive forms for your use. It also includes many references on landlording to help you increase your knowledge of the field.

Tenant Move-In Thank You Letter

Dear_____,

Thanks so much for choosing our facility! I appreciate your business and look forward to a long-lasting relationship. I believe that we have a special community, and it is all because of fine tenants like you who take pride in the building, the grounds, and the surrounding community. You're a great addition to a great community!

Sincerely,

[Your Name]

Holiday Letter

Dear_____,

I want to wish you and yours a happy holiday and a prosperous New Year!

At this time, I especially want to thank you for being such great and responsible tenants by paying your rent on time and keeping the property looking so neat. I appreciate your efforts!

The new year brings some changes for us all. First, we are dedicated to improving our maintenance-response record. We will respond to all service calls within 72 hours effective January 1. Please call us at _____ if you should need something repaired or replaced. If no one is in, leave your name, number, and address, and tell us what needs to be done.

A reminder: All rent is due on the 1st of the month. A late fee is charged after the 5th, and eviction papers must be filed if the rent is not paid by the 11th. This is necessary because all of *our* expenses (mortgages, taxes, and so on) are due on the 1st, and we aren't allowed any extensions for late payments. **So please be sure to send in your rent by the 1st of each month!**

Thanks again for choosing us! We hope the next year is the best ever for you!

Sincerely,

[Name]

Move-In Payment Schedule

Dear_____,

The following payments are due to cover the initial move-in charges for your address at:

_____ .

First month's rent: _____

Security deposit: _____

Application fee: _____

Key deposit: _____

Other deposits: _____

You have agreed to pay the total amount due in the following manner:

$_____ Date: _____

$_____ Date: _____

$_____ Date: _____

If payment is not made as agreed, then you understand that the rental/lease agreement becomes null and void. Any money then becomes non-refundable and is applied to rent for the number of days the premises are held or occupied. It is also applied to re-renting expenses. You further agree to immediately turn over the rental unit to the owner if he or she has already taken possession.

Tenant(s): _____

Permission granted: ☐ Yes   ☐ No

Owner: _____

By:_____

Move-In Inspection Report

Tenant Name: _____

Property Address: _____

KITCHEN

_____ Oven

_____ Refrigerator

_____ Cabinets

_____ Countertops

_____ Kitchen floor

_____ Other (specify) _____

Please initial: _____

BATHROOM

_____ Shower/Tub and sink

_____ Medicine cabinet

_____ Vanity

_____ Floor

_____ Mirrors

_____ Other (specify) _____

Please initial: _____

ALL ROOMS (general)

_____ Carpet/Floor

_____ Closets are clean

_____ Cabinets are clean

_____ Walls

_____ Windows

_____ Other (specify) _____

Please initial: _____

Tenant signature: _____ Date: _____

Landlord signature: _____ Date: _____

Monthly Inspection Report

Month of _____

Date	Location	Notes/Comments

Maintenance Guarantee

Dear_____,

I'm pleased to announce that we now offer a guarantee on all maintenance for your living space! We appreciate your business and would like to continue to ensure that your experience is as pleasant as possible.

As of _____(date), we guarantee that all repairs we are responsible for will be fixed within three days (72 hours) of notification of the problem minimizing your inconvenience.

What happens if we don't fix it within that time period? You will receive free rent on a per-day basis (after the three-day period) until the problem is corrected! You will receive this money in the form of a rent deduction following the next rent payment received.

We know you'll appreciate this new policy. Consider it our commitment to a wonderful tenant!

Resident: _____ **Approved by:** _____

Address: _____ **Move-in date**_____

(if applicable)

Returned Check Notice

Dear_____,

Today your bank informed me that your check for the amount of $_____ payable to our company is now being returned to us. We hope that this was a simple mistake and that you can quickly correct the error. However, at this point, your account balance is overdue and delinquent.

Therefore, I must request that you immediately make payment on this debt. Delivery of a money order or a certified check will bring your account up to date.

Here is the current standing of your account. The total amount due is:

Rent due: _____

Loss of discount (if any):   _____

Total amount now due: _____

This amount **must be paid** within ____ days! Please do not ignore this notice. Late payment can seriously affect your overall credit rating and limit your ability to borrow money from lenders. So, for your own protection, please pay as requested.

Sincerely,

[Your name]

Pay Rent or Quit Notice

[Name]

As repeated letters have reminded you, you are delinquent on payments to our company. This registered letter is an indication of how serious we consider this matter to be.

If you are not willing to pay the rent you owe in the amount of $_____ from the period of _____ to _____, plus a late fee of _____ for a total amount of $_____, then we will start legal proceedings. Legal fees can extremely expensive for you, costing thousands of dollars.

We have a signed rental agreement and insist that you live up to the terms of that agreement. If you do not provide us with proof that you are going to pay the amount due, then our attorney will cancel your rental agreement (as it so states), and you will be requested to leave the premises immediately.

We expect to hear from you by _____. Please contact us sooner if possible in order to make payment. It will save you much time and trouble.

[Your name]

30 Days' Notice to Terminate Tenancy

[Name]

This is a letter to notify you that your tenancy at _____
will end as of _____.

This letter provides a minimum of 30 days' advance notice requiring
you to give up possession, vacate the premises, and remove your
belongings on or before the date stated above.

Failure to vacate will result in legal proceedings against you. These
proceedings will recover possession as well as additional rent
and damages and court costs for unlawfully remaining within the
dwelling.

Please contact me or my office if you have any questions regarding
this notice and to receive information on getting back your security
deposit.

Thank you for your cooperation.

_____   _____
[Owner/Manager]   Dated

Reasons for Eviction Form

For nonpayment _____

(Suit on a lease for accrued rent, damages, late charges, and attorney's fee.)

For other breach of lease_____

(Suit on a lease for accrued rent, damages, late charges, and attorney's fee or the alternative on a three-/fourteen-day notice of termination of tenancy.)

Monies Due the Company

Did the lessee give 30 day's notice?   _____

Did the lessee return keys?   _____ Date returned _____

Date dwelling was vacated   _____

Rent paid through   _____

Date unit re-rented   _____

Security deposit _____   Amount _____

Cleaning fee _____   Amount _____

Pet fee _____   Amount _____

Other (specify) _____   Amount _____

Rent Owed _____ Month _____   Amount _____

Late Charges _____ Month _____ Amount _____

Other Charges _____ Month _____ Amount _____

Notes:

Tricia Orcutt
10 Woodruff Lake Way
Simpsonville, SC 29681
Home/Office: 864-288-3999
E-mail: triciaifc@aol.com
RE Investor & RE Wholesale Deals
R&O Corporation

I bought my first home as a foreclosure. It was a large home, on a golf course, that had been vacant for about a year. It needed some TLC and updating. Despite the work it needed, it was an excellent investment for the price. I was more than happy to walk into the deal with 35 percent extra equity. After that, I was hooked.

When I was just starting out, I trusted the word of contractors without checking references. That was my biggest mistake because I'd quickly discover their work was substandard. If the work is done improperly, time and money are lost, and the budget is blown. Budget and timing are everything in real estate investment.

Three of the most important things I learned starting out can really help new real estate investors:

1. Don't let analysis paralysis hold you back from moving quickly, or you'll lose the best deals. It only takes losing a couple of great deals to learn this lesson.

2. Do your due diligence well because poor information can be your worst enemy. If you haven't done your research well, your budget will be as unstable as a house of cards.

3. Know your market. You can't possibly know every market, so specialize in one market area. Get to know that market area like the back of your hand. Your confidence level will build, and

your knowledge will increase, enabling you to make faster and better investing decisions.

I also learned what investment strategies worked best for me. For example, I buy low, rehab well, and flip fast for a fair price. If you're in real estate investing, you want to use other people's (hard money lenders, banks, tenants, etc.) money whenever possible to make deals happen. Put less money down, and let your money work for you on more properties through leveraging, rather than trying to pay off one.

Finally, find tried-and-true formulas that really work; use them, and stick with them.

There are a variety of ways you can find potential investment properties, including going to foreclosure sales at your local courthouse; watching the investment club postings online; and looking for empty houses and tracking down the owner to make an offer. In addition to these strategies, I also have scouts looking for properties that fit within my parameters. Scouts can be Realtors, family members, or other investors. You might also want to place an ad in your local newspaper saying you buy houses for cash.

I like to flip properties after rehabbing them. All of my long-term investment rentals are commercial. It's easier to evict a business than a family, and it's also more profitable. I have an outstanding tax accountant/financial planner, who is also an investor, to handle the taxes on the rental properties.

Real estate offers a great investment opportunity. I definitely prefer real estate as my investment of choice as stocks can go up and down. Money market accounts yield small, continual growth. However, real estate can quickly surpass the investment potential if it's done skillfully.

The sky really is the limit with real estate. Whether it's a good market or a bad one, people will always need it. It's as much in demand as food. Real estate can allow for leveraging to quickly

grow your investment. If you hold your properties, you are using other people's (tenant) money to pay down the note, paying you cash flow each month while your equity is growing. If you flip your properties, it allows for a speedy accumulation of cash, which enables you to buy properties without mortgages if you so choose. It's an amazing way to invest.

CHAPTER

13

KEEPING RECORDS

In many ways, this is the most important chapter of the book. Recordkeeping is an essential part of keeping your investment properties profitable—and the IRS happy. Accounting skills, in particular, allow you to protect your investments and give you power over your money. If you do not understand accounting at a basic level, then you can be over your financial head in a hurry. If you are new to the real estate investment business (or any other business, for that matter), read Robert T. Kiyosaki's and Sharon Lechter's classic book, *Rich Dad, Poor Dad*. In clear language, it shows how to make money work for you—the central wisdom of any investor or entrepreneur.

RECORDKEEPING

It is a fact: Rental properties require a lot of paperwork, and records have to be easily accessible. If you are not an organized sort or you simply detest paperwork, then you may want to hire someone to do it for you. Fortunately, with the advent of the digital age, it is much easier to maintain records these days. Many software programs are available at a reasonable cost. You will need to keep complete and accurate records in three areas:

- **Financial management.** As stated above, basic financial skills are essential. If you do not acquire them, your investments will suffer. The "Accounting Skills" section later in this chapter will spell out the financial-management skills required to be a successful real estate investor.

- **Litigation.** You will be dealing with tenants—residential or commercial—so be prepared for occasional legal problems. In the tenant-owner relationship, the burden is often on you, as the owner, to provide documentation concerning the relationship or understanding you have with a tenant. If you cannot provide the necessary records, the tenant (as a consumer) will most always win any dispute.

- **Taxation.** All income and expenses for each rental property must be reported on IRS Form 1040 Schedule E. This form determines whether or not you had a taxable profit or loss. By law, you are required to verify all income and expenses through maintenance of proper records, including detailed receipts of all transactions. Always be able to support the accuracy of your tax records.

In general, keep a cash receipt journal, which lists the master rental income information as well as ledgers for individual rental units. Also, retain all bank deposit slips in case there is a discrepancy between your records and the bank records. Do not forget to keep written receipts for all expenses. Unless you have such a receipt, the Internal Revenue Service may not accept a check as proof of a deductible property expense. Here are some useful guidelines to follow in terms of keeping records:

- Keep a written record of all mileage if you use your car for rental property business. It is a deductible expense. Include the date, destination, purpose, and number of miles traveled.

- Keep all rental property records for three to five years. Check with your state regulatory commission for an exact period of time.

- Maintain records concerning the purchase and capital improvements made during ownership for as long as you own the property.

It is also important to set up a filing system to keep track of all important records. The system can be a simple manual one, a sophisticated electronic one, or a combination of both. At the overall property level, you should have separate files for ownership (loan documents, inspection reports, and so on), income and major expenses, and maintenance and capital improvements expenses. At the unit level, have a folder for tenants with separate files for each, including such items as the lease agreement, legal notices, charges, and payments). Keep copies of all these items and provide copies to the tenant as well. Also, keep a maintenance file on each unit along with the records and receipts for maintenance jobs and capital improvements. This way, you can track the condition of every unit and keep them in good condition to protect your investment.

OVERALL ACCOUNTING SKILLS

Nothing will kill a real estate investment career faster than a lack of a financial education. That does not mean you have to become a CPA or get an MBA. It means you have to acquire fundamental accounting skills so you will be able to make smart financial choices to advance your career. You must be able to read and understand such financial statements as the following:

- **Cash flow statement**—This reflects the real financial health of your investment. A cash flow analysis shows your revenues (cash inflow) and expenditures (cash outflow). In many ways, it is the most important financial statement because it lets you know exactly where you stand in terms of cash.

- **Balance sheet**—This tells you the value of your business at a particular point in time. The balance sheet formula is: Assets = Liabilities + Owner's Equity.

- **Income statement**—This tells you if your business made a profit or suffered a loss during a certain period of time. The income statement formula is: Revenues – Expenses = Net Profit or Loss.

- **Budget**—A budget is an estimate of future income and expenses from a property. It is important because it lets you anticipate and track the income and outgo from your investment. Budget planning for a single-family rental unit is pretty simple. However, the larger the property, the more complex budgeting becomes. In that case, you need to thoroughly review past expenses, check the current condition of the property, and establish trends in utilities usage. As part of budgeting, you should establish a cash reserve to cover unexpected expenses. This reserve is the safety net you need when cash flow from a property does not materialize at levels you expected. The reserve should be large enough to pay the mortgage and all property expenses for at least a month without relying on any rental income. A three- to six-month reserve would be even better. Do not forget to include funds in the reserve to cover such annual and semiannual expenses as property taxes and income tax. It is a wise idea to set up a separate account in which to deposit money for possible major capital improvements as well. After all, eventually roofs need re-shingling and plumbing needs replacement. It is better to save regularly for those rainy (and expensive) days than to face a bill that can overwhelm your financial condition.

As you can see, with good accounting skills, you can identify the strengths and weaknesses of your investments and of any future properties you consider.

At an advanced level, you may decide you want to shift into a more entrepreneurial mode and move into large property development projects. In that case, you will have to learn how to develop and write a feasibility study. This forces you to do an evaluation or analysis of the potential impact of your proposed property development project. As the name suggests, it tells you if your project is feasible or not by forcing you to make an assessment of projected income that will result from your development project. This analysis then prompts you to make an assessment of costs (cash flow) that includes everything to do with any premises you may need — loan costs, bank fees and charges, and so on. The feasibility study provides you with an automatic assessment of how much money you have projected to be spent and received on a monthly basis. Typically, a feasibility study also gives you a cumulative bottom line. It provides you with an idea of the cash that should be in your bank account at any point in time based on the projections you have made. If you are not happy with the cumulative totals, then re-evaluate projected income and all expenditures. That, in turn, forces you to look at the feasibility study again to decide if your project is realistic and achievable.

ACCOUNTING AT THE RENTAL LEVEL

As mentioned earlier, it is important to maintain proper financial records for tax and governmental purposes. Accounting is also a vital and dynamic means of making the most of your investment. And, beyond that, these records can help you sell a property at a better price because the documentation will ease any buyer's doubts about the quality of that property. The new digital technology makes accounting a much easier task. It also makes rent collection and reporting easier as well. You can offer residential or commercial tenants the option of paying by credit card, ACH (automatic clearing house), or by electronic fund transfers to your account on a specific date. The same is true for you. As a property owner, you can make payments to vendors and service providers electronically.

In terms of tenants, provide a receipt for rental or other payments no matter what method of payment is used. The same is true of your expenses. Use checks or credit accounts so you receive clear and unambiguous receipts for IRS purposes.

Also be sure to keep your rental financial matters separate from any personal transactions. When funds get mixed, it can be difficult to sort out which expenses are legitimate deductions and which are not.

Once you establish yourself as a real estate investor and decide to move into larger residential, commercial, or industrial properties, you will find that the accounting gets much more complicated. That is the time to consider the hiring of a property manager. A good professional manager will provide you with detailed monthly reporting and will work with your accountant to create a good tax plan and ensure proper reporting to the IRS. Also consider hiring a tax advisor. Tax laws can be complex and confusing, and it often takes a professional to interpret and apply them correctly. A tax advisor can help you take full legal advantage of owning real estate. For example, you can deduct all operating expenses from rental income. These include such expenses as property taxes, payroll, maintenance and repair costs, management fees, and utilities. You can also take advantage of depreciation. This is a non-cash expense (deduction) that reduces the value of a property as a result of wear and tear, age, or obsolescence. It reduces taxable income in the current year and is recaptured later. An accountant can also help you in the area of capital items. These typically include components (new roofs, HVAC systems, and so on) that extend the life of the building. The accountant will show you which items can be expenses and which must be capitalized. Rental property expenditures are accounted for separately. They are capitalized when their cost basis is depreciated or amortized over several years rather than deducted as an operating expense in the present year. This creates a situation in which you are not able to reduce taxable income by the full cost incurred, but rather by a prorated amount over multiple years. An accountant will be able to generate depreciation or cost recovery schedules, which will indicate the amount that can be deducted each year. Beyond tasks, your accountant can keep you up to date on any federal tax code changes that affect depreciation or other taxation issues.

Accounting Software

With a single property, you do not need software for accounting purposes. You can simply use a pad and a pencil. However, it is a good idea to be familiar with the software programs available on the market today. They will come in handy as you expand your investments, allowing you to handle more difficult accounting procedures. If you have a few rental properties, such spreadsheet programs as Microsoft Excel or general accounting packages like Quicken or QuickBooks can meet your needs for streamlining basic accounting requirements. Once you move beyond that level, however, you'll need software designed specifically for property management. It should include the following:

- A complete accounting package (general ledger, accounts receivable and accounts payable along with check writing, budgeting, and financial-reporting capabilities.

- The ability to track work orders and reminders, prints late notices, leases, checks, 1099s, and so on.

- Tenant and lease-management capabilities (including rental management forms).

- Pop-ups to remind you of late rent, expiring leases, and so forth, categorized by building, unit, owner, or tenant.

- Capabilities to organize tenants, contractors, and others.

- Templates for letters and forms.

A search on the Internet will reference many programs. Simply type "property management software" into the window. Below is a partial list of software package names and their URLs in alphabetical order. Many sites will provide a free trial period in which you can try out the software. Choose the one that best fits your needs and is easiest to understand:

- MRI Residential (**www.realestate.intuit.com**)

- RentRight (**www.rent-right.com**)

- Spectra (**www.spectraesolutions.com**)

- Tenant File (**www.tenantfile.com**)

- TenantPro (**www.propertyautomation.com**)

You should be able to customize any of these programs to fit your specific needs. Whichever program you use, carefully review the reports it generates. The information can help you spot problems and improve the overall profitability of your property.

If you choose to have a management company do your accounting, you should receive your reports a week or two after the end of each accounting month. Also review this information carefully, but do not think of it as a review; instead, you are learning on a continuous basis—learning how to cut costs and improve profitability—while storing knowledge that will become increasingly important as your real estate investments grow.

CHAPTER

14

TAX ADVANTAGES AND EXIT STRATEGIES

As stated earlier in this book, a great advantage of real estate investment is the tax benefits. Legally, you can shelter income and defer capital gains. By understanding the laws and following them, you can minimize taxation and maximize the money you keep on an after-tax basis. You must have complete knowledge of taxation rules and keep up to date on them because they are constantly changing. If you do not have that knowledge, then you should definitely have an accountant or a tax advisor who does. In fact, they should be specialists in the area of real estate so they can help you achieve the optimal financial position as well as aid you in choosing the best exit strategy.

OPTIMIZING TAX ADVANTAGES

The first advantage of real estate investment is depreciation (now called "cost recovery" in the tax code). This concept assumes that assets (buildings and so on) will lose an equal amount of value each year due to wear and tear. It is a "non-cash expense." That is, it does not actually take cash out of your pocket. Instead, it's treated as an expense or deduction when adding up your income. The result is that it decreases your taxable income, which, in turn, lets you shelter positive cash flow from taxation. In effect, depreciation lowers income taxes for the current year and defers them to a later date. The key word is "defer." Depreciation does not eliminate income taxes. Technically, an annual depreciation deduction is figured on a reduction in basis of the rental property. This is calculated as your original cost in the property plus capital improvements. This is then recaptured (added to your taxable profit) in full and taxed upon disposition or sale. At present, all tax deductions taken for depreciation are recaptured and taxed at a maximum rate of 25 percent when you sell the property. Remember that the land on which you have property is not depreciable. Buildings wear out; land does not. So, if you want to enjoy larger depreciation benefits, make improvements to your buildings.

You may wonder what assessment the Internal Revenue Service will accept in order to determine depreciation. There are two options: You can have an appraisal done, which can be expensive, or you can have a Comparative Market Analysis (CMA) completed by a broker, which is often done for free or at a low cost.

Keep in mind that there are different kinds of depreciation for real estate. Under present tax laws, straight-line depreciation is used for recently acquired rental properties. This form of depreciation uses a method of calculating the depreciation of a property that assumes the property will lose an equal amount of value each year. The annual depreciation is calculated by subtracting the salvage value (the estimated value of the property at the end of its useful life) of the asset from the purchase price, and then dividing this number by the estimated useful life of the property. The recovery period is the period of time during which the depreciation is taken. The IRS has specific rules for straight-line depreciation. The following regulations apply to properties placed in service or bought on or after May 13, 1993:

- **Commercial properties.** The recovery period is 39 years (or an annual cost recovery of 2.564 percent). The IRS classified mixed-use properties as commercial unless the income from the residential portion is 80 percent or more of the gross rental income.

- **Residential rental property.** The recovery period is 27.5 years (or a cost recovery of 3.636 percent on an annual basis). A property is qualified as residential if the tenants stay a minimum of 30 days or more and no substantial services are provided (health care, etc.).

A requirement of the Tax Reform Act of 1984 is that taxpayers use the 15th of the month to establish the date of acquisition and date of disposition when calculating cost recovery deductions. This is called the **midmonth convention requirement**. The act applies to real estate placed in service after June 22, 1984, with the exception of low-income housing. Simply put, this means that the transaction is presumed to have been completed on the 15th of the month, regardless of the actual day of sale. So the depreciation deduction is prorated, based on the number of full months of ownership plus one-half month for the month of purchase or sale.

The second tax advantage of real estate investment is the opportunity to minimize income taxes. In order to understand your ability to do this, you have to understand that there are two broad categories of income for taxpayers. The first is ordinary income. This category includes wages, bonuses, commissions, rents, and interest. Items in this category are taxed at the federal level. The rates can range up to 35 percent. When you have rental property, the taxable income you receive from it is subject to taxation as ordinary income. The second income is capital gains. This income is generated when investments (real estate, stocks, etc.) are sold for a profit. Any income you realize from a sale is subject to taxation as a capital gain. Capital gains are classified as:

- **Short-term.** Any property held for 12 months or less. The capital gains are taxed at the same rate as ordinary income.

- **Long-term.** Any property held longer than 12 months. The capital gains are taxed at lower rates than ordinary income. The current rate is 5 percent or 15 percent, depending on your overall tax bracket.

In order to figure out what part of your income will be taxed (and how), you will need to perform a cash flow analysis in order to determine the positive or negative cash flow from a property. Although cash flow statements can get complicated, their basic form is this:

Rental Income

-	Expenses	(operating expenses, debt service interest,
= Net Taxable Income		capital-improvement expenses, damages, theft,
x	Tax Rate	and rental income depreciation)
=	Tax Liability	

Passive and Active Activity

A further consideration is passive and active activity. In 1986, Congress passed passive income and loss provisions to prevent the abuse of real estate tax shelters. Before that time, it was perfectly legal for individuals (primarily, the rich) to find all kinds of loopholes to avoid paying taxes on income. Some bought investments that would generate artificial tax losses to shelter income and reduce taxes. Soon, greed reared its ugly head, and many of the tax shelters became outright scams. So Congress stepped in and passed the Tax Reform Law of 1986. Here is what that means for your investments:

By definition, rental properties are passive activities and are subject to complex passive activity loss rules. Generally speaking, the passive activity rules limit your ability to offset other types of income with net passive losses. That means: If you have losses from a rental property (passive activity), you cannot always take those losses on your tax return in the current year to reduce income from such non-passive activities as wages, salary, interest, dividends, or gains from sales of stocks. Passive losses can offset income from other passive activities. If you do have a net passive loss in any one year, then that loss is generally delayed to a later year until either you have passive income or you completely dispose of the property (the passive activity).

However, if you actively participate in a rental activity, you can deduct as much as $25,000 of the rental loss. To actively participate means that you own at least 10 percent of the property and you actively make management decisions (approving new tenants, setting rental terms, approving improvements, and so on). This exception is not available to everyone. For example, if you have modified adjusted gross income over $100,000, your maximum loss available decreases by 50 cents for every dollar above $100,000. The maximum loss is completely phased out when your modified adjusted gross income reaches $150,000. Modified adjusted gross income is determined by calculating adjusted gross income without regard to deductions (IRA contributions or pensions, taxable Social Security benefits, and so on). Beyond the requirements already listed, there are two others:

1. **The property must qualify.** There are certain types of properties not included in the active participation provision. These include net leased properties and vacation homes in a rental pool.

2. **You must file your tax return as an individual.** In other words, corporations, some trusts, and other ownership forms cannot take advantage of this special deduction.

If losses are disallowed in a year, they are called suspended losses. They can be saved and applied to reduce rental and other passive income in future years. If suspended losses cannot be used in this way, you, as a real estate investor, can use them when you sell the rental property. In effect, this reduces the capital gain. These losses ultimately give you a benefit. However, another consideration is the time value of money. In other words, if you can use those losses now rather than in the future, you can gain even more of a tax advantage.

The Active Path—Qualifying as a Real Estate Professional

There are two exceptions to the IRS's passive income rules regarding real estate rental activities. One is the $25,000 exception mentioned earlier in this chapter. The second is those individuals who can meet the IRS requirements regarding classification as real estate professionals. Starting in 1994, you are not subject to the $25,000 limitation if you meet the eligibility requirements relating to your real estate activities. If you are classified as a real estate professional, you are permitted to deduct all of your rental real estate losses from your ordinary income (wages, commissions), interest, short-term capital gains, and non-qualified dividends. How do you define yourself as a real estate professional? Here are the rules:

- You are a professional if more than 50 percent of your personal services or employment is performed in a real estate business or in rental real estate activities (acquisition, brokerage, operation, leasing, management, development, construction, or reconstruction).

- These activities represent at least 750 hours per tax year. If you're an employee, work hours don't count unless you're at least a 5 percent owner of the employer.

If you meet these criteria, then you are considered an active investor. You are allowed to claim all your real estate loss deductions incurred during the year in order to offset positive taxable income or offset gains at the time of sale. Being an active investor can be attractive, but meeting the IRS qualifications can be complicated. That is because the IRS considers each interest of a taxpayer in rental real estate to be a separate activity — unless you opt to treat all rental real estate interests as one activity. Because it is such a complicated process, it is best to consult with your tax advisor to see if it's the best choice.

EXIT STRATEGIES

As a real estate investor, you should always have an eye on the future and plans for what to do with your properties. After all, you are in it for a profit and to achieve a secure future for you and your family. So it pays not only to buy the best property at the best price, but to consider what you will do with that asset to achieve maximum income and minimum tax impact; in other words, formulate an exit strategy. There are several ideas to consider when choosing an exit strategy; knowing which is the best for you depends on the situation and its tax advantages for you.

SELLING OUTRIGHT

Outright sale is the most straightforward exit strategy. With this strategy, you simply sell the property and report the sale to the IRS, determining if there is a taxable gain or loss. If there is a gain, then you have to pay taxes. If the property has been held for a minimum of 12 months, then capital gains tax rates of 5 percent or 15 percent are in effect. Remember that seller financing is not considered an all-cash sale. Neither is an installment sale. Also remember that the sale will prompt the 5 percent, 15 percent, or 25 percent tax rate on cost recovery deduction. Outright sale can be a good option for investors who are near the end of their real estate careers or for those who want a simpler, less complicated life.

As part of the sale, you have to figure the gain or the loss. Several factors must be considered, including the following:

- Sales price

- Capital improvements

- Accumulated depreciation (when taken during the holding period, it increases your taxes when it is recaptured)

- Operating losses (if not taken in previous tax years, these can increase the adjusted basis and lower the potential taxable gain—or increase the loss available so you can shelter other income)

Step 1 in the process is to calculate net sales proceeds. These are the gross sales price minus the selling expenses, as shown below:

CALCULATING TOTAL GAIN OR LOSS ON A SALE

Gross Sales Price	**$1,750,000**
– Selling expenses	($50,000)
Net Sales Proceeds	$1,700,000
– Adjusted basis (see table in Step 2)	($750,000)
Total Gain (Loss) on Sale	$950,000

Step 2 is to calculate the adjusted basis for the property. Basis is defined as the original cost of the property (the equity down payment plus the total debt incurred to finance the property plus closing costs, appraisal, environmental reports, and so on.)

In cases in which the owner did not buy the property, the basis is figured differently in three instances:

1. Inheritance—The **fair market value** at the time of transfer for property received as an inheritance.

2. Gift—The **carryover basis** if the property is received as a gift.

3. Tax-deferred exchange—The **substituted basis** if the property was acquired in a tax-deferred exchange.

Keep in mind, however, that the basis changes during the ownership period. It is not static because of three factors:

1. **Capital improvements.** In many instances, when you acquire a property, you will want to make improvements that increase its value and ability to generate income. That is when you make capital improvements that are defined as money spent to improve the existing property or to construct new property. As you might expect, these improvements lead to increase in the adjusted basis because they are added to the original acquisition cost. Do not confuse repairs with capital improvements and try to figure them into your calculations. Replacing a few roof shingles is a repair; replacing an entire roof is a capital improvement because it qualifies as a major physical development or redevelopment to a property that extends the life of the property. The following costs are included in capital improvement: architect fees, building permits, construction materials, contractor payments, and labor costs.

2. **Straight-line depreciation.** Cost recovery taken each tax

year is accumulated. This reduces the adjusted basis of the property. You have to include the total accumulated depreciation in the overall calculation of the gain or loss upon sale as part of the adjusted basis, but it also must be reported separately, and it is taxed at a different rate on your return.

3. **Casualty losses.** You can include any losses from damage to your property or destruction of it due to natural disasters (earthquake, fire, flood, hurricane, tornado, and so on).

CALCULATION OF ADJUSTED BASIS

Original Acquisition/Basis	$800,000
+ Capital improvements	$55,000
− Accumulated cost recovery	($100,000)
− Casualty losses taken	($5,000)
Adjusted Basis	$750,000

Step 3 is to determine the total gain or loss on the sale. This is determined by taking the net sales price and subtracting the adjusted basis.

Step 4 is to adjust the total gain by accounting for accumulated cost recovery and suspended losses. When you have suspended losses reported on your tax returns during the ownership period, you can deduct them from the net sales proceeds. As you will recall, suspended losses are those that you could not use in previous tax years because you did not meet the IRS requirements.

CAPITAL GAIN DUE TO APPRECIATION

Total Sale Gain	$950,000
– Straight-line cost recovery	($105,000)
– Suspended losses	($70,000)
Capital Gain from Appreciation	$775,000

Step 5 is to calculate total tax liability. Unless your property was held for more than 12 months, the net gain on sale is taxed as ordinary income. In most cases, as an investor, you will hold a property for longer than a year, which means you can qualify for the lower long-term capital gains tax rates. In regard to taxes, the net gain on sale must be apportioned between the capital gain from appreciation and the recapture of the accumulated depreciation. In the table above, you can see that the total gain on the sale of $950,000 is reduced by a total of $175,000 ($105,000 in straight-line cost recovery plus $70,000 in suspended losses). This creates a gain of $775,000 from appreciation. Now, calculate the total tax liability as shown in the table below.

CALCULATION OF TOTAL TAX LIABILITY

Straight-Line Cost Recovery	$105,000
x Tax rate on recapture	25%
Total Tax Due for Recapture	$26,250
Capital Gain from Appreciation	$775,000
x Tax rate on capital gain	15%
Total Tax Due on Capital Gain	$116,250
Total Tax Liability	$142,500

The accumulated depreciation is recaptured at 25 percent. This results in a tax liability of $26,250. The appreciation gain was taxed at a maximum flat rate of 15 percent. This results in a tax liability of $116,250. The total tax liability ends up as $142,500.

Remember that if the sale of your property results in a net loss, then that loss must first be applied to offset net passive-activity income or gains. If there are no losses, the net can be applied to reduce the income or gains from non-passive activities such as earned income or wages.

The Installment Sale

The IRS states "An installment sale is a sale of property where you receive at least one payment after the tax year of the sale. If you dispose of property in an installment sale, you report part of your gain when you receive each installment payment. You cannot use the installment method to report a loss." This means that you can maximize the time value of your money by reporting your receipt of funds over a specified period of time rather than as one sum at the time of sale. This allows you to minimize or defer taxes. If you use the installment method, you have to report only a prorated portion of the proceeds actually received in the specific tax year. This means that your taxable gain is extended over several years. In addition, you can report it in years in which you may be in a lower tax bracket. If you are a seller who does not need to take your equity at the time of sale because you have other sources of income or want to minimize taxes (or both), this is an ideal method for you. The installment sale includes transactions in which the seller gives you financing and will receive payments over time. This can happen in markets where buyer financing is difficult to obtain. In these cases, sellers may take a mortgage note from the buyer for some or all of their equity in the property.

Tax-Deferred Exchanges

As mentioned earlier in the book, you can also take advantage of the Tax-Deferred 1031 Exchange law. This tax law allows you to sell one property and buy another without incurring capital gains taxes. You simply have to reinvest all your profits into the next property (or properties) within a specific timeline. However, the property must be "qualifying property," or property held for investment purposes or used in a taxpayer's trade or business. Investment property includes real estate, improved or unimproved, held for investment or income-producing purposes. Real estate must be replaced with "like-kind" real estate.

This means that like-kind replacement property can be any improved or unimproved real estate held for income, investment, or business use. Here are some examples:

- Improved real estate can be replaced with unimproved real estate and vice versa.

- A 100 percent interest can be exchanged for an undivided percentage interest with multiple owners and vice versa.

- One property can be exchanged for two or more properties.

- Two or more properties can be exchanged for one replacement property.

- A duplex can be exchanged for a fourplex.

- Investment property can be exchanged for business property and vice versa.

However, a taxpayer's personal residence cannot be exchanged for income property, nor can income or investment property be exchanged for a personal residence, in which the taxpayer will reside.

There are three types of 1031 tax-deferred exchanges that can take place:

1. **Straight exchanges,** in which two parties trade properties of equal or approximate value.

2. **Multi-party exchange** involves three or more parties buying, selling, or exchanging properties. These exchanges tend to be complex, and you will definitely need a tax professional to guide you through the process.

3. **Delayed exchange** allows the sale of the relinquished party and the buying of the replacement property to occur at different times as long as stringent rules are followed. This is the exchange most often used.

In these exchanges, the capital gains tax is deferred but not eliminated. Nevertheless, deferral is a great way to leverage small real estate holdings into larger ones. Because you can postpone gains, you can use a tax-deferred exchange strategy to transfer equity to a larger property — without paying taxes. In addition, there is no limit on exchanges. You can make as many exchanges as you want. So, over a lifetime, you can keep growing income and appreciation by adding new properties without having to pay the capital gains tax. This strategy is especially useful if you specialize in buying and renovating properties and want to keep reinvesting your profits into larger properties. Otherwise, you risk being classified as a real estate dealer by the IRS and will not be able to participate in exchanges.

There are some basic rules that must be followed in order to qualify for a 1031 Exchange:

- The properties to be exchanged must be located in the

United States. (You can exchange foreign property for foreign property and domestic for domestic. However, you cannot mix these exchanges together.)

- You must trade only like-kind real estate.

- An exchange must be made that is equal to or greater in both value and equity. Any cash or debt relief received above this amount is considered "boot" and is taxable. See explanation below for specifics.

- The like-kind property must be identified within 45 days of the closing on the initial property.

- All proceeds from the initial sale must be turned over to a "qualified intermediary" (QI, facilitator, exchanger, among others), who is the person or company that plays the role of middleman. Any of the proceeds not under the control of the middleman are subject to taxation. The middleman holds the funds from the initial property in escrow until such time as the closing on the second property occurs. The middleman also assists the owner with the preparation of paperwork and other services to ensure the transaction progresses smoothly.

- The closing on the second property must take place within 180 days following the close on the first property.

"Boot"

In order for a Section 1031 Exchange to be completely tax-free, you cannot receive any boot. **Boot** is a term you will not find in the Internal Revenue Code or Regulations, but it is commonly defined this way: Boot received is the money or the fair market value of "other property" received by the taxpayer in a 1031 exchange. **Money** includes all cash equivalents plus liabilities of the taxpayer assumed by the other party, or liabilities to which the property exchanged by the taxpayer is subject. **Other property** is property that is not like-kind. This includes personal property received in an exchange of real property, property used for personal purposes, or "non-qualified property." Other property also includes such things as a promissory note received from a buyer (seller financing). Any boot received is taxable (to the extent of gain realized on the exchange). Boot is not always intentionally received and can result from a variety of factors. That means it is important for you to understand what can result in boot if taxable income is to be avoided. The most common sources of boot include the following:

- **Cash boot** taken from the exchange. This is usually in the form of "net cash received," or the difference between cash received from the sale of the relinquished property and cash paid to acquire the replacement property or properties. Net cash received can result when a taxpayer is "trading down" in the exchange so that the replacement property doesn't cost as much as the amount for which the relinquished property sold.

- **Debt reduction boot** occurs when a taxpayer's debt on replacement property is less than the debt that was on the relinquished property. Debt reduction boot can occur when a taxpayer is "trading down" in the exchange, the same as with cash boot.

- **Sale proceeds** are funds used to service costs at closing that are not closing expenses. If proceeds of sale are used to service non-transaction costs at closing, the result is the same as if the taxpayer received cash from the exchange, and then used the cash to pay these costs. That means it would be wise for you to bring cash to the closing of the sale of your relinquished property to pay for the following non-transaction costs:

— Rent prorations

— Utility escrow charges

— Tenant damage deposits transferred to the buyer

— Any other charges unrelated to the closing

- **Excess borrowing.** If you borrow more money than is necessary to close on replacement property, this results in cash being held by a middleman to be excessive for the closing. Again, excess cash held by a middleman is distributed to the taxpayer, resulting in cash boot. You (or the other party) must use all cash being held by a middleman for replacement property. Additional financing must be no more than what is necessary, in addition to the cash, to close on the property.

- **Loan acquisition** refers to costs with respect to the replacement property that are serviced from exchange funds brought to the closing. Loan acquisition costs include origination fees and other fees related to acquiring the loan. Taxpayers usually take the position that loan acquisition costs are serviced from the proceeds of the loan. However, the IRS and the lender may take a different position that these costs are serviced from Exchange funds.

- **Non-like-kind property** that is received from the

exchange, in addition to like-kind property (real estate). Non-like-kind property could include such items as seller financing, promissory notes, and so on.

Here are the boot offset rules: Only the net boot received by a party is taxed. In determining the amount of net boot received, certain offsets are allowed and others are not, as follows:

- Cash boot paid (replacement property) always offsets cash boot received (relinquished property).

- Debt boot paid (replacement property) always offsets debt-reduction boot received (relinquished property).

- Cash boot paid always offsets debt-reduction boot received.

- Debt boot paid never offsets cash boot received (net cash boot received is always taxable).

- Exchange expenses (transaction and closing costs) paid (relinquished property and replacement property closings) always offset net cash boot received.

These rules are complicated, so make sure your tax advisor is up to date. However, here are some general rules regarding the boot:

- Always trade "across" or up; never trade down. Trading down always results in boot received, either cash, debt reduction, or both. The boot received can be mitigated by exchange expenses paid.

- Bring cash to the closing of the relinquished property to cover charges that are not transaction costs.

- Do not receive property that is not like-kind.

- Do not over-finance replacement property. Financing should be limited to the amount of money necessary to close on the replacement property in addition to exchange funds which will be brought to the replacement property closing.

All in all, a 1031 Exchange is a wonderful tool for deferring taxes; however, it also has its risks. For one thing, it can be difficult to complete the purchase agreement within 180 days in a highly competitive market. If you exceed the deadline, then you end up with a taxable transaction. Another disadvantage is that the exchange includes a reduced basis for depreciation in the replacement property. The tax basis of replacement property is essentially the purchase price of the replacement property minus the gain that was deferred on the sale of the relinquished property as a result of the exchange. In other words, the replacement property includes a deferred gain that will be taxed in the future if you cash out of your investment. A third disadvantage is that you may chase deferred capital gains so hard that you end up overpaying for a property and more taxes on it in the future.

A complication to be considered involves a **reverse exchange**, also called a Title-Holding Exchange. This is an exchange in which the replacement property is purchased and closed on before the relinquished property is sold. Usually the middleman takes title to the replacement property and holds title until the taxpayer can find a buyer for the relinquished property and close on the sale under an Exchange Agreement with the intermediary. Following the closing of the relinquished property (or simultaneous with this closing), the middleman conveys title to the replacement property to the taxpayer. The benefit of this exchange is that you are sure to have the replacement property in your possession, but the risk involves identifying the property within 45 days and completing the acquisition within the 180-day limitation. To help with reverse exchanges, the IRS issued a recent Revenue Procedure that established the notion of an Exchange Accommodation Title-Holder (EAT). This is just another name for a qualified intermediary (middleman). The EAT buys the replacement property using money that you advanced. He or she then holds the property for you. After that, you have the 180-day replacement period to find a buyer for the property that you wish to relinquish.

Capital Gains Exclusion

Another wonderful benefit for investors (and homeowners) is the capital gains exclusion (Internal Revenue Code 121). Under this plan, you are allowed to sell a principal residence once every two years and exclude up to $250,000 ($500,000 for a married couple) of the gain on the sale. And, as long as you meet the rules, you can do this as often as you please. Often known as serial home selling, this is a profitable, tax-free strategy. If you meet the two-year ownership and use tests for a principal residence, and if you do not sell more than one principal residence in any two-year period, then you can exclude any capital gain tax on the sale (up to the $250,000 or $500,000 limits). Of course, there are requirements to meet. In the case of married taxpayers who file jointly, the following rules apply:

- The sellers must own and have occupied (or used) the home as their principal residence for a total of 24 months (730 days) in the past 60 months — ending on the date of sale or exchange. At the time of the sale or exchange, the occupancy does not have to be continuous, and the home need not be the seller's principal residence. Only one spouse has to legally hold the title, but both must meet the use test. Here are the factors the IRS considers in order to determine if the principal residence meets the use test:

— Is the residence used as the address of record for such verifiable items as driver's licenses, credit card bills, tax returns, utilities, and so on?

— Is the residence the address of record for employment purposes?

— Is this the residence where you actually live and where your personal property (furniture, furnishings, clothes, and so on) were kept?

— Generally speaking, the seller can only use the exclusion every two years. Vacations and short absences do count as usage.

As of 2004, there are new IRS guidelines that provide partial principal residence exemptions for sellers who do not qualify for the full exemption. These exemptions are based on the number of actual months the seller lived in the home divided by 24 months. Partial exemptions are allowed in the following cases:

• **Health-related reasons.** Such a reason might be the need to move because of ill health or because you need to care for a family member. Consult with a tax advisor on this issue.

- **Unforeseen circumstances.** These categories can include a variety of reasons: divorce, death, incarceration, unemployment, and so on. Again, see your tax advisor for guidance.

- **Work reasons.** This exemption can apply when you have a change in employment in which your new job location is at least 50 miles farther away from the old principal residence than the former job location.

Here is an example of how the partial exemption is figured: Assuming you're the seller, you first calculate the fractional amount of time that you met the two-year use test. In this example, you are transferred to a job in another city and sell after being in your home for only a year and a half. That means you had an occupancy period of 18/24 (the number of months you lived in the home divided by 24 the number of months in the two-year occupancy requirement), or 0.75. When you multiplied the full $250,000 exclusion amount by 0.75, you would be eligible to exclude a sale gain of up to $187,500.

Special home considerations are extended to members of the military. Because of redeployments, soldiers often find it hard to meet the residency rule and end up owing taxes when they sell. However, a 2003 law change now exempts military personnel from the two-year use requirement for as long as ten years. This lets them qualify for the full exclusion whenever they must move to fulfill service commitments.

Of course, there is one obvious disadvantage to serial home selling: You have to repeatedly buy and sell homes approximately every 24 months and live with the continual improvements in a fixer-up type of home. There are also some pitfalls to avoid if you engage in this kind of selling:

- Do not buy homes in excellent condition. They lack profit potential from improvements.

- Do not buy run-down houses. Getting profit from these properties is difficult. If you do buy such a property, be sure you don't pay more than its land value alone.

- Do not buy condominiums and town houses. Normally, there is little opportunity for profit because the market value is held down by recent sales prices of comparable condos and town houses in the vicinity. If the surrounding units are run-down, you will not earn much profit even if you improve your unit.

- Do not buy houses in an undesirable location, high crime area, or an area with a reputation for poor-quality schools. You can pour all the money you want into these properties, but the resale value will still be low.

Lease Options

Lease options were covered earlier in the book, but a brief review is in order here plus some additional information on pitfalls of using this strategy. A lease option is a technique that combines aspects of real estate rental, sales, and finance. It is a property lease for a fixed time period, such as 12 months or 24 months, with an option for the tenant to buy the property at an agreed option price during the lease term. Lease optioning has benefits for both buyers and sellers as shown below. Sellers have the following advantages:

- As a seller, you have strong buyer demand.

- You get a top-dollar option price.

- You can get above-market rents.

- You retain the tax deductions.

Advantages for buyers include:

- You only need a small amount of upfront cash.

- Your monthly rent credit builds a down payment.

- You can try out the property before buying it.

- You can control property through leverage.

- Greater profitability results from longer terms.

Although lease optioning is a good strategy, there can be pitfalls so, if you are inexperienced in the real estate game, it is prudent to use a real estate attorney with a considerable amount of experience in lease options. His or her expertise can be invaluable in keeping you out of bad agreements. An attorney can help you avoid the following mistakes:

- The Due on Sale clause can go into effect with your lender. The result is that the lender can demand that you pay off the entire outstanding loan balance.

- If the IRS considers the property to be a sale, then you cannot use the tax benefits of depreciation and deductible expenses.

- Property taxes can be re-assessed, depending on the part of the country in which you live. Re-assessment is sometimes based on a change in ownership that means a tax assessor could use the lease option to increase the assessed value of your property.

- Failure to comply with seller disclosure laws can occur, leaving you with stiff penalties.

- A possibility exists that you can be prevented from evicting a tenant even if he or she defaults on the lease. There are instances when a court may consider the tenant as a buyer. The court reasons that an eviction notice does not apply because it considers the lease option a contract to buy real estate. The result is costly court proceedings.

Gifts and Bequests

Gifts of property carry the same tax basis from the seller to the new owner. For example, assume you want to gift a property that has a fair market value of $750,000, but the tax basis is $150,000. In that case, your tax basis remains at $150,000. However, if the gift recipient were to immediately sell the property, he or she would have a taxable gain of $600,000. One way to avoid this is to buy and hold properties for life. This takes advantage of the fact that death provides a tax-free transfer of real estate. Upon your death, the property is transferred tax-free to your heirs and receives a full step up in basis. In the example cited above, your estate with a fair market value of $750,000 will have a tax basis of $750,000. Thus, your heirs will owe taxes only on any future gain. This is a long-range strategy that pays dividends for many generations of your family.

Winston T. Rego is a multi-millionaire real estate investor. In the last four years he has increased his net worth 1600%. He is also a licensed commercial Realtor with Open House Realty and assists investors increase their income and grow their wealth through investing in real estate. His phone number is 864-235-5600.

I was a very successful attorney in Chicago, Illinois, making a very good income. At the same time, I was looking for a better return on my money than what I could get from traditional stocks, mutual funds, and savings accounts. So I turned to real estate.

I started by buying a four-unit apartment building in Chicago for $500,000. The tenants were good and paid on time. The maintenance was minimal, and we did fine. I then bought a 13-unit apartment complex in a poorer neighborhood of Chicago for $860,000. The tenants were horrible. They trashed their apartments and failed to pay rent on time. I had to spend a lot of time away from my busy law practice to manage that property. Fortunately, I managed to sell that property in nine months for $1,000,000, and I came out ahead. I then bought a 23-unit apartment complex in South Carolina. By that time, I had developed some ideas on how to run an apartment complex well. Again, this latest complex was in a poorer area, and the tenants were horrible. Using good management techniques, I turned the property around to where I had good tenants, and the property was making a profit.

In my opinion, residential rental properties are the worst investment. If mismanaged, they cost you a lot. If managed perfectly, they give you a maximum return of about 5 percent. If you factor in your time, and even if the complex is managed

perfectly, you will get a lower return than what you will get from putting your money in a CD in the bank. I managed residential rental property for three years. Now I own triple net commercial rental property that requires almost no management.

If you're a property manager or a prospective property manager, you must realize the market is the best way to determine rental rates. Check out what your competitors, near your property, are charging. Factor in whether those properties are better than yours, and that should help you figure out what to charge. Lower the rate if you have a lot of vacancies, and raise it if you have a waiting list.

I believe in keeping my tenants very happy, so I do not receive many complaints. However, it's expected that maintenance issues will crop up from time to time. I try to make my tenants understand that we have a partnership. If they treat me fairly, I will treat them fairly. I expect them to pay their rent on time and take care of the property as if it is their own home. In return, I fix all reasonable maintenance problems immediately. If it cannot be fixed immediately, I keep them informed as I am trying to get the problem fixed as soon as possible. The flip of this is, if the tenants fail to live up to this agreement, I will aggressively collect late fees and evict them.

Collecting rent and evicting nonpaying tenants were the biggest challenge I faced when I first started managing properties. Tenants are very smart and will take advantage of every weakness the landlord has. I am a kind-hearted person and believe in treating people fairly. It was hard for me to be strict with tenants when they gave me their sob stories on why they could not pay their rent, but I learned.

Accounting is another critical component of property management. While I have a CPA for accounting purposes, I use QuickBooks for in-house accounting needs. It's also important that you set up a reserve fund for payments that are annual or semi-annual, such as taxes and insurance.

If you're new to property management, you can start by having a good lease. Learn the local landlord and tenant laws and the process for evicting tenants. Immediately start the process for evicting nonpaying tenants when the grace period for paying the rent is up. Collect at least one month's security deposit. Treat tenants fairly, and fix all reasonable repairs promptly. If you treat the tenants well, they will reward you by paying their rent on time and by taking care of the property.

Having a professional rent collection, maintenance, and eviction system in place, and maintaining good documentation is the best way to minimize your risks. It is better to have a unit vacant than to put a bad tenant in there. Always do a credit check, and call references before you lease a unit to a tenant.

THE SECRET TO BUILDING REAL ESTATE WEALTH

The secret is that there is no secret — no matter what the self-styled gurus tell you on radio or television or in print. Real estate fortunes are built by knowledge, patience, and the application of common-sense guidelines. It is all a matter of thinking long range, not short range, keeping an eye out for opportunities, and knowing your niche within a market. In general, you can build your fortune over time through two ways. The first is to get the maximum return out of your properties. The second is to formulate an investment strategy.

MAXIMIZING RETURN ON YOUR PROPERTIES

Once you have bought properties, you need to continually ask yourself four questions:

1. How can I increase the cash flow?

2. How can I build equity?

3. How can I maximize my tax benefits?

4. How can I increase appreciation?

As you can see from these questions, real estate investment is not a passive activity. You have to be active and stay on top of your properties to get the most benefit out of them. There are a number of guidelines you can follow to achieve your goals.

Guideline 1: Raise Rents Gradually

It is a simple equation: increased rents = increased cash flow. Of course, it is not always easy to raise rents, depending on the market. Raise the rents too high, and you create turnover. On the other hand, if you keep them below market levels, you are not earning the maximum cash flow. Rely on your judgment, but, in general, it is a good idea not to surprise tenants with big increases. The best strategy is to raise rents gradually on a yearly basis. Psychologically, it is less stressful, and tenants are more accepting of gradual increases that result from higher operational costs.

Guideline 2: Keep Your Tenants Happy to Reduce Turnover

Here is another simple equation: a lost tenant = lost income. Worse, when a tenant moves out, you must pay for the cost of updating the space (maintenance, repair, improvements, and so on), resulting in lost rent and increased expenses. The key, of course, is to keep tenants satisfied by being accessible and by meeting their reasonable needs. It also helps to sign them to long-term leases, which lessens the potential for frequent turnover.

Guideline 3: "Niche" Yourself

Gary Keller, author of the highly successful *The Millionaire Real Estate Investor*, states in his book, "Our observation is that Millionaire Real Estate Investors tend to specialize in a niche they can learn well and identify fast—they 'niche to get rich.'" "Niche-ing" is a smart move simply because there are so many different areas of real estate, and no one can master them all. By mastering a niche, you become an expert, giving you an advantage over your competition. Possible niches include single-family, multi-family, undeveloped land, new homes, rehabs, foreclosures, senior housing, and many others.

Guideline 4: Reduce Expenses

There are number of ways to reduce operating expenses. When you acquire a property, evaluate every expense to see where cuts can be made. It may be that the previous owner has not kept a close eye on them, and he or she may have overpaid for utilities or other services. Here are number of ways in which you can curtail expenses:

- Arrange for an energy audit from the local utilities companies. If the audit indicates savings can be made, you can invest in new energy- and water-saving technologies. These are short-term expenses that can save substantial amounts in the long run.

- Evaluate the current contractors and service providers. Ask for bids or proposals from firms that are reputable, reliable, bonded, insured, and recognized for delivering quality work. Once you find these contractors and service providers, continue to give them business. Because you are an established customer, they are more likely to give you discounts, particularly as your volume grows.

- Shop and compare annual insurance premium rates to make sure you are not overpaying.

- If a property management firm is used, check with other firms to compare the service and rates you are getting from the present company.

- Review property tax expenses. In most areas of the country, property taxes are linked to the value of the real estate. So if real estate values decline, ask your local tax assessor and ask about a re-assessment. If you succeed, you will get a reduction in property taxes, resulting in an increase in your cash flow. When dealing with assessors, the best course is to back up your claim with facts presented clearly and persuasively.

Guideline 5: Maximize Curb Appeal

It is often been said that you never get a second chance to make a first impression. This is especially true of real estate. People tend to react emotionally toward properties, so it is critical to maintain and, if necessary, renovate your properties for maximum curb appeal. It may be simply a matter of cleaning up the yard and applying a fresh coat of paint. Landscape improvements, in particular, are a cost-effective way to increase curb appeal. Plantings (bushes, flowers, etc.) are inexpensive, yet they create a great impression. Depending on the property, it may be worth your while to improve the property through renovation. If that is the case, focus on inexpensive improvements that provide a relatively quick payback. Update baths and kitchens in single-family or multi-unit residential properties. If you have commercial properties, concentrate on the common areas, making them look fresh and inviting for the tenants and their customers.

Guideline 6: Refinance

One of the greatest expenses for many investors is mortgage interest, so it stands to reason that you can save a great deal by refinancing the mortgage. For example, assume it will cost you $2,000 to refinance your $300,000 loan, but you'll pay 1 percent less. After approximately eight months, you will be ahead. The other side of refinancing is that it builds equity faster. Remember, rent is paying your mortgage so, over time, you will end up owning a free and clear property. In the early years of owning property, you may need to use financing with 20-year-plus amortization terms because your net operating income will probably be stretched as you service the debt. However, once cash flow has improved, you may find that you can afford higher mortgage payments. In that case, you can refinance from long-term mortgages to shorter-term ones. The result is that the amount of principal reduction paid with each payment increases substantially. You can also adopt the strategy of making additional payments on the mortgage and designating them for principal reduction. Over time, this reduces the total amount of interest paid and, at the same time, brings the loan payoff date much closer. This occurs because the interest paid on the loan is a function of the outstanding principal balance. A final note: Make sure the refinance loan does not have a pre-payment penalty. As you might expect, lenders do not like early payoffs because it does not give them the full return.

Guideline 7: Do Not Forget Tax Benefits

Many tax benefits were covered earlier in the book, but remember that they can really boost your returns on a property. For example, the capital gains exclusion is a generous benefit. Used properly, you can eliminate any income tax on your gains. In addition, if you are willing to live in a property for two years during renovation, you can use the serial home selling strategy and end up with tax-free profits. Simultaneous or tax-deferred exchanges permit you to keep your money working rather than paying it in taxes, which adds up to another equation: More money in real estate = better cash flow + increased wealth accumulation. Finally, there is the depreciation benefit. You can take a reduction that lessens your taxable income from the property. All in all, tax benefits are highly effective tools for increasing returns on your investment. Learn to use them wisely.

Guideline 8: Change Your Property's Use

Earlier in the book, the concept of "highest and best use" of real estate was introduced. In a legal sense, it is the use of a property that makes it the most valuable to a buyer or to the market. In a business sense, it means one single use will result in maximum profitability through the best and most efficient use of the property. So why not achieve that maximum profitability by changing its use? There are many ways to do this.

- **Assemblage.** This is the combining of two or more adjoining lots into one larger tract to increase the total value. You can more efficiently develop the larger tract and increase its value through redevelopment. For example, you might buy several small tracts and combine them into one large lot in order to build a multi-unit apartment building.

- **Lot split.** This is the opposite strategy of assemblage. With this method, you divide a large tract of land into several smaller tracts. The result is that you receive a greater financial reward than if you kept the land "as is." You can also split a large tract into several tracts and put small multi-unit (one to four) residential properties on each, qualifying you for more favorable financing.

- **Use conversion.** This is simply taking the use of one property and converting it into another use. An example is taking an old factory, renovating it, and converting it into office space.

- **Zoning.** This is a profitable strategy in areas with growing populations, and it can be a win-win for both buyer and seller. Quite often, for example, as a city expands, agricultural land becomes less productive (in real estate terms). So once you buy this agricultural land, you can get it zoned or re-zoned for residential, commercial, or industrial use. Because it is in the path of progress, you reap the reward of dramatically increased value.

Guideline 9: Know When to Walk Away

Overall, real estate investment is one of the safest methods of building wealth. However, even in real estate, negative forces can affect your investment. Neighborhoods can deteriorate and economies can decline. These factors force property values down, reducing both your income and equity. You must stay informed about national, state, and local economies and trends. When you are an active investor, not a passive one, you can spot negative factors and stay ahead of the game by selling the property and reinvesting in more lucrative areas. So do not get emotionally tied to a property.

CHOOSE AN INVESTMENT STRATEGY

Different investors have different strategies in the real estate market, but they all boil down to two objectives: buying to build cash or buying to build equity and wealth. Either objective is fine. The important part is to choose a strategy early, follow it, and let it guide you in making your decisions.

For example, suppose you decide to pursue a cash strategy. You may decide on several methods to achieve your goals in this strategy. One method is to start out as a "scout," seeking good opportunities for investors and charging a finder's fee for doing so. This is strictly a cash strategy. A second method is to buy an option on an investment property and then try to find someone else to acquire it. Unlike the scout method, you will get negotiation leverage and a better profit margin. A third method is to acquire a property, leave it "as is," and then put it back on the market at a higher price. The profit margin is even better than with the buy-and-sell method, but it takes time and, because of that, volume may be low. The final method is to buy a property, improve it, and then sell it. Margins are even better with this method, but, of course, it takes a much bigger investment of time and money than the previous methods.

If you prefer to build long-term wealth, you can choose a different strategy — building cash flow and equity, choosing one of several methods to achieve your objectives for this strategy.

Lease options require little money and have several variations:

- You can negotiate to lease a property with the option to buy it at the end of the period at an agreed-upon price. You may or may not have to put money down. As part of the agreement, you reserve the right to "re-lease the property to another tenant," and that is exactly what you do, except you lease it at a higher price. This increases your cash flow. If you choose this method, be sure to have a renter before you lease-option the property.

- Another variation occurs when you rent a property you own to a tenant with the option to buy at the end of the lease period. If you negotiate the price well, you can gain increased cash flow during the lease period and improve equity as well.

- If you prefer a less complicated variation than the ones above, you can simply buy the property and lease it out, a method called "buy and hold." With this option, you can sell at any time or hold the property as long as you like for the cash flow and equity buildup.

- The long-term strategy is to buy, improve, and hold. It is a commitment to build cash flow and equity. Over time, you get higher rents and improved buildup of equity. You can also enjoy the benefits mentioned earlier, including reduction of taxes through improvements, zoning, and so on.

As we stated earlier, it does not matter which strategy you choose as long as you follow it consistently. There are two things to keep in mind, however. A cash strategy tends to be short-term; that is, your income goes away when you stop buying and selling. The "buy, improve, and hold" strategy is long-term and builds wealth over time. It offers you a more secure future.

ACTION PLAN!

One of the universal traits of successful people in every field is the ability to set goals and then to write action plans to carry out those goals. Action is the key word. One of the best ways to reap the rewards of investment is by using the SMART system. It has proven its worth over many years. SMART stands for:

S = Specific
M = Measurable
A = Action-oriented
R = Realistic
T = Timely

Take a closer look at each of these terms so you can understand exactly what they mean. For this example, assume you want to start your real estate investment career by buying a single-family residential home

Specific — A goal should define your dream in exact terms. A vague goal is, "I want to be a wealthy real estate investor." A specific goal, however, is, "I want to start on the path to real estate wealth by buying a single-family home." This kind of language defines your goal in specific terms.

Measurable — If you cannot measure your goal, how will you know when you have reached it? Build milestones into your goals. Again, a vague goal would be "I want to be a wealthy real estate investor soon!" A specific goal would be, "I want to start on the path to real estate wealth by buying a single-family home by June 2006." With this kind of detail, you can gauge your progres easily.

Action-oriented — Be sure to write out specific action steps so you can measure progress toward your goal. By action-oriented, it should be a physical action. For example, one good action step for starting your career would be, "I will view 20 residential properties by March 15 and begin contacting owners by March 20." By following this step, you are taking a concrete, physical action on a specific date instead of merely thinking, *Well, I'll view properties soon and contact owners pretty soon.*

Realistic — Make sure your goal is one that is doable. Be certain you have all the tools necessary to help you do the job — the right skills, the knowledge, and the attitude, or be willing to learn all those things. For example, it would not be a realistic goal to jump into the large multi-unit residential market with no knowledge of that market. You need to acquire experience and knowledge first.

Timely — Every goal you set should have a completion date. This prevents you from saying to yourself, *"Well, I'll get to it someday soon."* That kind of procrastination means that day will never arrive. An example of a timely goal would be: "I want to acquire one residential property by June 1 of 2006 and, I want to acquire one every two years following that date."

The most important step of all in the SMART system is to write it down on paper. This is absolutely necessary! Writing it down means you are making a commitment to the goal. It also means you can check your progress, helping you keep on track.

Now, it is time to get started by completing the first draft of an Action Plan on the following pages.

ACTION PLAN

Overall Goal: _____

_____

ACTION STEP	COMPLETION DATE

ACTION STEP	COMPLETION DATE

401(k)/403(b) An investment plan sponsored by an employer that enables individuals to set aside pre-tax income for retirement or emergency purposes. 401(k) plans are provided by private corporations. 403(b) plans are provided by non-profit organizations.

401(k)/403(b) Loan A type of financing using a loan against the money accumulated in a 401(k)/403(b) plan.

Abatement Sometimes referred to as free rent or early occupancy. A condition that could happen in addition to the primary term of the lease.

Above Building Standard Finishes and specialized designs that have been upgraded in order to accommodate a tenant's requirements.

Absorption Rate The speed and amount of time at which rentable space, in square feet, is filled.

Abstract or Title Search The process of reviewing all transactions that have been recorded publicly in order to determine whether any defects in the title exist that could interfere with a clear property ownership transfer.

Accelerated Cost Recovery System A calculation for taxes to provide more depreciation for the first few years of ownership.

Accelerated Depreciation A method of depreciation where the value of a property depreciates faster in the first few years after purchasing it.

Acceleration Clause A clause in a contract that gives the lender the right to demand immediate payment of the balance of the loan if the borrower defaults on the loan.

Acceptance The seller's written approval of a buyer's offer.

Ad Valorem A Latin phrase that translates as "according to value." Refers to a tax that is imposed on a property's value that is typically based on the local government's evaluation of the property.

Addendum An addition or update for an existing contract between parties.

Additional Principal Payment Additional money paid to the lender, apart from the scheduled loan payments, to pay more of the principal balance, shortening the length of the loan.

Adjustable-Rate Mortgage (ARM) A home loan with an interest rate that is adjusted periodically in order to reflect changes in a specific financial resource.

Adjusted Funds From Operations (AFFO) The rate of REIT performance or ability to pay dividends that is used by many analysts who have concerns about the quality of earnings as measured by Funds From Operations (FFO).

Adjustment Date The date at which the interest rate is adjusted for an adjustable-rate mortgage (ARM).

Adjustment Period The amount of time between adjustments for an interest rate in an ARM.

Administrative Fee A percentage of the value of the assets under management, or a fixed annual dollar amount charged to manage an account.

Advances The payments the servicer makes when the borrower fails to send a payment.

Adviser A broker or investment banker who represents an owner in a transaction and is paid a retainer and/or a performance fee once a financing or sales transaction has closed.

Agency Closing A type of closing in which a lender uses a title company or other firm as an agent to finish a loan.

Agency Disclosure A requirement in most states that agents who act for both buyers or sellers must disclose who they are working for in the transaction.

Aggregation Risk The risk that is associated with warehousing mortgages during the process of pooling them for future security.

Agreement of Sale A legal document the buyer and seller must approve and sign that details the price and terms in the transaction.

Alienation Clause The provision in a loan that requires the borrower to pay the total balance of the loan at once if the property is sold or the ownership transferred.

Alternative Mortgage A home loan that does not match the standard terms of a fixed-rate mortgage.

Alternative or Specialty Investments Types of property that are not considered to be conventional real estate investments, such as self-storage facilities, mobile homes, timber, agriculture, or parking lots.

Amortization The usual process of paying a loan's interest and principal via scheduled monthly payments.

Amortization Schedule A chart or table that shows the percentage of each

payment that will be applied toward principal and interest over the life of the mortgage and how the loan balance decreases until it reaches zero.

Amortization Tables The mathematical tables that are used to calculate what a borrower's monthly payment will be.

Amortization Term The number of months it will take to amortize the loan.

Anchor The business or individual who is serving as the primary draw to a commercial property.

Annual Mortgagor Statement A yearly statement to borrowers which details the remaining principal balance and amounts paid throughout the year for taxes and interest.

Annual Percentage Rate (APR) The interest rate that states the actual cost of borrowing money over the course of a year.

Annuity The regular payments of a fixed sum.

Application The form a borrower must complete in order to apply for a mortgage loan, including information such as income, savings, assets, and debts.

Application Fee A fee some lenders charge that may include charges for items such as property appraisal or a credit report unless those fees are included elsewhere.

Appraisal The estimate of the value of a property on a particular date given by a professional appraiser, usually presented in a written document.

Appraisal Fee The fee charged by a professional appraiser for his estimate of the market value of a property.

Appraisal Report The written report presented by an appraiser regarding the value of a property.

Appraised Value The dollar amount a professional appraiser assigned to the value of a property in his report.

Appraiser A certified individual who is qualified by education, training, and experience to estimate the value of real and personal property.

Appreciation An increase in the home's or property's value.

Appreciation Return The amount gained when the value of the real estate assets increases during the current quarter.

Arbitrage The act of buying securities in one market and selling them immediately in another market in order to profit from the difference in price.

ARM Index A number that is publicly published and used as the basis for interest rate adjustments on an ARM.

As-Is Condition A phrase in a purchase or lease contract in which the new tenant accepts the existing condition of the premises as well as any physical defects.

Assessed Value The value placed on a home that is determined by a tax assessor in order to calculate a tax base.

Assessment (1) The approximate value of a property. (2) A fee charged in addition to taxes in order to help pay for items such as water, sewer, street improvements, etc.

Assessor A public officer who estimates the value of a property for the purpose of taxation.

Asset A property or item of value owned by an individual or company.

Asset Management Fee A fee that is charged to investors based on the amount of money they have invested into real estate assets for the particular fund or account.

Asset Management The various tasks and areas around managing real estate assets from the initial investment until the time it is sold.

Asset Turnover The rate of total revenues for the previous 12 months divided by the average total assets.

Assets Under Management The amount of the current market value of real estate assets that a manager is responsible to manage and invest.

Assignee Name The individual or business to whom the lease, mortgage, or other contract has been re-assigned.

Assignment The transfer of rights and responsibilities from one party to another for paying a debt. The original party remains liable for the debt should the second party default.

Assignor The person who transfers the rights and interests of a property to another.

Assumable Mortgage A mortgage that is capable of being transferred to a different borrower.

Assumption The act of assuming the mortgage of the seller.

Assumption Clause A contractual provision that enables the buyer to take responsibility for the mortgage loan from the seller.

Assumption Fee A fee charged to the buyer for processing new records when they are assuming an existing loan.

Attorn To agree to recognize a new owner of a property and to pay rent to the new landlord.

Average Common Equity The sum of the common equity for the last five quarters divided by five.

Average Downtime The number of months that are expected between a lease's expiration and the beginning of a replacement lease under the current market conditions.

Average Free Rent The number of months the rent abatement concession is expected to be granted to a tenant as part of an incentive to lease under current market conditions.

Average Occupancy The average rate of each of the previous 12 months that a property was occupied.

Average Total Assets The sum of the total assets of a company for the

previous five quarters divided by five.

Back Title Letter A letter that an attorney receives from a title insurance company before examining the title for insurance purposes.

Back-End Ratio The calculation lenders use to compare a borrower's gross monthly income to their total debt.

Balance Sheet A statement that lists an individual's assets, liabilities, and net worth.

Balloon Loan A type of mortgage in which the monthly payments are not large enough to repay the loan by the end of the term, and the final payment is one large payment of the remaining balance.

Balloon Payment The final huge payment due at the end of a balloon mortgage.

Balloon Risk The risk that a borrower may not be able to come up with the funds for the balloon payment at maturity.

Bankrupt The state an individual or business is in if they are unable to repay their debt when it is due.

Bankruptcy A legal proceeding where a debtor can obtain relief from payment of certain obligations through restructuring their finances.

Base Loan Amount The amount that forms the basis for the loan payments.

Base Principal Balance The original loan amount once adjustments for subsequent fundings and principal payments have been made without including accrued interest or other unpaid debts.

Base Rent A certain amount that is used as a minimum rent, providing for rent increases over the term of the lease agreement.

Base Year The sum of actual taxes and operating expenses during a given year, often that in which a lease begins.

Basis Point A term for 1/100 of one percentage point.

Before-Tax Income An individual's income before taxes have been deducted.

Below-Grade Any structure or part of a structure that is below the surface of the ground that surrounds it.

Beneficiary An employee who is covered by the benefit plan his or her company provides.

Beta The measurement of common stock price volatility for a company in comparison to the market.

Bid The price or range an investor is willing to spend on whole loans or securities.

Bill of Sale A written legal document that transfers the ownership of personal property to another party.

Binder (1) A report describing the conditions of a property's title. (2) An early agreement between seller and buyer.

Biweekly Mortgage A mortgage repayment plan that requires payments every two weeks to help repay the loan over a shorter amount of time.

Blanket Mortgage A rare type of mortgage that covers more than one of the borrower's properties.

Blind Pool A mixed fund that accepts capital from investors without specifying property assets.

Bond Market The daily buying and selling of thirty-year treasury bonds that also affects fixed rate mortgages.

Book Value The value of a property based on its purchase amount plus upgrades or other additions with depreciation subtracted.

Break-Even Point The point at which a landlord's income from rent matches expenses and debt.

Bridge Loan A short-term loan for individuals or companies that are still seeking more permanent financing.

Broker A person who serves as a go-between for a buyer and seller.

Brokerage The process of bringing two or more parties together in exchange for a fee, commission, or other compensation.

Buildable Acres The portion of land that can be built on after allowances for roads, setbacks, anticipated open spaces, and unsuitable areas have been made.

Building Code The laws set forth by the local government regarding end use of a given piece of property. These law codes may dictate the design, materials used, and/or types of improvements that will be allowed.

Building Standard Plus Allowance A detailed list provided by the landlord stating the standard building materials and costs necessary to make the premises inhabitable.

Build-Out Improvements to a property's space that have been implemented according to the tenant's specifications.

Build-to-Suit A way of leasing property, usually for commercial purposes, in which the developer or landlord builds to a tenant's specifications.

Buydown A term that usually refers to a fixed-rate mortgage for which additional payments can be applied to the interest rate for a temporary period, lowering payments for a period of one to three years.

Buydown Mortgage A style of home loan in which the lender receives a higher payment in order to convince them to reduce the interest rate during the initial years of the mortgage.

Buyer's Remorse A nervousness that first-time homebuyers tend to feel after signing a sales contract or closing the purchase of a house.

Call Date The periodic or continuous right a lender has to call for payment of the total remaining balance prior to the date of maturity.

Call Option A clause in a loan agreement that allows a lender to demand repayment of the entire principal balance at any time.

Cap A limit on how much the monthly payment or interest rate is allowed to increase in an adjustable-rate mortgage.

Capital Appreciation The change in a property's or portfolio's market value after it has been adjusted for capital improvements and partial sales.

Capital Expenditures The purchase of long-term assets, or the expansion of existing ones, that prolongs the life or efficiency of those assets.

Capital Gain The amount of excess when the net proceeds from the sale of an asset are higher than its book value.

Capital Improvements Expenses that prolong the life of a property or add new improvements to it.

Capital Markets Public and private markets where individuals or businesses can raise or borrow capital.

Capitalization The mathematical process that investors use to derive the value of a property using the rate of return on investments.

Capitalization Rate The percentage of return as it is estimated from the net income of a property.

Carryback Financing A type of funding in which a seller agrees to hold back a note for a specified portion of the sales price.

Carrying Charges Costs incurred to the landlord when initially leasing out a property and then during the periods of vacancy.

Cash Flow The amount of income an investor receives on a rental property after operating expenses and loan payments have been deducted.

Cashier's Check A check the bank draws on its own resources instead of a depositor's account.

Cash-on-Cash Yield The percentage of a property's net cash flow and the average amount of invested capital during the specified operating year.

Cash-Out Refinance The act of refinancing a mortgage for an amount that is higher than the original amount for the purpose of using the leftover cash for personal use.

Certificate of Deposit A type of deposit that is held in a bank for a limited time and pays a certain amount of interest to the depositor.

Certificate of Deposit Index (CODI) A rate that is based on interest rates of six-month CDs and is often used to determine interest rates for some ARMs.

Certificate of Eligibility A type of document that the Department of Veterans Affairs issues to verify the eligibility of a veteran for a VA loan.

Certificate of Occupancy (CO) A written document issued by a local government or building agency that states that a home or other building is inhabitable after meeting all building codes.

Certificate of Reasonable Value (CRV) An appraisal presented by the Department of Veterans Affairs that shows the current market value of a property.

Certificate of Veteran Status A document veterans or reservists receive if they have served 90 days of continuous active duty (including training time).

Chain of Title The official record of all transfers of ownership over the history of a piece of property.

Chapter 11 The part of the federal bankruptcy code that deals with reorganizations of businesses.

Chapter 7 The part of the federal bankruptcy code that deals with liquidations of businesses.

Circulation Factor The interior space that is required for internal office circulation and is not included in the net square footage.

Class A A property rating that is usually assigned to those that will generate the maximum rent per square foot, due to superior quality and/or location.

Class B A good property that most potential tenants would find desirable but lacks certain attributes that would bring in the top dollar.

Class C A building that is physically acceptable but offers few amenities, thereby becoming cost-effective space for tenants who are seeking a particular image.

Clear Title A property title that is free of liens, defects, or other legal encumbrances.

Clear-Span Facility A type of building, usually a warehouse or parking garage, consisting of vertical columns on the outer edges of the structure and clear spaces between the columns.

Closed-End Fund A mixed fund with a planned range of investor capital and a limited life.

Closing The final act of procuring a loan and title in which documents are signed between the buyer and seller and/or their respective representation and all money concerned in the contract changes hands.

Closing Costs The expenses that are related to the sale of real estate including loan, title, and appraisal fees and are beyond the price of the property itself.

Closing Statement See: Settlement Statement.

Cloud on Title Certain conditions uncovered in a title search that present a negative impact to the title for the property.

Commercial Mortgage-Backed Securities (CMBS) A type of securities that is backed by loans on commercial real estate.

Collateralized Mortgage Obligation (CMO) Debt that is fully based on a pool of mortgages.

Co-Borrower Another individual who is jointly responsible for the loan and is on the title to the property.

Cost of Funds Index (COFI) An index used to determine changes in the interest rates for certain ARMs.

Co-Investment Program A separate account for an insurance company or investment partnership in which two or more pension funds may co-invest their capital in an individual property or a portfolio of properties.

Co-Investment The condition that occurs when two or more pension funds or groups of funds are sharing ownership of a real estate investment.

Collateral The property for which a borrower has obtained a loan, thereby assuming the risk of losing the property if the loan is not repaid according to the terms of the loan agreement.

Collection The effort on the part of a lender, due to a borrower defaulting on a loan, which involves mailing and recording certain documents in the event that the foreclosure procedure must be implemented.

Commercial Mortgage A loan used to purchase a piece of commercial property or building.

Commercial Mortgage Broker A broker specialized in commercial mortgage applications.

Commercial Mortgage Lender A lender specialized in funding commercial mortgage loans.

Commingled Fund A pooled fund that enables qualified employee benefit plans to mix their capital in order to achieve professional management, greater diversification, or investment positions in larger properties.

Commission A compensation to salespeople that is paid out of the total amount of the purchase transaction.

Commitment The agreement of a lender to make a loan with given terms for a specific period.

Commitment Fee The fee a lender charges for the guarantee of specified loan terms, to be honored at some point in the future.

Common Area Assessments Sometimes called Homeowners' Association Fees. Charges paid to the homeowners' association by the individual unit owners, in a condominium or planned unit development (PUD), that are usually used to maintain the property and common areas.

Common Area Maintenance The additional charges the tenant must pay in addition to the base rent to pay for the maintenance of common areas.

Common Areas The portions of a building, land, and amenities, owned or managed by a planned unit development (PUD) or condominium's homeowners' association, that are used by all of the unit owners who share in the common expense of operation and maintenance.

Common Law A set of unofficial laws that were originally based on English customs and used to some extent in several states.

Community Property Property that is acquired by a married couple during the course of their marriage and is considered in many states to be owned jointly, unless certain circumstances are in play.

Comparable Sales Also called Comps or Comparables. The recent selling prices of similar properties in the area that are used to help determine the market value of a property.

Compound Interest The amount of interest paid on the principal balance of a mortgage in addition to accrued interest.

Concessions Cash, or the equivalent, that the landlord pays or allows in the form of rental abatement, additional tenant finish allowance, moving expenses, or other costs expended in order to persuade a tenant to sign a lease.

Condemnation A government agency's act of taking private property, without the owner's consent, for public use through the power of eminent domain.

Conditional Commitment A lender's agreement to make a loan providing the borrower meets certain conditions.

Conditional Sale A contract to sell a property that states that the seller will retain the title until all contractual conditions have been fulfilled.

Condominium A type of ownership in which all of the unit owners own the property, common areas, and buildings jointly, and have sole ownership in the unit to which they hold the title.

Condominium Conversion Changing an existing rental property's ownership to the condominium form of ownership.

Condominium Hotel A condominium project that involves registration desks, short-term occupancy, food and telephone services, and daily cleaning services, and is generally operated as a commercial hotel even though the units are individually owned.

Conduit A strategic alliance between lenders and unaffiliated organizations that acts as a source of funding by regularly purchasing loans, usually with a goal of pooling and securitizing them.

Conforming Loan A type of mortgage that meets the conditions to be purchased by Fannie Mae or Freddie Mac.

Construction Documents The drawings and specifications an architect and/ or engineer provides to describe construction requirements for a project.

Construction Loan A short-term loan to finance the cost of construction, usually dispensed in stages throughout the construction project.

Construction Management The process of ensuring that the stages of the construction project are completed in a timely and seamless manner.

Construction-to-Permanent Loan A construction loan that can be converted to a longer-term traditional mortgage after construction is complete.

Consultant Any individual or company that provides the services to institutional investors, such as defining real estate investment policies, making recommendations to advisers or managers, analyzing existing real estate portfolios, monitoring and reporting on portfolio performance, and/or reviewing specified investment opportunities.

Consumer Price Index (CPI) A measurement of inflation, relating to the change in the prices of goods and services that are regularly purchased by a specific population during a certain period of time.

Contiguous Space Refers to several suites or spaces on a floor (or connected floors) in a given building that can be combined and rented to a single tenant.

Contingency A specific condition that must be met before either party in a contract can be legally bound.

Contract An agreement, either verbal or written, to perform or not to perform a certain thing.

Contract Documents See: Construction Documents.

Contract Rent Also known as Face Rent. The dollar amount of the rental obligation specified in a lease.

Conventional Loan A long-term loan from a non-governmental lender that a borrower obtains for the purchase of a home.

Convertible Adjustable-Rate Mortgage A type of mortgage that begins as a traditional ARM but contains a provision to enable the borrower to change to a fixed-rate mortgage during a certain period of time.

Convertible Debt The point in a mortgage at which the lender has the option to convert to a partially or fully owned property within a certain period of time.

Convertible Preferred Stock Preferred stock that can be converted to common stock under certain conditions that have been specified by the issuer.

Conveyance The act of transferring a property title between parties by deed.

Cooperative Also called a Co-op. A type of ownership by multiple residents of a multi-unit housing complex in which they all own shares in the cooperative corporation that owns the property, thereby having the right to occupy a particular apartment or unit.

Cooperative Mortgage Any loan that is related to a cooperative residential project.

Core Properties The main types of property, specifically office, retail, industrial, and multi-family.

Co-Signer A second individual or party who also signs a promissory note or loan agreement, thereby taking responsibility for the debt in the event that the primary borrower cannot pay.

Cost-Approach Improvement Value The current expenses for constructing a copy or replacement for an existing structure, but subtracting an estimate of the accrued depreciation.

Cost-Approach Land Value The estimated value of the basic interest in the land, as if it were available for development to its highest and best use.

Cost-of-Sale Percentage An estimate of the expenses of selling an investment that represents brokerage commissions, closing costs, fees, and other necessary sales costs.

Coupon The token or expected interest rate the borrower is charged on a promissory note or mortgage.

Courier Fee The fee that is charged at closing for the delivery of documents between all parties concerned in a real estate transaction.

Covenant A written agreement, included in deeds or other legal documents, that defines the requirements for certain acts or use of a property.

Credit An agreement in which a borrower promises to repay the lender at a later date and receives something of value in exchange.

Credit Enhancement The necessary credit support, in addition to mortgage collateral, in order to achieve the desired credit rating on mortgage-backed securities.

Credit History An individual's record which details his current and past financial obligations and performance.

Credit Life Insurance A type of insurance that pays the balance of a mortgage if the borrower dies.

Credit Rating The degree of creditworthiness a person is assigned based on his credit history and current financial status.

Credit Report A record detailing an individual's credit, employment, and residence history used to determine the individual's creditworthiness.

Credit Repository A company that records and updates credit applicants' financial and credit information from various sources.

Credit Score Sometimes called a Credit Risk Score. The number contained in a consumer's credit report that represents a statistical summary of the information.

Creditor A party to whom other parties owe money.

Cross-Collateralization A group of mortgages or properties that jointly secures one debt obligation.

Cross-Defaulting A provision that allows a trustee or lender to require full payment on all loans in a group, if any single loan in the group is in default.

Cumulative Discount Rate A percentage of the current value of base rent with all landlord lease concessions taken into account.

Current Occupancy The current percentage of units in a building or property that is leased.

Current Yield The annual rate of return on an investment, expressed as a percentage.

Deal Structure The type of agreement in financing an acquisition. The deal can be un-leveraged, leveraged, traditional debt, participating debt, participating/convertible debt, or joint ventures.

Debt Any amount one party owes to another party.

Debt Service Coverage Ratio (DSCR) A property's yearly net operating income divided by the yearly cost of debt service.

Debt Service The amount of money that is necessary to meet all interest and principal payments during a specific period.

Debt-to-Income Ratio The percentage of a borrower's monthly payment on long-term debts divided by his gross monthly income.

Dedicate To change a private property to public ownership for a particular public use.

Deed A legal document that conveys property ownership to the buyer.

Deed in Lieu of Foreclosure A situation in which a deed is given to a lender in order to satisfy a mortgage debt and to avoid the foreclosure process.

Deed of Trust A provision that allows a lender to foreclose on a property in the event that the borrower defaults on the loan.

Default The state that occurs when a borrow fails to fulfill a duty or take care of an obligation, such as making monthly mortgage payments.

Deferred Maintenance Account A type of account that a borrower must fund to provide for maintenance of a property.

Deficiency Judgment The legal assignment of personal liability to a borrower for the unpaid balance of a mortgage, after foreclosing on the property has failed to yield the full amount of the debt.

Defined-Benefit Plan A type of benefit provided by an employer that defines an employee's benefits either as a fixed amount or a percentage of the beneficiary's salary when he retires.

Defined-Contribution Plan A type of benefit plan provided by an employer in which an employee's retirement benefits are determined by the amount that has been contributed by the employer and/or employee during the time of employment, and by the actual investment earnings on those contributions over the life of the fund.

Delinquency A state that occurs when the borrower fails to make mortgage payments on time, eventually resulting in foreclosure, if severe enough.

Delinquent Mortgage A mortgage in which the borrower is behind on payments.

Demising Wall The physical partition between the spaces of two tenants or from the building's common areas.

Deposit Also referred to as Earnest Money. The funds that the buyer provides when offering to purchase property.

Depreciation A decline in the value of property or an asset, often used as a tax-deductible item.

Derivative Securities A type of securities that has been created from other financial instruments.

Design/Build An approach in which a single individual or business is responsible for both the design and construction.

Disclosure A written statement, presented to a potential buyer, that lists information relevant to a piece of property, whether positive or negative.

Discount Points Fees that a lender charges in order to provide a lower interest rate.

Discount Rate A figure used to translate present value from future payments or receipts.

Discretion The amount of authority an adviser or manager is granted for investing and managing a client's capital.

Distraint The act of seizing a tenant's personal property when the tenant is in default, based on the right the landlord has in satisfying the debt.

Diversification The act of spreading individual investments out to insulate a portfolio against the risk of reduced yield or capital loss.

Dividend Yield The percentage of a security's market price that represents the annual dividend rate.

Dividend Distributions of cash or stock that stockholders receive.

Dividend-Ex Date The initial date on which a person purchasing the stock can no longer receive the most recently announced dividend.

Document Needs List The list of documents a lender requires from a potential borrower who is submitting a loan application.

Documentation Preparation Fee A fee that lenders, brokers, and/or settlement agents charge for the preparation of the necessary closing documents.

Dollar Stop An agreed amount of taxes and operating expenses each tenant must pay out on a prorated basis.

Down Payment The variance between the purchase price and the portion that the mortgage lender financed.

DOWNREIT A structure of organization that makes it possible for REITs to purchase properties using partnership units.

Draw A payment from the construction loan proceeds made to contractors, subcontractors, home builders, or suppliers.

Due Diligence The activities of a prospective purchaser or mortgager of real property for the purpose of confirming that the property is as represented by the seller and is not subject to environmental or other problems.

Due on Sale Clause The standard mortgage language that states the loan must still be repaid if the property is resold.

Earnest Money See: Deposit.

Earthquake Insurance A type of insurance policy that provides coverage against earthquake damage to a home.

Easement The right given to a non-ownership party to use a certain part of the property for specified purposes, such as servicing power lines or cable lines.

Economic Feasibility The viability of a building or project in terms of costs and revenue where the degree of viability is established by extra revenue.

Economic Rent The market rental value of a property at a particular point in time.

Effective Age An estimate of the physical condition of a building presented by an appraiser.

Effective Date The date on which the sale of securities can commence once a registration statement becomes effective.

Effective Gross Income (EGI) The total property income that rents and other sources generate after subtracting a vacancy factor estimated to be appropriate for the property.

Effective Gross Rent (EGR) The net rent that is generated after adjusting for tenant improvements and other capital costs, lease commissions, and other sales expenses.

Effective Rent The actual rental rate that the landlord achieves after deducting the concession value from the base rental rate a tenant pays.

Electronic Authentication A way of providing proof that a particular electronic document is genuine, has arrived unaltered, and came from the indicated source.

Eminent Domain The power of the government to pay the fair market value for a property, appropriating it for public use.

Encroachment Any improvement or upgrade that illegally intrudes onto another party's property.

Encumbrance Any right or interest in a property that interferes with using it or transferring ownership.

End Loan The result of converting to permanent financing from a construction loan.

Entitlement A benefit of a VA home loan. Often referred to as eligibility.

Environmental Impact Statement Legally required documents that must accompany major project proposals where there will likely be an impact on the surrounding environment.

Equal Credit Opportunity Act (ECOA) A federal law that requires a lender or other creditor to make credit available for applicants regardless of sex, marital status, race, religion, or age.

Equifax One of the three primary credit-reporting bureaus.

Equity The value of a property after existing liabilities have been deducted.

Employee Retirement Income Security Act (ERISA) A legislation that controls the investment activities, mainly of corporate and union pension plans.

Errors and Omissions Insurance A type of policy that insures against the mistakes of a builder or architect.

Escalation Clause The clause in a lease that provides for the rent to be increased to account for increases in the expenses the landlord must pay.

Escrow A valuable item, money, or documents deposited with a third party for delivery upon the fulfillment of a condition.

Escrow Account Also referred to as an Impound Account. An account established by a mortgage lender or servicing company for the purpose of holding funds for the payment of items, such as homeowner's insurance and property taxes.

Escrow Agent A neutral third party who makes sure that all conditions of a real estate transaction have been met before any funds are transferred or property is recorded.

Escrow Agreement A written agreement between an escrow agent and the contractual parties that defines the basic obligations of each party, the money (or other valuables) to be deposited in escrow, and how the escrow agent is to dispose of the money on deposit.

Escrow Analysis An annual investigation a lender performs to make sure they are collecting the appropriate amount of money for anticipated expenditures.

Escrow Closing The event in which all conditions of a real estate transaction have been met, and the property title is transferred to the buyer.

Escrow Company A neutral company that serves as a third party to ensure that all conditions of a real estate transaction are met.

Escrow Disbursements The dispensing of escrow funds for the payment of real estate taxes, hazard insurance, mortgage insurance, and other property expenses as they are due.

Escrow Payment The funds that are withdrawn by a mortgage servicer from a borrower's escrow account to pay property taxes and insurance.

Estate The total assets, including property, of an individual after he has died.

Estimated Closing Costs An estimation of the expenses relating to the sale of real estate.

Estimated Hazard Insurance An estimation of hazard insurance, or homeowner's insurance, that will cover physical risks.

Estimated Property Taxes An estimation of the property taxes that must be paid on the property, according to state and county tax rates.

Estoppel Certificate A signed statement that certifies that certain factual statements are correct as of the date of the statement and can be relied upon by a third party, such as a prospective lender or purchaser.

Eviction The legal removal of an occupant from a piece of property.

Examination of Title A title company's inspection and report of public records and other documents for the purpose of determining the chain of ownership of a property.

Exclusive Agency Listing A written agreement between a property owner and a real estate broker in which the owner promises to pay the broker a commission if certain property is leased during the listing period.

Exclusive Listing A contract that allows a licensed real estate agent to be the only agent who can sell a property for a given time.

Executed Contract An agreement in which all parties involved have fulfilled their duties.

Executor The individual who is named in a will to administer an estate.

Executrix is the feminine form.

Exit Strategy An approach investors may use when they wish to liquidate all or part of their investment.

Experian One of the three primary credit-reporting bureaus.

Face Rental Rate The rental rate that the landlord publishes.

Facility Space The floor area in a hospitality property that is dedicated to activities, such as restaurants, health clubs, and gift shops, that interactively service multiple people and is not directly related to room occupancy.

Funds Available for Distribution (FAD) The income from operations, with cash expenditures subtracted, that may be used for leasing commissions and tenant improvement costs.

FAD Multiple The price per share of a REIT divided by its funds available for distribution.

Fair Credit Reporting Act (FCRA) The federal legislation that governs the processes credit reporting agencies must follow.

Fair Housing Act The federal legislation that prohibits the refusal to rent or sell to anyone based on race, color, religion, sex, family status, or disability.

Fair Market Value The highest price that a buyer would be willing to pay, and the lowest a seller would be willing to accept.

Fannie Mae See: Federal National Mortgage Association.

Fannie Mae's Community Home Buyer's Program A community lending model based on borrower income in which mortgage insurers and Fannie Mae offer flexible underwriting guidelines in order to increase the buying power for a low- or moderate-income family and to decrease the total amount of cash needed to purchase a home.

Farmer's Home Administration (FMHA) An agency within the U.S. Department of Agriculture that provides credit to farmers and other rural residents.

Federal Home Loan Mortgage Corporation (FHLMC) Also known as Freddie Mac. The company that buys mortgages from lending institutions, combines them with other loans, and sells shares to investors.

Federal Housing Administration (FHA) A government agency that provides low-rate mortgages to buyers who are able to make a down payment as low as 3 percent.

Federal National Mortgage Association (FNMA) Also known as Fannie Mae. A congressionally chartered, shareholder-owned company that is the nation's largest supplier of home mortgage funds. The company buys mortgages from lenders and resells them as securities on the secondary mortgage market.

Fee Simple The highest possible interest a person can have in a piece of real estate.

Fee Simple Estate An unconditional, unlimited inheritance estate in which the owner may dispose of or use the property as desired.

Fee Simple Interest The state of owning all the rights in a real estate parcel.

Funds From Operations (FFO) A ratio that is meant to highlight the amount of cash a company's real estate portfolio generates relative to its total operating cash flow.

FFO Multiple The price of a REIT share divided by its funds from operations.

FHA Loans Mortgages that the Federal Housing Administration (FHA) insures.

FHA Mortgage Insurance A type of insurance that requires a fee to be paid at closing in order to insure the loan with the Federal Housing Administration (FHA).

Fiduciary Any individual who holds authority over a plan's asset management, administration or disposition, or renders paid investment advice regarding a plan's assets.

Finance Charge The amount of interest to be paid on a loan or credit card balance.

Firm Commitment A written agreement a lender makes to loan money for the purchase of property.

First Mortgage The main mortgage on a property.

First Refusal Right/ Right of First Refusal A lease clause that gives a tenant the first opportunity to buy a property or to lease additional space in a property at the same price and terms as those contained in an offer from a third party that the owner has expressed a willingness to accept.

First-Generation Space A new space that has never before been occupied by a tenant and is currently available for lease.

First-Loss Position A security's position that will suffer the first economic loss if the assets below it lose value or are foreclosed on.

Fixed Costs Expenses that remain the same despite the level of sales or production.

Fixed Rate An interest rate that does not change over the life of the loan.

Fixed Time The particular weeks of a year that the owner of a timeshare arrangement can access his or her accommodations.

Fixed-Rate Mortgage A loan with an unchanging interest rate over the life of the loan.

Fixture Items that become a part of the property when they are permanently attached to the property.

Flat Fee An amount of money that an adviser or manager receives for managing a portfolio of real estate assets.

Flex Space A building that provides a flexible configuration of office or showroom space combined with manufacturing, laboratory, warehouse, distribution, etc.

Float The number of freely traded shares owned by the public.

Flood Certification The process of analyzing whether a property is located in a known flood zone.

Flood Insurance A policy that is required in designated flood zones to protect against loss due to flood damage.

Floor Area Ratio (FAR) A measurement of a building's gross square footage compared to the square footage of the land on which it is located.

For Sale By Owner (FSBO) A method of selling property in which the property owner serves as the selling agent and directly handles the sales process with the buyer or buyer's agent.

Force Majeure An external force that is not controlled by the contractual parties and prevents them from complying with the provisions of the contract.

Foreclosure The legal process in which a lender takes over ownership of a property once the borrower is in default in a mortgage arrangement.

Forward Commitments Contractual agreements to perform certain financing duties according to any stated conditions.

Four Quadrants of the Real Estate Capital Markets The four market types that consist of Private Equity, Public Equity, Private Debt, and Public Debt.

Freddie Mac See: Federal Home Loan Mortgage Corporation.

Front-End Ratio The measurement a lender uses to compare a borrower's monthly housing expense to gross monthly income.

Full Recourse A loan on which the responsibility of a loan is transferred to an endorser or guarantor in the event of default by the borrower.

Full-Service Rent A rental rate that includes all operating expenses and real estate taxes for the first year.

Fully Amortized ARM An ARM with a monthly payment that is sufficient to amortize the remaining balance at the current interest accrual rate over the amortization term.

Fully Diluted Shares The number of outstanding common stock shares if all convertible securities were converted to common shares.

Future Proposed Space The space in a commercial development that has been proposed but is not yet under construction, or the future phases of a multi-phase project that has not yet been built.

General Contractor The main person or business that contracts for the construction of an entire building or project, rather than individual duties.

General Partner The member in a partnership who holds the authority to bind the partnership and shares in its profits and losses.

Gift Money a buyer has received from a relative or other source that will not have to be repaid.

Ginnie Mae See: Government National Mortgage Association.

Going-In Capitalization Rate The rate that is computed by dividing the expected net operating income for the first year by the value of the property.

Good Faith Estimate A lender's or broker's estimate that shows all costs associated with obtaining a home loan including loan processing, title, and inspection fees.

Government Loan A mortgage that is insured or guaranteed by the FHA, the Department of Veterans Affairs (VA), or the Rural Housing Service (RHS).

Government National Mortgage Association (GNMA) Also known as Ginnie Mae. A government-owned corporation under the U.S. Department of Housing and Urban Development (HUD) that performs the same role as Fannie Mae and Freddie Mac in providing funds to lenders for making home loans, but only purchases loans that are backed by the federal government.

Grace Period A defined time period in which a borrower may make a loan payment after its due date without incurring a penalty.

Graduated Lease A lease, usually long-term, in which rent payments vary in accordance with future contingencies.

Graduated Payment Mortgage A mortgage that requires low payments during the first years of the loan, but eventually requires larger monthly payments over the term of the loan that become fixed later in the term.

Grant To give or transfer an interest in a property by deed or other documented method.

Grantee The party to whom an interest in a property is given.

Grantor The party who is transferring an interest in a property.

Gross Building Area The sum of areas at all floor levels, including the basement, mezzanine, and penthouses included in the principal outside faces of the exterior walls without allowing for architectural setbacks or projections.

Gross Income The total income of a household before taxes or expenses have been subtracted.

Gross Investment in Real Estate (Historic Cost) The total amount of equity and debt that is invested in a piece of real estate minus proceeds from sales or partial sales.

Gross Leasable Area The amount of floor space that is designed for tenants' occupancy and exclusive use.

Gross Lease A rental arrangement in which the tenant pays a flat sum for rent, and the landlord must pay all building expenses out of that amount.

Gross Real Estate Asset Value The total market value of the real estate investments under management in a fund or individual accounts, usually including the total value of all equity positions, debt positions, and joint venture ownership positions.

Gross Real Estate Investment Value The market value of real estate investments that are held in a portfolio without including debt.

Gross Returns The investment returns generated from operating a property without adjusting for adviser or manager fees.

Ground Lease Land being leased to

an individual that has absolutely no residential dwelling on the property; or if it does, the ground (or land) is the only portion of the property being leased.

Ground Rent A long-term lease in which rent is paid to the land owner, normally to build something on that land.

Growing-Equity Mortgage A fixed-rate mortgage in which payments increase over a specified amount of time with the extra funds being applied to the principal.

Guarantor The part who makes a guaranty.

Guaranty An agreement in which the guarantor promises to satisfy the debt or obligations of another, if and when the debtor fails to do so.

Hard Cost The expenses attributed to actually constructing property improvements.

Hazard Insurance Also known as Homeowner's Insurance or Fire Insurance. A policy that provides coverage for damage from forces such as fire and wind.

Highest and Best Use The most reasonable, expected, legal use of a piece of vacant land or improved property that is physically possible, supported appropriately, financially feasible, and that results in the highest value.

High-Rise In a suburban district, any building taller than six stories. In a business district, any building taller than 25 stories.

Holdbacks A portion of a loan funding that is not dispersed until an additional condition is met, such as the completion of construction.

Holding Period The expected length of time, from purchase to sale, that an investor will own a property.

Hold-Over Tenant A tenant who retains possession of the leased premises after the lease has expired.

Home Equity Conversion Mortgage (HECM) Also referred to as a Reverse Annuity Mortgage. A type of mortgage in which the lender makes payments to the owner, thereby enabling older homeowners to convert equity in their homes into cash in the form of monthly payments.

Home Equity Line An open-ended amount of credit based on the equity a homeowner has accumulated.

Home Equity Loan A type of loan that allows owners to borrow against the equity in their homes up to a limited amount.

Home Inspection A pre-purchase examination of the condition a home is in by a certified inspector.

Home Inspector A certified professional who determines the structural soundness and operating systems of a property.

Home Price The price that a buyer and seller agree upon, generally based on the home's appraised market value.

Homeowners' Association (HOA) A group that governs a community, condominium building, or neighborhood and enforces the covenants, conditions, and restrictions set by the developer.

Homeowners' Association Dues The monthly payments that are paid to the homeowners' association for maintenance and communal expenses.

Homeowner's Insurance A policy that includes coverage for all damages that may affect the value of a house as defined in the terms of the insurance policy.

Homeowner's Warranty A type of policy homebuyers often purchase to cover repairs, such as heating or air-conditioning, should they stop working within the coverage period.

Homestead The property an owner uses as his primary residence.

Housing Expense Ratio The percentage of gross income that is devoted to housing costs each month.

HUD (Housing and Urban Development) A federal agency that oversees a variety of housing and community development programs, including the FHA.

HUD Median Income The average income for families in a particular area, which is estimated by HUD.

HUD-1 Settlement Statement Also known as the Closing Statement or Settlement Sheet. An itemized listing of the funds paid at closing.

HUD-1 Uniform Settlement Statement A closing statement for the buyer and seller that describes all closing costs for a real estate transaction or refinancing.

HVAC Heating, ventilating, and air-conditioning.

Hybrid Debt A position in a mortgage that has equity-like features of participation in both cash flow and the appreciation of the property at the point of sale or refinance.

Implied Cap Rate The net operating income divided by the sum of a REIT's equity market capitalization and its total outstanding debt.

Impounds The part of the monthly mortgage payment that is reserved in an account in order to pay for hazard insurance, property taxes, and private mortgage insurance.

Improvements The upgrades or changes made to a building to improve its value or usefulness.

Incentive Fee A structure in which the fee amount charged is based on the performance of the real estate assets under management.

Income Capitalization Value The figure derived for an income-producing property by converting its expected benefits into property value.

Income Property A particular property that is used to generate income but is not occupied by the owner.

Income Return The percentage of the total return generated by the income from property, fund, or account operations.

Index A financial table that lenders use for calculating interest rates on ARMs.

Indexed Rate The sum of the published index with a margin added.

Indirect Costs Expenses of development other than the costs of direct material and labor that are related directly to the construction of improvements.

Individual Account Management The process of maintaining accounts that have been established for individual plan sponsors or other investors for investment in real estate, where a firm acts as an adviser in obtaining and/or managing a real estate portfolio.

Inflation Hedge An investment whose value tends to increase at a greater rate than inflation, contributing to the preservation of the purchasing power of a portfolio.

Inflation The rate at which consumer prices increase each year.

Initial Interest Rate The original

interest rate on an ARM which is sometimes subject to a variety of adjustments throughout the mortgage.

Initial Public Offering (IPO) The first time a previously private company offers securities for public sale.

Initial Rate Cap The limit specified by some ARMs as the maximum amount the interest rate may increase when the initial interest rate expires.

Initial Rate Duration The date specified by most ARMs at which the initial rate expires.

Inspection Fee The fee that a licensed property inspector charges for determining the current physical condition of the property.

Inspection Report A written report of the property's condition presented by a licensed inspection professional.

Institutional-Grade Property A variety of types of real estate properties usually owned or financed by tax-exempt institutional investors.

Insurance Binder A temporary insurance policy that is implemented while a permanent policy is drawn up or obtained.

Insurance Company Separate Account A real estate investment vehicle only offered by life insurance companies, which enables an ERISA-governed fund to avoid creating unrelated taxable income for certain types of property investments and investment structures.

Insured Mortgage A mortgage that is guaranteed by the FHA or by private mortgage insurance (PMI).

Interest Accrual Rate The rate at which a mortgage accrues interest.

Interest-Only Loan A mortgage for which the borrower pays only the interest that accrues on the loan balance

each month.

Interest Paid over Life of Loan The total amount that has been paid to the lender during the time the money was borrowed.

Interest Rate The percentage that is charged for a loan.

Interest Rate Buy-Down Plans A plan in which a seller uses funds from the sale of the home to buy down the interest rate and reduce the buyer's monthly payments.

Interest Rate Cap The highest interest rate charge allowed on the monthly payment of an ARM during an adjustment period.

Interest Rate Ceiling The maximum interest rate a lender can charge for an ARM.

Interest Rate Floor The minimum possible interest rate a lender can charge for an ARM.

Interest The price that is paid for the use of capital.

Interest-Only Strip A derivative security that consists of all or part of the portion of interest in the underlying loan or security.

Interim Financing Also known as Bridge or Swing Loans. Short-term financing a seller uses to bridge the gap between the sale of one house and the purchase of another.

Internal Rate of Return (IRR) The calculation of a discounted cash flow analysis that is used to determine the potential total return of a real estate asset during a particular holding period.

Inventory The entire space of a certain proscribed market without concern for its availability or condition.

Investment Committee The governing

body that is charged with overseeing corporate pension investments and developing investment policies for board approval.

Investment Manager An individual or company that assumes authority over a specified amount of real estate capital, invests that capital in assets using a separate account, and provides asset management.

Investment Policy A document that formalizes an institution's goals, objectives, and guidelines for asset management, investment advisory contracting, fees, and utilization of consultants and other outside professionals.

Investment Property A piece of real estate that generates some form of income.

Investment Strategy The methods used by a manager in structuring a portfolio and selecting the real estate assets for a fund or an account.

Investment Structures Approaches to investing that include un-leveraged acquisitions, leveraged acquisitions, traditional debt, participating debt, convertible debt, triple-net leases, and joint ventures.

Investment-Grade CMBS Commercial mortgage-backed securities that have ratings of AAA, AA, A, or BBB.

Investor Status The position an investor is in, either taxable or tax-exempt.

Joint Liability The condition in which responsibility rests with two or more people for fulfilling the terms of a home loan or other financial debt.

Joint Tenancy A form of ownership in which two or more people have equal shares in a piece of property, and rights pass to the surviving owner(s) in the event of death.

Joint Venture An investment business formed by more than one party for the purpose of acquiring or developing and managing property and/or other assets.

Judgment The decision a court of law makes.

Judicial Foreclosure The usual foreclosure proceeding some states use, which is handled in a civil lawsuit.

Jumbo Loan A type of mortgage that exceeds the required limits set by Fannie Mae and Freddie Mac each year.

Junior Mortgage A loan that is a lower priority behind the primary loan.

Just Compensation The amount that is fair to both the owner and the government when property is appropriated for public use through eminent domain.

Landlord's Warrant The warrant a landlord obtains to take a tenant's personal property to sell at a public sale to compel payment of the rent or other stipulation in the lease.

Late Charge The fee that is imposed by a lender when the borrower has not made a payment when it was due.

Late Payment The payment made to the lender after the due date has passed.

Lead Manager The investment banking firm that has primary responsibility for coordinating the new issuance of securities.

Lease A contract between a property owner and tenant that defines payments and conditions under which the tenant may occupy the real estate for a given period of time.

Lease Commencement Date The date at which the terms of the lease are implemented.

Lease Expiration Exposure Schedule

A chart of the total square footage of all current leases that expire in each of the next five years, without taking renewal options into account.

Lease Option A financing option that provides for homebuyers to lease a home with an option to buy, with part of the rental payments being applied toward the down payment.

Leasehold The limited right to inhabit a piece of real estate held by a tenant.

Leasehold State A way of holding a property title in which the mortgagor does not actually own the property but has a long-term lease on it.

Leasehold Interest The right to hold or use property for a specific period of time at a given price without transferring ownership.

Lease-Purchase A contract that defines the closing date and solutions for the seller in the event that the buyer defaults.

Legal Blemish A negative count against a piece of property such as a zoning violation or fraudulent title claim.

Legal Description A way of describing and locating a piece of real estate that is recognized by law.

Legal Owner The party who holds the title to the property, although the title may carry no actual rights to the property other than as a lien.

Lender A bank or other financial institution that offers home loans.

Letter of Credit A promise from a bank or other party that the issuer will honor drafts or other requests for payment upon complying with the requirements specified in the letter of credit.

Letter of Intent An initial agreement defining the proposed terms for the end contract.

Leverage The process of increasing the return on an investment by borrowing some of the funds at an interest rate less than the return on the project.

Liabilities A borrower's debts and financial obligations, whether long- or short-term.

Liability Insurance A type of policy that protects owners against negligence, personal injury, or property damage claims.

London InterBank Offered Rate (LIBOR) The interest rate offered on Eurodollar deposits traded between banks and used to determine changes in interest rate for ARMs.

Lien A claim put by one party on the property of another as collateral for money owed.

Lien Waiver A waiver of a mechanic's lien rights that is sometimes required before the general contractor can receive money under the payment provisions of a construction loan and contract.

Life Cap A limit on the amount an ARM's interest rate can increase during the mortgage term.

Lifecycle The stages of development for a property: pre-development, development, leasing, operating, and rehabilitation.

Lifetime Payment Cap A limit on the amount that payments can increase or decrease over the life of an ARM.

Lifetime Rate Cap The highest possible interest rate that may be charged, under any circumstances, over the entire life of an ARM.

Like-Kind Property A term that refers to real estate that is held for productive use in a trade or business or for investment.

Limited Partnership A type of

partnership in which some partners manage the business and are personally liable for partnership debts, but some partners contribute capital and share in profits without the responsibility of management.

Line of Credit An amount of credit granted by a financial institution up to a specified amount for a certain period of time to a borrower.

Liquid Asset A type of asset that can be easily converted into cash.

Liquidity The ease with which an individual's or company's assets can be converted to cash without losing their value.

Listing Agreement An agreement between a property owner and a real estate broker that authorizes the broker to attempt to sell or lease the property at a specified price and terms in return for a commission or other compensation.

Loan An amount of money that is borrowed and usually repaid with interest.

Loan Application A document that presents a borrower's income, debt, and other obligations to determine credit worthiness, as well as some basic information on the target property.

Loan Application Fee A fee lenders charge to cover expenses relating to reviewing a loan application.

Loan Commitment An agreement by a lender or other financial institution to make or ensure a loan for the specified amount and terms.

Loan Officer An official representative of a lending institution who is authorized to act on behalf of the lender within specified limits.

Loan Origination The process of obtaining and arranging new loans.

Loan Origination Fee A fee lenders charge to cover the costs related to arranging the loan.

Loan Servicing The process a lending institution goes through for all loans it manages. This involves processing payments, sending statements, managing the escrow/impound account, providing collection services on delinquent loans, ensuring that insurance and property taxes are made on the property, handling pay-offs and assumptions, as well as various other services.

Loan Term The time, usually expressed in years, that a lender sets in which a buyer must pay a mortgage.

Loan-to-Value (LTV) The ratio of the amount of the loan compared to the appraised value or sales price.

Lock-Box Structure An arrangement in which the payments are sent directly from the tenant or borrower to the trustee.

Lock-In A commitment from a lender to a borrower to guarantee a given interest rate for a limited amount of time.

Lock-In Period The period of time during which the borrower is guaranteed a specified interest rate.

Lockout The period of time during which a loan may not be paid off early.

Long-Term Lease A rental agreement that will last at least three years from initial signing to the date of expiration or renewal.

Loss Severity The percentage of lost principal when a loan is foreclosed.

Lot One of several contiguous parcels of a larger piece of land.

Low-Documentation Loan A mortgage that requires only a basic verification of income and assets.

Low-Rise A building that involves fewer than four stories above the ground level.

Lump-Sum Contract A type of construction contract that requires the general contractor to complete a building project for a fixed cost that is usually established beforehand by competitive bidding.

Magic Page A story of projected growth that describes how a new REIT will achieve its future plans for funds from operations or funds available for distribution.

Maintenance Fee The charge to homeowners' association members each month for the repair and maintenance of common areas.

Maker One who issues a promissory note and commits to paying the note when it is due.

Margin A percentage that is added to the index and fixed for the mortgage term.

Mark to Market The act of changing the original investment cost or value of a property or portfolio to the level of the current estimated market value.

Market Capitalization A measurement of a company's value that is calculated by multiplying the current share price by the current number of shares outstanding.

Market Rental Rates The rental income that a landlord could most likely ask for a property in the open market, indicated by the current rents for comparable spaces.

Market Study A forecast of the demand for a certain type of real estate project in the future that includes an estimate of the square footage that could be absorbed and the rents that could be charged.

Market Value The price a property would sell for at a particular point in time in a competitive market.

Marketable Title A title that is free of encumbrances and can be marketed immediately to a willing purchaser.

Master Lease The primary lease that controls other subsequent leases and may cover more property than all subsequent leases combined.

Master Servicer An entity that acts on behalf of a trustee for security holders' benefit in collecting funds from a borrower, advancing funds in the event of delinquencies and, in the event of default, taking a property through foreclosure.

Maturity Date The date at which the total principal balance of a loan is due.

Mechanic's Lien A claim created for securing payment priority for the price and value of work performed and materials furnished in constructing, repairing, or improving a building or other structure.

Meeting Space The space in hotels that is made available to the public to rent for meetings, conferences, or banquets.

Merged Credit Report A report that combines information from the three primary credit-reporting agencies including: Equifax, Experian, and TransUnion.

Metes and Bounds The surveyed boundary lines of a piece of land described by listing the compass directions (bounds) and distances (metes) of the boundaries.

Mezzanine Financing A financing position somewhere between equity and debt, meaning that there are higher-priority debts above and equity below.

Mid-Rise Usually, a building which shows four to eight stories above ground level. In a business district, buildings up to 25 stories may also be included.

Mixed-Use A term referring to space within a building or project which can be used for more than one activity.

Modern Portfolio Theory (MPT) An approach of quantifying risk and return in an asset portfolio which emphasizes the portfolio rather than the individual assets and how the assets perform in relation to each other.

Modification An adjustment in the terms of a loan agreement.

Modified Annual Percentage Rate (APR) An index of the cost of a loan based on the standard APR but adjusted for the amount of time the borrower expects to hold the loan.

Monthly Association Dues A payment due each month to a homeowners' association for expenses relating to maintenance and community operations.

Mortgage An amount of money that is borrowed to purchase a property using that property as collateral.

Mortgage Acceleration Clause A provision enabling a lender to require that the rest of the loan balance is paid in a lump sum under certain circumstances.

Mortgage Banker A financial institution that provides home loans using its own resources, often selling them to investors such as insurance companies or Fannie Mae.

Mortgage Broker An individual who matches prospective borrowers with lenders that the broker is approved to deal with.

Mortgage Broker Business A company that matches prospective borrowers with lenders that the broker is approved to deal with.

Mortgage Constant A figure comparing an amortizing mortgage payment to the outstanding mortgage balance.

Mortgage Insurance (MI) A policy, required by lenders on some loans, that covers the lender against certain losses that are incurred as a result of a default on a home loan.

Mortgage Insurance Premium (MIP) The amount charged for mortgage insurance, either to a government agency or to a private MI company.

Mortgage Interest Deduction The tax write-off that the IRS allows most homeowners to deduct for annual interest payments made on real estate loans.

Mortgage Life and Disability Insurance A type of term life insurance borrowers often purchase to cover debt that is left when the borrower dies or becomes too disabled to make the mortgage payments.

Mortgagee The financial institution that lends money to the borrower.

Mortgagor The person who requests to borrow money to purchase a property.

Multi-Dwelling Units A set of properties that provide separate housing areas for more than one family but only require a single mortgage.

Multiple Listing Service A service that lists real estate offered for sale by a particular real estate agent that can be shown or sold by other real estate agents within a certain area.

National Association of Real Estate

Investment Trusts (NAREIT) The national, non-profit trade organization that represents the real estate investment trust industry.

National Council of Real Estate Investment Fiduciaries (NCREIF) A group of real estate professionals who serve on committees; sponsor research articles, seminars and symposiums; and produce the NCREIF Property Index.

NCREIF Property Index (NPI) A quarterly and yearly report presenting income and appreciation components.

Negative Amortization An event that occurs when the deferred interest on an ARM is added, and the balance increases instead of decreases.

Net Asset Value (NAV) The total value of an asset or property minus leveraging or joint venture interests.

Net Asset Value Per Share The total value of a REIT's current assets divided by outstanding shares.

Net Assets The total value of assets minus total liabilities based on market value.

Net Cash Flow The total income generated by an investment property after expenses have been subtracted.

Net Investment in Real Estate Gross investment in properties minus the outstanding balance of debt.

Net Investment Income The income or loss of a portfolio or business minus all expenses, including portfolio and asset management fees, but before gains and losses on investments are considered.

Net Operating Income (NOI) The pre-tax figure of gross revenue minus operating expenses and an allowance for expected vacancy.

Net Present Value (NPV) The sum of the total current value of incremental future cash flows plus the current value of estimated sales proceeds.

Net Purchase Price The gross purchase price minus any associated financed debt.

Net Real Estate Investment Value The total market value of all real estate minus property-level debt.

Net Returns The returns paid to investors minus fees to advisers or managers.

Net Sales Proceeds The income from the sale of an asset, or part of an asset, minus brokerage commissions, closing costs, and market expenses.

Net Square Footage The total space required for a task or staff position.

Net Worth The worth of an individual or company figured on the basis of a difference between all assets and liabilities.

No-Cash-Out Refinance Sometimes referred to as a Rate and Term Refinance. A refinancing transaction that is intended only to cover the balance due on the current loan and any costs associated with obtaining the new mortgage.

No-Cost Loan A loan for which there are no costs associated with the loan that are charged by the lender, but with a slightly higher interest rate.

No-Documentation Loan A type of loan application that requires no income or asset verification, usually granted based on strong credit with a large down payment.

Nominal Yield The yield investors receive before it is adjusted for fees, inflation, or risk.

Non-Assumption Clause A provision in a loan agreement that prohibits transferring a mortgage to another borrower without approval from the lender.

Non-Compete Clause A provision in a lease agreement that specifies that the tenant's business is the only one that may operate in the property in question, thereby preventing a competitor moving in next door.

Non-Conforming Loan Any loan that is too large or does not meet certain qualifications to be purchased by Fannie Mae or Freddie Mac.

Non-Discretionary Funds The funds that are allocated to an investment manager who must have approval from the investor for each transaction.

Non-Investment-Grade CMBS Also referred to as High-Yield CMBS. Commercial mortgage-backed securities that have ratings of BB or B.

Non-Liquid Asset A type of asset that is not turned into cash very easily.

Non-Performing Loan A loan agreement that cannot meet its contractual principal and interest payments.

Non-Recourse Debt A loan that limits the lender's options to collect on the value of the real estate in the event of a default by the borrower.

Nonrecurring Closing Costs Fees that are only paid one time in a given transaction.

Note A legal document requiring a borrower to repay a mortgage at a specified interest rate over a certain period of time.

Note Rate The interest rate that is defined in a mortgage note.

Notice of Default A formal written notification a borrower receives once the borrower is in default stating that legal action may be taken.

Offer A term that describes a specified price or spread to sell whole loans or securities.

One-Year Adjustable-Rate Mortgage An ARM for which the interest rate changes annually, generally based on movements of a published index plus a specified margin.

Open Space A section of land or water that has been dedicated for public or private use or enjoyment.

Open-End Fund A type of commingled fund with an infinite life, always accepting new investor capital and making new investments in property.

Operating Cost Escalation A clause that is intended to adjust rents to account for external standards such as published indexes, negotiated wage levels, or building-related expenses.

Operating Expense The regular costs associated with operating and managing a property.

Opportunistic A phrase that generally describes a strategy of holding investments in underperforming and/or under-managed assets with the expectation of increases in cash flow and/or value.

Option A condition in which the buyer pays for the right to purchase a property within a certain period of time without the obligation to buy.

Option ARM Loan A type of mortgage in which the borrower has a variety of payment options each month.

Original Principal Balance The total principal owed on a mortgage before a borrower has made a payment.

Origination Fee A fee that most lenders charge for the purpose of covering the costs associated with arranging the loan.

Originator A company that underwrites loans for commercial and/or multi-family properties.

Out-Parcel The individual retail sites located within a shopping center.

Overallotment A practice in which the underwriters offer and sell a higher number of shares than they had planned to purchase from the issuer.

Owner Financing A transaction in which the property seller agrees to finance all or part of the amount of the purchase.

Parking Ratio A figure, generally expressed as square footage, that compares a building's total rentable square footage to its total number of parking spaces.

Partial Payment An amount paid that is not large enough to cover the normal monthly payment on a mortgage loan.

Partial Sales The act of selling a real estate interest that is smaller than the whole property.

Partial Taking The appropriating of a portion of an owner's property under the laws of Eminent Domain.

Participating Debt Financing that allows the lender to have participatory rights to equity through increased income and/or residual value over the balance of the loan or original value at the time the loan is funded.

Party in Interest Any party that may hold an interest, including employers, unions, and, sometimes, fiduciaries.

Pass-Through Certificate A document that allows the holder to receive payments of principal and interest from the underlying pool of mortgages.

Payment Cap The maximum amount a monthly payment may increase on an ARM.

Payment Change Date The date on which a new payment amount takes effect on an ARM or GPM, usually in the month directly after the adjustment date.

Payout Ratio The percentage of the primary earnings per share, excluding unusual items, that are paid to common stockholders as cash dividends during the next 12 months.

Pension Liability The full amount of capital that is required to finance vested pension fund benefits.

Percentage Rent The amount of rent that is adjusted based on the percentage of gross sales or revenues the tenant receives.

Per-Diem Interest The interest that is charged or accrued daily.

Performance Bond A bond that a contractor posts to guarantee full performance of a contract in which the proceeds will be used for completing the contract or compensating the owner for loss in the event of nonperformance.

Performance Measurement The process of measuring how well an investor's real estate has performed regarding individual assets, advisers/managers, and portfolios.

Performance The changes each quarter in fund or account values that can be explained by investment income, realized or unrealized appreciation, and the total return to the investors before and after investment management fees.

Performance-Based Fees The fees that advisers or managers receive that are based on returns to investors.

Periodic Payment Cap The highest amount that payments can increase or decrease during a given adjustment period on an ARM.

Periodic Rate Cap The maximum amount that the interest rate can increase or decrease during a given adjustment period on an ARM.

Permanent Loan A long-term property mortgage.

Personal Property Any items belonging to a person that is not real estate.

PITI Principal, Interest, Taxes, Insurance. The items that are included in the monthly payment to the lender for an impounded loan, as well as mortgage insurance.

PITI Reserves The amount in cash that a borrower must readily have after the down payment and all closing costs are paid when purchasing a home.

Plan Assets The assets included in a pension plan.

Plan Sponsor The party that is responsible for administering an employee benefit plan.

Planned Unit Development (PUD) A type of ownership where individuals actually own the building or unit they live in, but common areas are owned jointly with the other members of the development or association. Contrast with condominium, where an individual actually owns the airspace of his unit, but the buildings and common areas are owned jointly with the others in the development or association.

Plat A chart or map of a certain area showing the boundaries of individual lots, streets, and easements.

Pledged Account Mortgage (PAM) A loan tied to a pledged savings account for which the fund and earned interest are used to gradually reduce mortgage payments.

Point Also referred to as a Discount Point. A fee a lender charges to provide a lower interest rate, equal to 1 percent of the amount of the loan.

Portfolio Management A process that involves formulating, modifying, and implementing a real estate investment strategy according to an investor's investment objectives.

Portfolio Turnover The amount of time averaged from the time an investment is funded until it is repaid or sold.

Power of Attorney A legal document that gives someone the authority to act on behalf of another party.

Power of Sale The clause included in a mortgage or deed of trust that provides the mortgagee (or trustee) with the right and power to advertise and sell the property at public auction if the borrower is in default.

Pre-Approval The complete analysis a lender makes regarding a potential borrower's ability to pay for a home as well as a confirmation of the proposed amount to be borrowed.

Pre-Approval Letter The letter a lender presents that states the amount of money they are willing to lend a potential buyer.

Preferred Shares Certain stocks that have a prior distributions claim up to a defined amount before the common shareholders may receive anything.

Pre-Leased A certain amount of space in a proposed building that must be leased before construction may begin or a certificate of occupancy may be issued.

Prepaid Expenses The amount of money that is paid before it is due, including taxes, insurance, and/or assessments.

Prepaid Fees The charges that a borrower must pay in advance regarding certain recurring items, such as interest, property taxes, hazard insurance, and PMI, if applicable.

Prepaid Interest The amount of interest that is paid before its due date.

Prepayment The money that is paid to reduce the principal balance of a loan before the date it is due.

Prepayment Penalty A penalty that may be charged to the borrower when he pays off a loan before the planned maturity date.

Prepayment Rights The right a borrower is given to pay the total principal balance before the maturity date free of penalty.

Prequalification The initial assessment by a lender of a potential borrower's ability to pay for a home as well as an estimate of how much the lender is willing to supply to the buyer.

Price-to-Earnings Ratio The comparison that is derived by dividing the current share price by the sum of the primary earnings per share from continuing operations over the past year.

Primary Issuance The preliminary financing of an issuer.

Prime Rate The best interest rate reserved for a bank's preferred customers.

Prime Space The first-generation space that is available for lease.

Prime Tenant The largest or highest-earning tenant in a building or shopping center.

Principal The amount of money originally borrowed in a mortgage, before interest is included and with any payments subtracted.

Principal Balance The total current balance of mortgage principal not including interest.

Principal Paid over Life of Loan The final total of scheduled payments to the principal that the lender calculates to equal the face amount of the loan.

Principal Payments The lender's return of invested capital.

Principle of Conformity The concept that a property will probably increase in value if its size, age, condition, and style are similar to other properties in the immediate area.

Private Debt Mortgages or other liabilities for which an individual is responsible.

Private Equity A real estate investment that has been acquired by a noncommercial entity.

Private Mortgage Insurance (PMI) A type of policy that a lender requires when the borrower's down payment or home equity percentage is under 20 percent of the value of the property.

Private Placement The sale of a security in a way that renders it exempt from the registration rules and requirements of the SEC.

Private REIT A real estate investment company that is structured as a real estate investment trust that places and holds shares privately rather than publicly.

Pro Rata The proportionate amount of expenses per tenant for the property's maintenance and operation.

Processing Fee A fee some lenders charge for gathering the information necessary to process the loan.

Production Acres The portion of land that can be used directly in agriculture or timber activities to generate income, but not areas used for such things as machinery storage or support.

Prohibited Transaction Certain

transactions that may not be performed between a pension plan and a party in interest, such as the following: the sale, exchange or lease of any property; a loan or other grant of credit; and furnishing goods or services.

Promissory Note A written agreement to repay the specific amount over a certain period of time.

Property Tax The tax that must be paid on private property.

Prudent Man Rule The standard to which ERISA holds a fiduciary accountable.

Public Auction An announced public meeting held at a specified location for the purpose of selling property to repay a mortgage in default.

Public Debt Mortgages or other liabilities for which a commercial entity is responsible.

Public Equity A real estate investment that has been acquired by REITs and other publicly traded real estate operating companies.

Punch List An itemized list that documents incomplete or unsatisfactory items after the contractor has declared the space to be mostly complete.

Purchase Agreement The written contract the buyer and seller both sign defining the terms and conditions under which a property is sold.

Purchase Money Transaction A transaction in which property is acquired through the exchange of money or something of equivalent value.

Purchase-Money Mortgage (PMM) A mortgage obtained by a borrower that serves as partial payment for a property.

Qualified Plan Any employee benefit plan that the IRS has approved as a tax-exempt plan.

Qualifying Ratio The measurement a lender uses to determine how much they are willing to lend to a potential buyer.

Quitclaim Deed A written document that releases a party from any interest they may have in a property.

Rate Cap The highest interest rate allowed on a monthly payment during an adjustment period of an ARM.

Rate Lock The commitment of a lender to a borrower that guarantees a certain interest rate for a specific amount of time.

Rate-Improvement Mortgage A loan that includes a clause that entitles a borrower to a one-time-only cut in the interest rate without having to refinance.

Rating Agencies Independent firms that are engaged to rate securities' creditworthiness on behalf of investors.

Rating A figure that represents the credit quality or creditworthiness of securities.

Raw Land A piece of property that has not been developed and remains in its natural state.

Raw Space Shell space in a building that has not yet been developed.

Real Estate Agent An individual who is licensed to negotiate and transact the real estate sales.

Real Estate Fundamentals The factors that drive the value of property.

Real Estate Settlement Procedures Act (RESPA) A legislation for consumer protection that requires lenders to notify borrowers regarding closing costs in advance.

Real Property Land and anything else

of a permanent nature that is affixed to the land.

Real Rate of Return The yield given to investors minus an inflationary factor.

Realtor A real estate agent or broker who is an active member of a local real estate board affiliated with the National Association of Realtors.

Recapture The act of the IRS recovering the tax benefit of a deduction or a credit that a taxpayer has previously taken in error.

Recorder A public official who records transactions that affect real estate in the area.

Recording The documentation that the registrar's office keeps of the details of properly executed legal documents.

Recording Fee A fee real estate agents charge for moving the sale of a piece of property into the public record.

Recourse The option a lender has for recovering losses against the personal assets of a secondary party who is also liable for a debt that is in default.

Red Herring An early prospectus that is distributed to prospective investors that includes a note in red ink on the cover stating that the SEC-approved registration statement is not yet in effect.

Refinance Transaction The act of paying off an existing loan using the funding gained from a new loan that uses the same property as security.

Regional Diversification Boundaries that are defined based on geography or economic lines.

Registration Statement The set of forms that are filed with the SEC (or the appropriate state agency) regarding a proposed offering of new securities or the listing of outstanding securities on a national exchange.

Regulation Z A federal legislation under the Truth in Lending Act that requires lenders to advise the borrower in writing of all costs that are associated with the credit portion of a financial transaction.

Rehab Short for Rehabilitation. Refers to an extensive renovation intended to extend the life of a building or project.

Rehabilitation Mortgage A loan meant to fund the repairing and improving of a resale home or building.

Real Estate Investment Trust (REIT) A trust corporation that combines the capital of several investors for the purpose of acquiring or providing funding for real estate.

Remaining Balance The amount of the principal on a home loan that has not yet been paid.

Remaining Term The original term of the loan after the number of payments made has been subtracted.

Real Estate Mortgage Investment Conduit (REMIC) An investment vehicle that is designed to hold a pool of mortgages solely to issue multiple classes of mortgage-backed securities in a way that avoids doubled corporate tax.

Renewal Option A clause in a lease agreement that allows a tenant to extend the term of a lease.

Renewal Probability The average percentage of a building's tenants who are expected to renew terms at market rental rates upon the lease expiration.

Rent Commencement Date The date at which a tenant is to begin paying rent.

Rent Loss Insurance A policy that covers loss of rent or rental value for a landlord due to any condition that renders the leased premises inhabitable, thereby excusing the tenant from paying rent.

Rent The fee paid for the occupancy and/or use of any rental property or equipment.

Rentable/Usable Ratio A total rentable area in a building divided by the area available for use.

Rental Concession See: Concessions.

Rental Growth Rate The projected trend of market rental rates over a particular period of analysis.

Rent-Up Period The period of time following completion of a new building when tenants are actively being sought and the project is stabilizing.

Real Estate Owned (REO) The real estate that a savings institution owns as a result of foreclosure on borrowers in default.

Repayment Plan An agreement made to repay late installments or advances.

Replacement Cost The projected cost by current standards of constructing a building that is equivalent to the building being appraised.

Replacement Reserve Fund Money that is set aside for replacing of common property in a condominium, PUD, or cooperative project.

Request for Proposal (RFP) A formal request that invites investment managers to submit information regarding investment strategies, historical investment performance, current investment opportunities, investment management fees, and other pension fund client relationships used by their firm.

Rescission The legal withdrawing of a contract or consent from the parties involved.

Reserve Account An account that must be funded by the borrower to protect the lender.

Resolution Trust Corp. (RTC) The congressional corporation established for the purpose of containing, managing, and selling failed financial institutions, thereby recovering taxpayer funds.

Retail Investor An investor who sells interests directly to consumers.

Retention Rate The percentage of trailing year's earnings that have been dispersed into the company again. It is calculated as 100 minus the trailing 12-month payout ratio.

Return on Assets The measurement of the ability to produce net profits efficiently by making use of assets.

Return on Equity The measurement of the return on the investment in a business or property.

Return on Investments The percentage of money that has been gained as a result of certain investments.

Reverse Mortgage See: Home Equity Conversion Mortgage.

Reversion Capitalization Rate The capitalization rate that is used to derive reversion value.

Reversion Value A benefit that an investor expects to receive as a lump sum at the end of an investment.

Revolving Debt A credit arrangement that enables a customer to borrow against a predetermined line of credit when purchasing goods and services.

Revenue per Available Room (RevPAR) The total room revenue for a particular period divided by the average number of rooms available in a hospitality facility.

Right of Ingress or Egress The option

to enter or to leave the premises in question.

Right of Survivorship The option that survivors have to take on the interest of a deceased joint tenant.

Right to Rescission A legal provision that enables borrowers to cancel certain loan types within three days after they sign.

Risk Management A logical approach to analyzing and defining insurable and non-insurable risks while evaluating the availability and costs of purchasing third-party insurance.

Risk-Adjusted Rate of Return A percentage that is used to identify investment options that are expected to deliver a positive premium despite their volatility.

Road Show A tour of the executives of a company that is planning to go public, during which the executives travel to a variety of cities to make presentations to underwriters and analysts regarding their company and IPO.

Roll-Over Risk The possibility that tenants will not renew their lease.

Sale-Leaseback An arrangement in which a seller deeds a property, or part of it, to a buyer in exchange for money or the equivalent, then leases the property from the new owner.

Sales Comparison Value A value that is calculated by comparing the appraised property to similar properties in the area that have been recently sold.

Sales Contract An agreement that both the buyer and seller sign defining the terms of a property sale.

Second Mortgage A secondary loan obtained on a piece of property.

Secondary Market A market in which existing mortgages are bought and sold

as part of a mortgages pool.

Secondary (Follow-On) Offering An offering of stock made by a company that is already public.

Second-Generation or Secondary Space Space that has been occupied before and becomes available for lease again, either by the landlord or as a sublease.

Secured Loan A loan that is secured by some sort of collateral.

Securities and Exchange Commission (SEC) The federal agency that oversees the issuing and exchanging of public securities.

Securitization The act of converting a non-liquid asset into a tradable form.

Security The property or other asset that will serve as a loan's collateral.

Security Deposit An amount of money a tenant gives to a landlord to secure the performance of terms in a lease agreement.

Seisen (Seizen) The ownership of real property under a claim of freehold estate.

Self-Administered REIT A REIT in which the management are employees of the REIT or similar entity.

Self-Managed REIT See: Self-Administered REIT.

Seller Carry-Back An arrangement in which the seller provides the financing to purchase a home.

Seller Financing A type of funding in which the borrower may use part of the equity in the property to finance the purchase.

Senior Classes The security classes who have the highest priority for receiving payments from the underlying mortgage loans.

Separate Account A relationship in which a single pension plan sponsor is used to retain an investment manager or adviser under a stated investment policy exclusively for that sponsor.

Servicer An organization that collects principal and interest payments from borrowers and manages borrowers' escrow accounts on behalf of a trustee.

Servicing The process of collecting mortgage payments from borrowers as well as related responsibilities.

Setback The distance required from a given reference point before a structure can be built.

Settlement or Closing Fees Fees that the escrow agent receives for carrying out the written instructions in the agreement between borrower and lender and/or buyer and seller.

Settlement Statement See: HUD-1 Settlement Statement.

Shared-Appreciation Mortgage A loan that enables a lender or other party to share in the profits of the borrower when the borrower sells the home.

Shared-Equity Transaction A transaction in which two people purchase a property, one as a residence and the other as an investment.

Shares Outstanding The number of shares of outstanding common stock minus the treasury shares.

Site Analysis A determination of how suitable a specific parcel of land is for a particular use.

Site Development The implementation of all improvements that are needed for a site before construction may begin.

Site Plan A detailed description and map of the location of improvements to a parcel.

Slab The flat, exposed surface that is laid over the structural support beams to form the building's floor(s).

Social Investing A strategy in which investments are driven in partially or completely by social or non-real estate objectives.

Soft Cost The part of an equity investment, aside from the literal cost of the improvements, that could be tax-deductible in the first year.

Space Plan A chart or map of space requirements for a tenant that includes wall/door locations, room sizes, and even furniture layouts.

Special Assessment Certain charges that are levied against real estates for public improvements to benefit the property in question.

Special Servicer A company that is hired to collect on mortgages that are either delinquent or in default.

Specified Investing A strategy of investment in individually specified properties, portfolios, or commingled funds are fully or partially detailed prior to the commitment of investor capital.

Speculative Space Any space in a rental property that has not been leased prior to construction on a new building begins.

Stabilized Net Operating Income Expected income minus expenses that reflect relatively stable operations.

Stabilized Occupancy The best projected range of long-term occupancy that a piece of rental property will achieve after existing in the open market for a reasonable period of time with terms and conditions that are comparable to similar offerings.

Step-Rate Mortgage A loan that allows for a gradual interest rate increase during the first few years of the loan.

Step-Up Lease (Graded Lease) A lease agreement that specifies certain increases in rent at certain intervals during the complete term of the lease.

Straight Lease (Flat Lease) A lease agreement that specifies an amount of rent that should be paid regularly during the complete term of the lease.

Strip Center Any shopping area that is made up of a row of stores but is not large enough to be anchored by a grocery store.

Subcontractor A contractor who has been hired by the general contractor, often specializing in a certain required task for the construction project.

Subdivision The most common type of housing development created by dividing a larger tract of land into individual lots for sale or lease.

Sublessee A person or business that holds the rights of use and occupancy under a lease contract with the original lessee, who still retains primary responsibility for the lease obligations.

Subordinate Financing Any loan with a priority lower than loans that were obtained beforehand.

Subordinate Loan A second or third mortgage obtained with the same property being used as collateral.

Subordinated Classes Classes that have the lowest priority of receiving payments from underlying mortgage loans.

Subordination The act of sharing credit loss risk at varying rates among two or more classes of securities.

Subsequent Rate Adjustments The interest rate for ARMs that adjusts at regular intervals, sometimes differing from the duration period of the initial interest rate.

Subsequent Rate Cap The maximum amount the interest rate may increase at each regularly scheduled interest rate adjustment date on an ARM.

Super Jumbo Mortgage A loan that is over $650,000 for some lenders or $1,000,000 for others.

Surety A person who willingly binds himself to the debt or obligation of another party.

Surface Rights A right or easement that is usually granted with mineral rights that enables the holder to drill through the surface.

Survey A document or analysis containing the precise measurements of a piece of property as performed by a licensed surveyor.

Sweat Equity The non-cash improvements in value that an owner adds to a piece of property.

Synthetic Lease A transaction that is considered to be a lease by accounting standards but a loan by tax standards.

Taking Similar to condemning, or any other interference with rights to private property, but a physical seizure or appropriation is not required.

Tax Base The determined value of all property that lies within the jurisdiction of the taxing authority.

Tax Lien A type of lien placed against a property if the owner has not paid property or personal taxes.

Tax Roll A record that contains the descriptions of all land parcels and their owners that is located within the county.

Tax Service Fee A fee that is charged for the purpose of setting up monitoring of the borrower's property tax payments by a third party.

Teaser Rate A small, short-term interest

rate offered on a mortgage in order to convince the potential borrower to apply.

Tenancy by the Entirety A form of ownership held by spouses in which they both hold title to the entire property with right of survivorship.

Tenancy in Common A type of ownership held by two or more owners in an undivided interest in the property with no right of survivorship.

Tenant (Lessee) A party who rents a piece of real estate from another by way of a lease agreement.

Tenant at Will A person who possesses a piece of real estate with the owner's permission.

Tenant Improvement (TI) Allowance The specified amount of money that the landlord contributes toward tenant improvements.

Tenant Improvement (TI) The upgrades or repairs that are made to the leased premises by or for a tenant.

Tenant Mix The quality of the income stream for a property.

Term The length that a loan lasts or is expected to last before it is repaid.

Third-Party Origination A process in which another party is used by the lender to originate, process, underwrite, close, fund, or package the mortgages it expects to deliver to the secondary mortgage market.

Timeshare A form of ownership involving purchasing a specific period of time or percentage of interest in a vacation property.

Time-Weighted Average Annual Rate of Return The regular yearly return over several years that would have the same return value as combining the actual annual returns

for each year in the series.

Title The legal written document that provides someone ownership in a piece of real estate.

Title Company A business that determines that a property title is clear and that provides title insurance.

Title Exam An analysis of the public records in order to confirm that the seller is the legal owner, and there are no encumbrances on the property.

Title Insurance A type of policy that is issued to both lenders and buyers to cover loss due to property ownership disputes that may arise at a later date.

Title Insurance Binder A written promise from the title insurance company to insure the title to the property, based on the conditions and exclusions shown in the binder.

Title Risk The potential impediments in transferring a title from one party to another.

Title Search The process of analyzing all transactions existing in the public record in order to determine whether any title defects could interfere with the clear transfer of property ownership.

Total Acres The complete amount of land area that is contained within a real estate investment.

Total Assets The final amount of all gross investments, cash and equivalents, receivables, and other assets as they are presented on the balance sheet.

Total Commitment The complete funding amount that is promised once all specified conditions have been met.

Total Expense Ratio The comparison of monthly debt obligations to gross monthly income.

Total Inventory The total amount of

square footage commanded by property within a geographical area.

Total Lender Fees Charges that the lender requires for obtaining the loan, aside from other fees associated with the transfer of a property.

Total Loan Amount The basic amount of the loan plus any additional financed closing costs.

Total Monthly Housing Costs The amount that must be paid each month to cover principal, interest, property taxes, PMI, and/or either hazard insurance or homeowners' association dues.

Total of All Payments The total cost of the loan after figuring the sum of all monthly interest payments.

Total Principal Balance The sum of all debt, including the original loan amount adjusted for subsequent payments and any unpaid items that may be included in the principal balance by the mortgage note or by law.

Total Retail Area The total floor area of a retail center that is currently leased or available for lease.

Total Return The final amount of income and appreciation returns per quarter.

Townhouse An attached home that is not considered to be a condominium.

Trade Fixtures Any personal property that is attached to a structure and used in the business but is removable once the lease is terminated.

Trading Down The act of purchasing a property that is less expensive than the one currently owned.

Trading Up The act of purchasing a property that is more expensive than the one currently owned.

Tranche A class of securities that may

or may not be rated.

TransUnion Corporation One of the primary credit-reporting bureaus.

Transfer of Ownership Any process in which a property changes hands from one owner to another.

Transfer Tax An amount specified by state or local authorities when ownership in a piece of property changes hands.

Treasury Index A measurement that is used to derive interest rate changes for ARMs.

Triple Net Lease A lease that requires the tenant to pay all property expenses on top of the rental payments.

Trustee A fiduciary who oversees property or funds on behalf of another party.

Truth-in-Lending The federal legislation requiring lenders to fully disclose the terms and conditions of a mortgage in writing.

TurnKey Project A project in which all components are within a single supplier's responsibility.

Two- to Four-Family Property A structure that provides living space for two to four families while ownership is held in a single deed.

Two-Step Mortgage An ARM with two different interest rates: one for the loan's first five or seven years and another for the remainder of the loan term.

Under Construction The time period that exists after a building's construction has started but before a certificate of occupancy has been presented.

Under Contract The period of time during which a buyer's offer to purchase a property has been accepted, and the buyer is able to finalize financing arrangements without the concern of the seller making a deal with another buyer.

Underwriter A company, usually an investment banking firm, that is involved in a guarantee that an entire issue of stocks or bonds will be purchased.

Underwriters' Knot An approved knot according to code that may be tied at the end of an electrical cord to prevent the wires from being pulled away from their connection to each other or to electrical terminals.

Underwriting The process during which lenders analyze the risks a particular borrower presents and set appropriate conditions for the loan.

Underwriting Fee A fee that mortgage lenders charge for verifying the information on the loan application and making a final decision on approving the loan.

Unencumbered A term that refers to property free of liens or other encumbrances.

Unimproved Land See: Raw Land.

Unrated Classes Usually the lowest classes of securities.

Unrecorded Deed A deed that transfers right of ownership from one owner to another without being officially documented.

Umbrella Partnership Real Estate Investment Trust (UPREIT) An organizational structure in which a REIT's assets are owned by a holding company for tax reasons.

Usable Square Footage The total area that is included within the exterior walls of the tenant's space.

Use The particular purpose for which a property is intended to be employed.

VA Loan A mortgage through the VA program in which a down payment is not necessarily required.

Vacancy Factor The percentage of gross revenue that pro-forma income statements expect to be lost due to vacancies.

Vacancy Rate The percentage of space that is available to rent.

Vacant Space Existing rental space that is presently being marketed for lease minus space that is available for sublease.

Value-Added A phrase advisers and managers generally use to describe investments in underperforming and/ or under-managed assets.

Variable Rate Mortgage (VRM) A loan in which the interest rate changes according to fluctuations in particular indexes.

Variable Rate Also called adjustable rate. The interest rate on a loan that varies over the term of the loan according to a predetermined index.

Variance A permission that enables a property owner to work around a zoning ordinance's literal requirements which cause a unique hardship due to special circumstances.

Verification of Deposit (VOD) The confirmation statement a borrower's bank may be asked to sign in order to verify the borrower's account balances and history.

Verification of Employment (VOE) The confirmation statement a borrower's employer may be asked to sign in order to verify the borrower's position and salary.

Vested Having the right to draw on a portion or on all of a pension or other retirement fund.

Veterans Affairs (VA) A federal government agency that assists veterans in purchasing a home without a down payment.

Virtual Storefront A retail business presence on the Internet.

Waiting Period The period of time between initially filing a registration statement and the date it becomes effective.

Warehouse Fee A closing cost fee that represents the lender's expense of temporarily holding a borrower's loan before it is sold on the secondary mortgage market.

Weighted-Average Coupon The average, using the balance of each mortgage as the weighting factor, of the gross interest rates of the mortgages underlying a pool as of the date of issue.

Weighted-Average Equity The part of the equation that is used to calculate investment-level income, appreciation, and total returns on a quarter-by-quarter basis.

Weighted-Average Rental Rates The average ratio of unequal rental rates across two or more buildings in a market.

Working Drawings The detailed blueprints for a construction project that comprise the contractual documents which describe the exact manner in which a project is to be built.

Workout The strategy in which a borrower negotiates with a lender to attempt to restructure the borrower's debt rather than go through the foreclosure proceedings.

Wraparound Mortgage A loan obtained by a buyer to use for the remaining balance on the seller's first mortgage, as well as an additional amount requested by the seller.

Write-Down A procedure used in accounting when an asset's book value is adjusted downward to reflect current market value more accurately.

Write-Off A procedure used in accounting when an asset is determined to be uncollectible and is therefore considered to be a loss.

Yield Maintenance Premium A penalty the borrower must pay in order to make investors whole in the event of early repayment of principal.

Yield Spread The difference in income derived from a commercial mortgage and from a benchmark value.

Yield The actual return on an investment, usually paid in dividends or interest.

Zoning Ordinance The regulations and laws that control the use or improvement of land in a particular area or zone.

Zoning The act of dividing a city or town into particular areas and applying laws and regulations regarding the architectural design, structure, and intended uses of buildings within those areas.

Recommended Reading

Landlording, Leigh Robinson. Ninth Edition. ©2004. Express

The Millionarie Real Estate Investor, Gary Keller, ©2005. McGraw-Hill

The Power of Focus, Jack Canfield, Mark Victor Hansen, Les Hewitt. ©2004. Health Communications, Inc.

Rich Dad, Poor Dad. Robert T. Kiyosaki. ©1997, 1998. Warner Business Books

Secrets of a Millionaire Landlord, Robert Shemin, Esq. ©2002. Dearborn Trade Publishing.

INDEX

S

FIABCI-USA Membership Benefits

- **You are listed as FIABCI-USA Member in three searchable locations.** The FIABCI-USA home page (**www.fiabci-usa.com**) allows Internet users to search and find you by your geographic location, professional specialization and countries in which you have indicated expertise. Your contact info is all on-line. You are also able to link your own home page to FIABCI-USA's for free or add your photo or a small fee. In addition to the FIABCI-USA website, FIABCI International also has a website (**www.fiabci.org**) which lists all members of FBABCI worldwide. This website is also completely searchable to members and non-members looking for people to do business with. FIABCI International also prints the annual World Directory, which is sent to all FIABCI members worldwide.

- **Use technology to your advantage** buy using the online tools made available to you. Broadcast e-mail allows you to send e-mails to specific, targeted FIABCI members by using chosen criteria to search the online membership directory. Work from the Member's Only section of both **www.fiabci.org** and **www.fiabci-usa.com** to target your audience. Broadcast e-mail can be used to advertise a property, highlight a marketable skill you have, or just introduce yourself.

- **Referrals!** FIABCI-USA provides free referrals of names and contact information of FIABCI-USA members to companies who are seeking international expertise and connections. Make sure you list your six countries of expertise and the activities and property types you work with. That makes you available to receive a referral.

- **Network at local, national and international meetings.** Exclusive international meetings- such as our annual FIABCI World Congress (May 2006 in Bangkok, Thailand), the FIABCI Regional and the FIABCI December Business meeting -- offer unique opportunities to network with our peers in international real estate, learn about new business, and market yourself and your comapny. This year, the FIABCI Regional Americas Congress and the FIABCI Business Meetings will be held together in Palm Beach, Florida, Dec. 7-10, 2006. This is unique to be host to the world audience. *Most of our members report doing the majority of their international deals through networking while at FIABCI meetings.*

- **Identify your FIABCI affilation and international capabilty** by using the FIABCI-USA logo on your business cards, on your letterhead and in advertising. A logo sheet comes with our new member kit, or logos can be downloaded from **www.fiabci.org.**

- **Promote yourself** by using the provided press release, which explains your connection to our elite group of members around the world The press release can be modified to reflect your expertise and accomplishments. Also available for purchase is the customized Personal Presentation Piece.

- **FIABCI membership sets you apart** locally from your competition and can lead to increased local and national business, as well as international.

- **Come to Unique FIABCI Events** to make the most of your membership. Our Trade Missions establish relationships with foreign dignitaries and important foreign players. Or, set up your own meetings using our Member Directory next time you travel abroad.

- **Market yourself and your company more effectively** through sponsorship or marketing. Our members report having great success with marketing sessions at the World Congress, Regional Congress, and national meetings, to fellow FIABCI members.

Contact FIABCI-USA if you want to know more about the benefits you could be receiving!
Phone 703-524-4279 • fax 703-991-6256 • info@fiabci-usa.com • www.fiabci-usa.com

FIABCI-USA
M E M B E R S H I P   A P P L I C A T I O N

FIABCI

Name _____

Firm _____

Address _____

City _____ State_____ Zip_____

Phone _____ Fax_____

E-Mail and/or Home Page Address _____

Please indicate to which of the following Principal Members you currently belong:

☐ AFIRE   ☐ Appraisal Institute   ☐ ARRELO   ☐ BOMA   ☐ CCIM

☐ CORFAC   ☐ HBI   ☐ IREM   ☐ NAR   ☐ SIOR

Membership Category: ☐ Regular ($595 annual dues + $250 application fee = $845)

☐ Special ($645 annual dues + $250 application fee = $895)

Note: To qualify as a regular member you must be a member of one of the Principal Members of FIABCI listed above. Practitioners and those who serve the realestate industry and who do not qualify for regular membership are special members. Special members must be list a current member as a sponsor and be approved by FIABCI-USA.

Member Sponsor: Eugenia Foxworth, NYC Local Council President
(required for special membership)

FIABCI Language Spoken: ☐ English ☐ French ☐ German ☐ Japanese ☐ Spanish

Charge $_____ to your VISA, MasterCard, AMEX or make your check payable to FIABCI-USA.

Credit Card Number _____ if corp. card, please add CODE#_____

Expiration Date _____   Signature _____

Areas of Specialization
Specialty Codes Rank up to 5 or check All

☐ ADM - Property Management   ☐ TRA - Transaction/Brokerage
☐ CNS - Consulting   ☐ PRO - Development
☐ EXP - Valuation/Appraisal   ☐ FIN - Financing
☐ ARC/URB - Architecture/Urban Plan   ☐ LEG/TAX - Legal/tax
☐ ALL - All the Above
Order of importance:
1st _____ 2nd _____ 3rd _____ 4th _____ 5th _____ 6th _____

Property Types Rank up to 6 or check All
☐ RUR - Rural   ☐ COM - Retail   ☐ OFF - Office
☐ RES - Residential ☐ REC - Leisure   ☐ IND - Industrial
☐ ALL - All the Above
Order of importance:
1st _____ 2nd _____ 3rd _____ 4th _____ 5th _____ 6th _____

Please list up to six foreign countries in which you do business.

_____
_____
_____
_____
_____
_____

Membership Policy: We will begin servinyou upon receipt of your completed application and will continue to serve you unless you advise us in writing that you wish to cancel your membership. Membership is for the 12-month period. Join by December 31 to be listed in the following year's FIABCI World Directory. Effective date 1/1/06.

Return with your $845 or $895 payment to:
FIABCI-USA • 2000 North 15th Street • Suite 101 • Arlington, VA 22201 • Fax: (703) 991-6256
E-mail: info@fiabci-usa.com • http://www.fiabci-usa.com
Questions? Call (703) 524-4279

MORE GREAT TITLES FROM ATLANTIC PUBLISHING

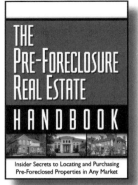
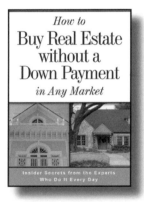
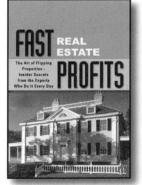